THE OFFICIAL
FARCRY®
SURVIVAL MANUAL

THE OFFICIAL
FARCRY®
SURVIVAL MANUAL

JOSH PARKER

TITAN BOOKS

LONDON

AN INSIGHT EDITIONS BOOK

CONTENTS

HOPE COUNTY, MONTANA

THE NATION OF YARA

PREHISTORY, POSTAPOCALYPSE, & THE FUTURE
(OR A FARTHER CRY BEYOND)

INTRODUCTION

My father was a doomsday-prepper survivalist or, as all the other kids on my block called him, Hunter's crazy dad. He taught me everything I know about preparing for and surviving the worst-case scenario. When I was nine, he showed me how to take someone down by applying a lollipop stick to a trachea, and, the year after that, how to "upgrade" a cigarette lighter to a blowtorch. Because of the intelligence he collected over his forty-year career as a CIA janitor, my dad was always convinced something major was going to happen. Doctors said his doomsday premonitions were likely paranoid delusions caused by working with cleaning chemicals all those years. He took a settlement and was grateful for it, but I'll never forget the cold, visceral pulse in my gut telling me something wasn't right and that I needed to look into it. Then again, it could have been the gas station curry I'd eaten earlier that day not agreeing with my stomach. Either way, that was the moment I realized I wanted to dedicate my life to uncovering the truth and discovering better food.

When I was young, I decorated my laptop with stickers featuring my favorite artists so they would inspire me every time I opened it—the *Purple Rain* album cover, *Abbey Road, Rain Dogs* by Tom Waits, the cover of *Fear and Loathing in Las Vegas*, the poster for Michael Biehn's movie *Blood Dragon*. After I graduated with a journalism degree and was about to head out on my first paid writing gig that would take me to an Indonesian archipelago, my crazy old prepper dad slapped a big sticker of a gun right in the center of my laptop case as a reminder to use my writing as a weapon, gifting me these parting words of advice: "Don't just use your keyboard to write. Use your keyboard to capture souls."

Because of the spotty power and internet connections on the Rook Islands, I went analog and ditched the laptop for a typewriter after my first week there. By the time I left the Islands, I had a M1911 pistol covered in album stickers hidden in my typewriter case. What was left of me realized that the more people you've been forced to kill with your typewriter, the more haunted your prose gets. I think that's what my crazy prepper dad meant by the whole "capturing souls with a keyboard" thing. Turned out to be solid writing and survival advice.

So, after five dizzying world tours of insanity, I figured it was time to put the crazy to paper. And if you're now reading this in the commanding voice of Rex "Power" Colt, don't worry—it's totally normal! Michael Biehn could totally play me in a movie. I'm the adventure-drinking gonzo journalist foodie Hunter Nash. My name is my occupation. The denizens and locals of the world's most dangerous and remote places know me for my mastery of extreme survival and my peerless ability to bullseye a James Beard Award–winning food review on a keyboard. The prestigious *Survival and Stew Review* once wrote of my work: *Nash is a four-star chef of a writer with impeccable taste buds for pistol triggers and prose on his remaining nine fingertips.*

I risk my life to tell the world's most dangerous stories, in the world's most dangerous places, ruled by the world's most deranged people—and have the occasional plate of crab rangoon along the way. I'm the most comfortable around insanity because I was raised in it; I can speak and translate its language. My dad taught me at an early age that sometimes the world can come at you with fangs, claws, and rifles when you least expect it, and you have to be prepared to bludgeon it to death with a typewriter to survive.

Stay frosty out there,
Nash

BECOME A
GONZO JOURNALIST

Gonzo journalist *(n)*
Someone who risks their life to write about muppet shows.

When my feet finally touched the ground and I returned to reality from my long, strange trip of drugs, crab rangoon, and insanity, I finally saw a realized vision of what I had been searching the world to write: this survival guide. Turns out Dad was right after all. The world is a crazy place, and you'll need everything in this book to make it out alive. So if you've finished reading and think you have what it takes to embark on a globe-trotting adventure to explore the world's most dangerous locations and try your hand at gonzo food criticism, here's a list of essentials to get you started. Sure, having field experience is valuable, but it also doesn't hurt to be raised by a crazy doomsday prepper for a father to show you the survival ropes (and how to tie them into knots).

Some say good journalism requires objectivity. As someone who's been there, embedding yourself in the story guarantees the closest possible perspective you can get without being the subject itself. So, what do you need in order to take on any story, anywhere, anytime? You need a desire for truth and facts, and the drive to get them to your editor by press time. You need the guts to tolerate bloodshed and mayhem, and a fifth of bourbon afterward. I learned the hard way that it takes a sober eye and a steady aim to spot important details, document them, and shoot your way out of a dangerous situation. It also doesn't hurt to have press credentials, a degree in journalism, and a touch of crazy. I do recommend learning at least one version of shorthand—long-form writing under fire is illegible and life-threatening anyway—and carry some tools of the trade. Here are the ones I typically have in my journalistic Everyday Carry (EDC) kit.

CREDENTIALS

- Passport
- Journalist credentials
- Travel insurance card
- Abduction insurance card

INVESTIGATIVE TOOLS

- Satellite smartphone
- Mini DSLR camera
- Mini audio recorder
- Bribe Money /Roll of cash
- Lockpicks

WRITING MATERIALS

- Notepad
- Pen and Pencil
- Slimline portable typewriter
  (you can't count on a tablet to hold
  a charge in the middle of a jungle!)

PERSONAL PROTECTION

- M1911 .45 ACP handgun
- Fountain Pen with concealed
  knife blade

FAR CRY 3

THE ROOK ISLANDS

THE ROOK ISLANDS

I heard reports of tourists going missing near an Indonesian archipelago so naturally I decided that would be a good first writing gig to take on. It took me a while, but after a few weeks of poking around I got the name of the hidden location: the Rook Islands. A tropical paradise with a little something for adventure seekers of all types: miles of shimmering beaches and raging waterways for the watersport enthusiasts; an endless horizon of forests for the outdoorsy types; rustic island cuisine for the foodies; monolithic mountain ranges and mazes of underground caves for extreme sports fans; and ancient shrines swallowed by centuries of nature hiding untold secrets, waiting to be discovered by globe-trotting archeologist types. But everyone who ends up here will eventually come face-to-face with the real Rook Islands: pirates and drug-smuggling camps, active mines from World War II, poisonous flora, and bloodthirsty apex predators, all vying to injure or kill you.

This chapter will teach you all I learned about how to survive on this beautiful and deadly island, from basic first aid to identifying poisonous wild flora, to silently escaping captivity in case your ransom insurance payout is delayed. But don't just think of these pages as a single chapter in a book; treat them as weapons in an arsenal of knowledge written to save your life in an emergency. You must wield the information on these pages with speed and accuracy, and you just might need it. Pirates and mercenaries have long infested the Islands, taking territory from the native Rakyat—skilled warriors with roots in the Island running as deep as their hatred for such interlopers. They're such an invaluable resource for weapons, shelter, and supplies that your odds of survival will increase just by getting on their good side. The pirates, of course, have no good sides; led by unhinged psychopaths like Vaas Montenegro, their brutality may mean your job of surviving is a challenging one indeed.

A smart man once said the definition of insanity is repeating the same thing over and over again and expecting different results, yet outsiders still choose to ignore the countless warning signs. Survival on the Rook Islands is just as much about resisting its temptation as it is enduring its chaos. You must maintain mental and emotional fitness to prevent infection from insanity. People can be so easily distracted by the allure of the Rook Islands' tropical paradise, they never see its fangs and claws hiding just beneath the surface until it's too late. I was both lucky and strong enough to survive—and, fortunately for you, also smart enough to take detailed mental notes along the way. So if after reading this introduction you still want to attempt your very own Rook Islands adventure, study these pages like holy scripture, be prepared, watch your back (and your step), trust few, and stay frosty out there.

Welcome to the Rook Islands!

001 BUILD YOUR FIRST AID KIT

I've encountered a lot of strange things in strange places, often with a risk of injury. But with all the dangers I heard of or encountered on the Islands, I found the likelihood of injury is more a certainty here, so you'll want to do as I did: Reserve some space in your rucksack for medical supplies. There are no drugstores on Rook Island (or in plenty of other places in the world) so you should prepare ahead of time. Carry at least these basics with you—and pack sunscreen while you're at it. The tropical sun is just as brutal as an angry pirate here.

MEDICAL SHEARS

All reliable first aid kits should have a good pair of trauma shears sturdy enough to cut through clothing, belts, and boots in an emergency. If you need to improvise, a combat knife might do, though it's a bit oversized.

TWEEZERS

Another first aid kit Hall of Famer, essential for removing splinters and foreign materials from wounds. You're going to be doing a lot of crawling through brush to avoid being detected by pirates; trust me when I say you'll need tweezers.

WOUND CARE

It wouldn't be a first aid kit without a good disinfectant, and you're not likely to loot a bottle of peroxide. Instead, bring a pack of disinfectant wipes; they're handy and easy to carry. Though, speaking as a writer, you can't beat the wound-numbing capabilities of a good whiskey in a pinch.

PAINKILLER

Now that you've disinfected your splinter-free flesh wounds, you're going to need a painkiller chaser. Ibuprofen or other NSAIDS will be king of the pill. If you didn't bring any, simply take whiskey disinfectant internally.

WOUND DRESSING

Gauze roller bandages, 1-inch (2.5 cm) medical tape, and triangle bandages for use as an arm sling (or tourniquet) are great all-rounders to cover the injuries you're likely to get while in the Rook Islands or elsewhere.

002 CHECK VITAL SIGNS

As both a survivalist and aspiring poet, my dad taught me that breathing and heartbeat are the two most important aspects of a person's vitals. Whether you're checking a pulse, or striking a chord on heartstrings with a sonnet, you have to master the alphabet before you can spell—and "Airway, Breathing, Circulation" are the ABCs of survival. There are several viable methods to accomplish this; which one you choose will depend on your unique situation. (You may find it challenging to listen for breathing as the rooster-crowing of gunfire tears the jungle around you to shreds.)

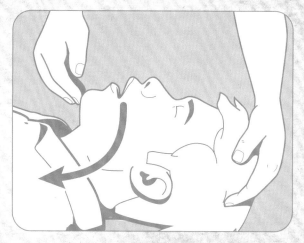

COUNT BREATHS

Watch the victim's chest for fifteen seconds and count the expansions. Multiply that number by four. (Twelve to twenty breaths per minute is the range you're looking for.)

LISTEN FOR BREATHING

If you're in a quiet enough location, you can also perform the above method by listening to the victim's breathing for fifteen seconds. If you've ever heard the phrase "island time," then you know it means the local clock is never really in sync with yours. Fifteen seconds hiding on Rook Islands can feel like an eternity in the wrong circumstances, but stay frosty.

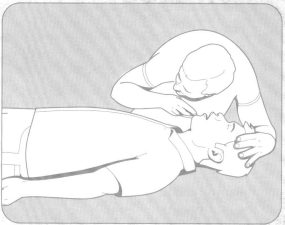

FINGER ON THE PULSE

Press two fingers gently against the inside of the forearm on the thumb side of the wrist. Count the number of beats in fifteen seconds and multiply that by four. (Sixty to one hundred per minute is the range you want to be in.) Checking a pulse isn't all in the wrists; you can also place two fingers on the Adam's apple and move to the side of the throat just under the jaw. Press gently and measure the beats, using the same method above.

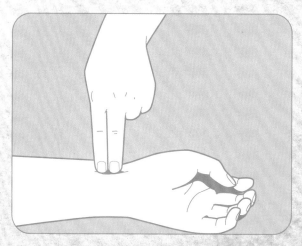

003 STOP BLEEDING

Most people find themselves in trouble on the Rook Islands because they're too distracted by its beauty to see the claws and teeth. From the peaks of Murder Summit to the beaches of Broken Neck Home, these two islands are a pair of jaws thirsty for blood. The more violent inhabitants are icing on the cake—and after witnessing a barroom knife fight or two, I learned not to discount them either. To keep that precious red gold from spilling on the floor, first determine the severity of the blood flow coming from the wound—and always tend to the most serious injuries first.

OOZING BLOOD

Typically from minor abrasions like scrapes and scratches that open capillaries. Clean and disinfect the wound, then apply dressing. Change the dressing daily, and if you see any signs of infection seek medical treatment immediately.

FLOWING BLOOD

This form of bleeding is typically associated with a punctured vein. First, elevate the injury above the heart and apply direct pressure on the wound. Continue to add more bandages until the bleeding stops, then dress the wound.

SPURTING BLOOD

If the blood is spurting, that means arterial damage, which is extremely life-threatening. Elevate the injury and apply firm direct pressure, adding more bandages as needed. If the bleeding won't stop, get out that fancy tourniquet in your first aid kit and tie it on; if you don't have one, cinch a belt or rope tight as you can just above the bleed and seek medical attention immediately.

INTERNAL BLEEDING

A "carpet-friendly hemorrhage" is still a hemorrhage. Injuries to organs and vessels can send someone into shock—and both shock and the injury that caused it can be extremely life-threatening. Ensure the victim is reclining and raise the injured area to restrict blood flow. Find medical help immediately, especially if the internal injury is in the torso. (See item 195 for more information.)

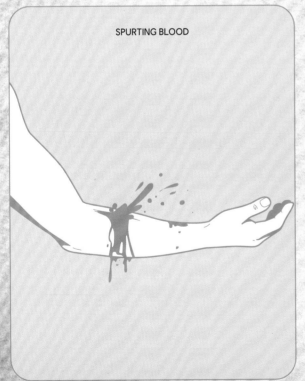

SPURTING BLOOD

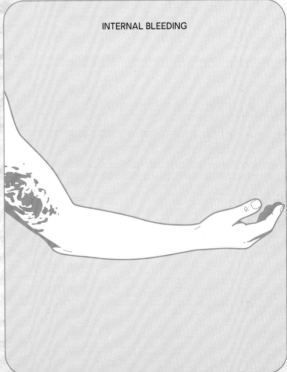

INTERNAL BLEEDING

004 SURVIVE A GUNSHOT WOUND

On the Rook Islands, flying bullets are the equivalent of mosquitoes: You're likely to be nicked by one at some point, so you may as well be prepared! Don't get any wild ideas of cauterizing wounds with a heated combat knife like an '80s action hero (that comes later; see item 199), instead, keep it simple: Stop the bleeding. Dress the wound. Let medical professionals remove bullets. But since doctors—and help in general—are hard to come by on the Rook Islands, you may have to give treating bullet wounds your best shot. Here's what to do (and not do).

CHECK FOR EXIT WOUNDS

If the bullet has successfully escaped the bloody labyrinth of meat and bone that is the human body, apply direct and firm pressure to the wounds to stop the bleeding and stabilize the victim. (See items 003 and 005 for more.)

DON'T EXTRACT BULLETS

If the bullet hasn't passed through your flesh and it's embedded deeply, it's best just to leave it alone; you risk introducing infection if your tools aren't sterile. As if that weren't bad enough, the projectile can cause even more bleeding and other internal damage if it's improperly disturbed.

GET MEDICAL ATTENTION

No matter where in your body you just picked up your new lead implant, you will definitely want to let medical professionals remove bullets or buckshot for the reasons mentioned above, especially since you may need antibiotics and other care along with the surgery. (If it's a sucking chest wound, see item 142 for more on how to handle the injury in question—and if your medical care is by Doctor Earnhardt, just hope he's having a sober day.)

005 TREAT FOR SHOCK

The bleeding may have stopped, but the trauma party isn't over yet! As the circulatory system diverts the body's blood supply to the vital organs during trauma, the redistribution of oxygen in this process can ultimately lead to shock. Pain and fear are two of the biggest contributing factors that compound the danger of shock—and they coincidentally just happen to be two of Vaas Montenegro's biggest claims to fame—so you may have your work cut out for you.

RECOGNIZE THE SYMPTOMS

A rapid pulse is a sign of trauma, so recite your ABCs and check the victim's pulse (see item 002 for more on how to check vital signs). Other signs of shock include grey or pale skin (especially around the lips) and cold or clammy skin on which the sweat doesn't evaporate.

LAY THE VICTIM DOWN

Recline the victim, keep their head down (which I learned was a good survival tip in general here), and treat any visible injuries. Slightly elevate the victim's feet, mindful of any leg injuries.

MONITOR BREATHING

Remove all packs and equipment from their body and loosen any restrictive clothing to help the victim breathe freely.

STABLIZE TEMPERATURE

Wrap them in blankets, coats, or any viable substitutes. Nothing available? Cuddle up and share some of that body heat.

TALK THEIR EARS OFF

Once the victim has been stabilized, strike up a conversation to keep their mind focused and to let them know everything is going to be just fine. Talking points well removed from their current situation would be the recommended topics of discussion.

006 GET JUNGLE SAVVY

A professional traveler like myself can still get lost—and one or two missteps (and a bad couple of hours wandering one evening just outside Amanaki Town) taught me some caution. The bad news: Jungles are some of the most dangerous environments with everything from poisonous insects and poisonous snakes to poisonous flora and crocodile-infested waters. The good news? Crocodiles aren't venomous! Your awareness must be heightened as you traverse a jungle to avoid danger, so keep your eyes sharp as machetes and keep a few tips in mind.

TRAVEL BY DAY

At night, it isn't so much a jungle as it is a horror film. Some of the more hazardous creatures come out at night and you may not be able to see them, but they will definitely see you.

BRING A MACHETE

When they built the jungle, they forgot to put in hiking trails, so you'll need to hack pathways through thick vegetation.

CROSS WATER WITH CAUTION

Cross shallow, cross slowly, and check for leeches when you emerge. (See item 007 for more information on crossing fast-moving water.)

AVOID ENTANGLEMENT

Even the jungle vegetation wants you dead. If you find yourself snared on plants, step backwards to get out of an entanglement rather than pushing ahead or sidestepping—you can get stuck even more.

PROTECT AGAINST BED BUGS

You haven't lived until you've discovered a scorpion in your boot. And depending on the species, you won't live long after. Seal your boots, gloves, and all loose garments in a tent or bag overnight.

STEP AWAY FROM SNAKES

You're more likely to get bitten by a snake if you try to disturb it or get close to it. If you see one, go around it. If an aggressive species is moving towards you, run like you just escaped a pirate camp!

BE SWAMP WARY

Given that it's home to crocodiles, constrictors, and venomous snakes, the survival tip here is simple: Stay out of swamps. But if it's your only viable path, observe the wildlife before wading or swimming. If waterfowl won't go there, it's a good sign you shouldn't either.

NAVIGATE WITH CAUTION

Use a long stick or branch to probe the ground ahead of you and to check water depth. If you get lost, pick a direction you feel is safest and maintain that course.

NAVIGATE TALL GRASS

The taller the grass, the less you can see where you're going, so bring a compass. Carry a staff to probe the path ahead and make noise to tell the resident snakes, insects, and spiders to scoot. Tuck your pants into your boots and wear a hat and gloves to protect against bug bites.

007 CROSS FAST-MOVING WATER SAFELY

Like virtually all mountainous islands, the Rooks are absolutely covered in streams flowing from high hills and peaks. Traversing any of those fast-moving bodies of water is a game of inches—that's all it takes to drown, and all it takes to knock someone down if it's moving fast enough. That's the problem with rivers and large bodies of water: millions of raging gallons to fill your lungs and sweep you off your feet. But death is also a game of inches on the Rook Islands, and crossing a feral waterway with sharp rocks for teeth is actually a safer bet than crossing paths with a clutch of pirates.

GO WADING

Reduce drag by removing your clothing before entering the water. Keep your boots or shoes on to protect against sharp rocks or other potential hazards. Carry your clothing over your head so you'll have dry clothes when you reach the other side and wade against the flow at a 45-degree angle—this will help you maintain balance and keep you on your feet. Use a pole to stabilize yourself and probe the water in front of you to feel for solid footing or other obstructions that may be in your path. (A friendly reminder: Pirates have been known to discard bodies in the local waterways. Try not to panic if you come across one.)

SWIM FOR IT (SAFELY)

Swimming plus clothing typically doesn't equal survival, so strip down to avoid being weighed down by wet clothes. A plastic bag or rain poncho is a good way to keep the stuff you've looted nice and dry, while also making for a handy flotation device. Swim on your back with your feet facing downstream to protect against impact with obstructions like rocks or other submerged debris. Paddle with your hands to guide yourself toward the far bank. Despite the speed of the surging water, swimming across a river safely is a slow process. Yes, you'll make landfall a long way down the river from your intended destination, but being dead is a bigger inconvenience in this humble observer's opinion. If all else fails and your safe attempt at a river crossing devolves into an off-the-rails water ride, see the next section—and hold on tight!

008 RIDE A RAGING RIVER

Caution should always be taken when crossing any body of moving water, and in the Rook Islands' untamed wilds I found both plenty of moving water and a need for caution. The speed of a current can be visually deceiving and if you're not properly prepared, even knee-deep water can knock you off your feet, throw you against rocks, toss you over waterfalls, and send you out to sea into the dominion of great white sharks and pirate boat patrols. Here are a few tips to help you pilot a river if you find yourself at the mercy of an angry current. Hopefully, your excursion is relatively piranha-free!

GO FEET FIRST

Position your feet facing downstream to use your legs as shock absorbers. Yes, a hard impact on your legs could be bone-shattering painful, but at least your brains will still be in your head.

GET WATER WINGS

Hold on to anything you have that floats and don't fight the current (or you'll tire quickly and get TKO'd). Ride it out and observe the way it flows while keeping an eye out for opportunities to get yourself to shore.

READ THE RIVER

The current is fastest in the narrow parts of the river and slows as it widens. Deep pools form on outside river bends and water flows slower through them, giving you a fighting chance to get to shore.

RIDE OR DIE

Currents flowing around a bend will naturally force you toward the shoreline; use this opportunity to look for a tree branch or overhang to grab onto. The Island jungles are dense with tall, long-rooted trees and vines, so the good news is you should have ample opportunities.

AVOID EDDIES

Avoiding eddies only applies to the life-threatening water phenomenon, not the Rakyat fisherman I met. (If you do see Eddie, say hello. Nice guy.) Eddies are rogue back currents that can tumble you like rag doll physics in a video game. Try and kick yourself away from eddies on the downstream side of a boulder. Swim downstream to get away from overfalls as they also create back currents.

009 SOFTEN YOUR LANDING

Between the tropical plant detritus, mud, and worse, it's a wonder I didn't take a header my very first day on the Islands. (It happened on the second day.) Despite the cavalier encouragement of Sir David Lee Roth to just "go ahead and jump," remember that he wasn't the lead singer of *Survivor*—a fall of just ten feet can cause serious injury, and falls from greater heights can be fatal. So if you find yourself needing to de-elevate, and quickly, here are a few ways to improve your survival chances so you can get back to dancing the night away—or at least maintaining your speed while you run through the jungle from whatever threatens you.

HAVE A LOOK DOWN

Scope out your landing options. This is the real world, not an Abstergo simulation, so it goes without saying you want to aim for soft, even ground like grass, sand, or mud.

YOUR LIFE IN YOUR FOOT'S HANDS

If you've properly prepared in advance for the Rook Islands, you're already wearing rugged, comfortable shoes or boots (preferably with soft insoles). These will come in handy for the hard part: the landing.

DO A PREFLIGHT CHECK

Try to stay as relaxed as possible before jumping—you want your body to be loose to better absorb the impact. Bend your knees, keep your elbows close to your body, and tuck your chin into your neck. Keep your legs together to maximize your chances of landing on your feet.

EYE OF THE TIGER

It's time to trust-fall into the slippery arms of gravity. Keep your eyes focused on your landing spot on the way down as it will help keep your body stabilized during the fall.

STICK THE LANDING

Do your best to land on both feet and let your weight collapse by bending your knees. If you had to jump from a significant height, go into a diagonal roll as you come down—this is the best way to absorb shock, and it also makes you look like a badass action hero.

010 JUMP INTO A CENOTE

For all the ways you can endanger yourself on the Islands, there are just as many ways to beat the sweltering, tropical heat: lakes, rivers, and the fact that the Islands are surrounded by ocean! They also have cenotes—a fancy word for "big sinkholes full of water." They're also the pirate's preferred body of water for disposing of bodies . . . not all of them dead. These geological formations pock the face of the Island and are great for cooling off, but not so great if you find yourself with a cinderblock tied to your ankles, about to be slam-dunked in a sadistic pickup game of pirate hostage basketball. (I heard tell of one crew spray-painting victims' heads orange.) Here are a few tips to help you survive.

KNOW THE MATH

Be aware of heights. Hitting water from even a 30-foot (10 m) fall is the equivalent of getting hit by a car traveling 25 mph (40 kmh). And whether it's a rusty Stryus or a clear deep pool in the bottom of a cenote, if you don't take both seriously, you'll be in a world of hurt very shortly.

CROSS YOUR HEART AND HOPE TO DIVE

The only guaranteed way to survive a plunge like this is . . . to take the stairs instead. But a few WWII-era bunkers aside, the Islands are not blessed overmuch with those; much like love and shoe shopping, you'll want to go in feetfirst. (My first ex-wife always did the higher jumps.)

BRACE FOR IMPACT

Much like when jumping down to solid ground, prep your body for a rough landing: knees slightly bent, arms across your chest, and elbows in. Think of it as doing one last chicken dance before getting turned into dipping sauce. And one more thing: Take a deep breath! (See next item.)

011 HOLD YOUR BREATH

If you survive a fall into water (hopefully with the advice in the previous item), congratulations! Now you might have other problems: You might be injured and have difficulty swimming. You might also find yourself underwater longer than expected—especially if one of Vaas's former crew gave you the gift of a cinderblock corsage and took you to the Enchantment Under the Sea dance! Consider these breathing techniques the currency to buy yourself some more time underwater, whether you safely ascend to friendly company or wait for not-so-friendly company to leave.

RELAX

It's easier said than done, but try to stay calm. Panicking increases your heart rate and your fight-or-flight reflex will demand oxygen, preventing you from being able to hold your breath.

STAY HUNGRY

Your body needs oxygen to digest food. As tempting as it might be to get another serving of roast pork at the Gaztown market, save it for after your swim. Try not to eat anything for a couple of hours before taking a dip and that sweet, sweet extra oxygen can be all yours!

EXPAND YOUR LUNG HORIZONS

You can increase your lung capacity and condition your body to function on lower levels of oxygen with static apnea training—simply put, breathing exercises. Hold your breath for fifteen seconds, then rest for one minute. Repeat this five more times, adding five seconds to each time you hold your breath.

KEEP UP THE CARDIO

Cardiovascular exercises (running, cycling, swimming, and the like) improve how efficiently your body uses oxygen. Keep in shape with at least a half hour of activity daily! In all the time I spent on the Rook Islands, I couldn't always find a ride from place to place—and I'll admit I did a lot of running for nonhitchhiking reasons—so if you keep it up as I did, holding your breath underwater should be no problem at all!

012 PUNCH OUT A SHARK

The Rook Islands have a bit of a shark problem. Marine biologists say the high great white population around the Islands is just from natural migration patterns. Locals say it's because pirates dispose of so many dead bodies in the ocean that they attract great whites like they were chumming in *Jaws*. I don't know who's right, but I can give you a few tips to help you out in a shark fight—no bigger boat needed.

AVOID REEFS

The vibrant marine life in reefs tends to draw great white sharks like pumpkin spice season pulls in crowds at Starbucks. These aquatic predators also lurk in the shallows near food sources. Try to avoid these areas if you're afloat in open water.

HEAD TO THE BASEMENT

Sometimes the safest option is nonconfrontation—at least if you have the air to spare. If you're on a dive and you're confronted by a shark, descend to the seabed and wait until the shark leaves the area.

GO FOR THE NOSE AND EYES

The easiest way to successfully punch out a shark is to be Dave Bautista. But since you're probably not him, try to remember the nose, eyes, and gills. According to marine biologists, a shark's nose is covered in microscopic sensing organs that let them detect other organisms in the dark (my local buddy Eddie confirmed this), and a gentle nose massage may be all you need to sedate this curious killer fish. (He did not confirm that part). If Bruce isn't buying it or if you don't feel like playing nice, then go for the eyes or gills; a swift blow, especially if you have a dive knife, could send it swimming home crying to its shark mom!

013 TAKE OUT A TAPIR WITH A KNIFE

Tapirs: the Rook Islands' tiny elephant swine! With an abundant population of these part pig, part potential wallet, all-delicious animals, a tasty meal (and perhaps a leather accessory or two) is usually never far away. But bringing one down means knowing how to perform emergency tapir shoulder surgery with a big scalpel. Luckily, my good friend Eddie the fisherman showed me how to do it.

MAKE A SNEAK ATTACK

You don't want to go head-on with a beast like this, so sneak up behind the tapir while it's distracted with rooting around in the local shrubbery. But be careful as you get close; they get mean if they feel threatened. Make sure you're able to back away in case you end up in a tapir gang fight.

GET A LEG UP

Grab the hind legs above the hooves, hold tight, and lift the tapir like a wheelbarrow. If you take away their ability to use their back legs, you take away their strength. Now you're in control! The meat and hide are valuable on the Rook Islands: Start thinking about what camo paint job you want to pimp out your personal firearm with!

KNIFE TO MEET YOU, TAPIR

Flip the tapir over on its side as if you were dumping that imaginary wheelbarrow and place your knee on the animal's shoulder. Thrust the knife as hard as you can, low and behind the shoulder, and sink the blade up to the hilt to pierce heart, lung, or hopefully both. Keep your weight on until the animal is still and be sure it's dead-dead before you get up and prepare for skinning.

014 ESCAPE JELLYFISH

Ah, the immortal jellyfish, the graceful medusae of the sea! While not all species of jellyfish are lethal, the venom in the harpoon-like organelles of those in this part of the world can turn your heart to stone in a single sting (killing you, in other words). So, keep your eyes open for these brainless bags of briny ocean preserves, as you shark-box and play Marco Polo with pirates in the pristine Rook Island waters. Sea creatures of all viscosities will soon fear you!

SPOT THE WATER

As if jellyfish weren't horrifying enough in general as mindless colony organisms, many also have long, venomous tentacles. These will float on the surface if one is nearby so leave the area if you spot any of these toxic tendrils. Jellyfish species can be colorful or clear and come in varying sizes. The Portuguese man-of-war, for example, can be spotted by the inflated blue and purple "sail" floating on the water. Nature often uses bright colors as warning signs, so listen to what she tells you: Avoid these things!

DRESS FOR THE OCCASION

The easiest way to deal with a sting is never to be stung at all. Wear a full body wet suit to protect against jellyfish stings; the thick artificial fabric will armor you up. Add booties, gloves, and a hood or goggles.

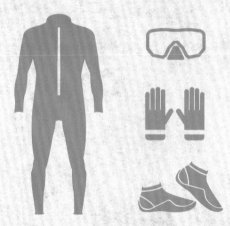

015 TREAT JELLYFISH STINGS

Once, as a freelancer writing an article for an educational magazine, I overdosed on mescaline at an aquarium and ended up in the jellyfish tank in my underwear, wielding a mop like a trident. Searing pain radiated from stings on my arms for hours afterward. Noting the reddish tentacle marks that ran up my arm, my burly cellmate in the drunk tank that night chastised me for doing heroin wrong. This particular species wasn't fatal, but even with some nonlethal jellyfish, pain lingers for days—weeks, even. When it finally does subside, you still feel the phantom pains of those graceful yet deadly jellyfish.

AVOID THE NUMBER ONE ADVICE

Contrary to popular belief, peeing on jellyfish stings doesn't help to heal them, nor does peeing directly on jellyfish. I tried both options after preparing with a few painkilling medicinal beers and the stings only burned worse. Skip this option; with all the dangers you'll encounter in these waters, you'll pee yourself at some point regardless.

GIVE A LITTLE TLC

Use a pair of tweezers to remove barbs or any tentacle remnants stuck on your skin. Flush the affected area with vinegar or salt water but do not scrub or scrape it! The friction will trigger any remaining microscopic barbs still stuck in your skin. Rinse with hot water around 113°F (45°C) for at least twenty minutes; the washing action will help soothe skin and dislodge stingers, while the high heat—nearly unbearable as it is—will help deactivate some of the proteins in the venom. Take some anti-inflammatory pain meds and maybe consider a medicinal beer or three.

MONITOR SYMPTOMS

Most people will recover from a sting, albeit with a bit more respect for jellyfish afterward. But if you've been stung and you're experiencing more severe symptoms like difficulty breathing, chest pains, throat swelling, or serious nausea or vomiting, then get medical attention immediately.

016 GET FAMILIAR WITH THE FLORA

In the wrong circumstances, a trip to the Rook Islands will mean dodging pirates and apex predators. Even in the right circumstances, you can still get hurt, like on one of my fishing trips with Eddie: A nasty scrape on a rocky reef left a nastier inflamed rash down my entire arm—until he applied a paste of aloe and goat's foot, and the pain and swelling gradually subsided. The Islands have a vast taxonomy of exotic floral species that can be great resources for crafting pain relievers, wound remedies, or boiling into cold-fighting teas. Keep this guide handy as you travel so you don't accidentally ingest the wrong plant, and drop dead on the Rooks Island's exotic floor-a.

When it comes to identifying poisonous flora species, you get by with a little help from your senses.

LOOK

The best way to avoid contact with poison flora is knowing what to look for so study pictures of plant life indigenous to the region. I've even done some of the leg work for you!

SMELL

Give it a good whiff: Much like most things, a pungent odor is a good indicator to not put it in your mouth.

TOUCH

Test for contact poisoning: Hold a small piece of the plant on your inner elbow for a few minutes. Burning, itches, or rashes means the plant hates you.

TASTE

Tear off a very small piece and chew it in your mouth for approximately fifteen minutes. If it tastes bitter or soapy, spit it out and forage insects instead.

GOLDEN BEEHIVE
(*Zingiber spectabile*)
Native; inedible. Grounds into poultice for inflammatory eyes and food preservation.

ALOE (*Aloe vera*)
Non-native; edible. Originally from the Arabian Peninsula, aloe now grows worldwide, and is used in foods, as a topical medicine (just ask Eddie!), and as a laxative. Pick your own on the Islands; some pirates like to dose open jars of aloe with battery acid for the worst chemical peel "prank" ever.

ARROWROOT
(*Tacca leontopetaloides*)
Native, edible, and easily digestible. Can be used in cooking as a starch, or added to homemade ice cream—like the stuff I bought at Amanaki market for Eddie's fishing trip—to thicken it up and reduce freezer-burn.

SCREWPINE
(*Pandanus tectorius*)
Native; inedible. Grows in subtropical locations or higher tropical elevations. The sturdy leaves can be used in crafting and are in abundant supply on the Island. Plus it has a hilarious name.

GOOD LUCK PLANT
(*Cordyline fruticosa*)
Native; edible. Also called cabbage palm (which sounds like a very unlucky skin rash), and used as medicine, food, and decoration. Also used to make the Hawai'ian alcoholic drink Okolehao—good luck indeed!

RHODODENDRON
(*Rhododendron sp.*)
Native; inedible. Grows in higher altitudes. Toxic to certain species of wildlife and can cause illness if ingested. (And it never fought a famous movie monster.)

TORCH GINGER
(*Etlingera elatior*)
Native; edible. Mostly used for decorative purposes. Ripe seed pods are used for cooking fish. Also makes a great burlesque name.

HELICONIA (*Heliconia rostrata*)
Native; inedible. Its brightly colored red and yellow-green flowers make a striking decorative plant all over the Islands.

HIBISCUS (*Hibiscus rosa-sinensis*)
Native; leaves edible when dried. Grows in subtropical and tropical regions. Locals drink hibiscus honey tea with a touch of lemon and more than a touch of whiskey as a traditional cold remedy.

PALANI
(*Hedychium coccineum*)
Non-native; edible. Also called ginger lily, palani is actually hybridized from a Hawai'ian lily. Growing tall and beautiful, its roots are edible but tasteless; the flowers hold essential oils used in Island remedies, like Palani Cocaine.

YELLOW SAGE (*Salvia officinalis*)
Non-native; inedible. Capable of growing in beaches and grasslands, with berries toxic to humans. Pirates sometimes like to mess with hostages by offering them Yellow Sage tea.

KELP (*Sargassum mangarevense*)
Native; edible. Grows offshore of the Islands in underwater "forests" and in tropical regions worldwide, kelp is packed with vitamins and the Rakyat believe it helps dieters shed weight.

BLUE ALGAE
(*Arthrospira platensis*)
Native; edible. Found in underwater caves on the Islands, blue algae is actually a bacterium, but this version is still edible and has a high protein content—but avoid bright blue algae and other toxic types.

BREEZE WAKAME
(*Undaria pinnatifida*)
Transient species; edible. Used in soups and salads, wakame has an enzyme that can help burn away fatty tissue. Still just an invasive seaweed species despite the cool name.

LOTUS FLOWER
(*Nelumbo nucifera*)
Native; edible. Aquatic flora species also known as water lily. Often considered sacred, and used by holy men to adorn temples and graves.

GOAT'S FOOT
(*Ipomoea pes-caprae*)
Native; medicinal; salt-tolerant and grows near beaches—good thing because it's used in poultices, including for jellyfish stings. The name suggests it's probably also used by witch doctors and warlocks.

TIARE (*Gardenia taitensis*)
Native; inedible. Often worn by young women, it's called a "jealous flower" for its solitary growing space—apt, considering how young Rakyat women will cut you if you intrude on their space.

017 CATCH MONKEYS WITH COCONUTS

I met quite a supporting cast of colorful characters in my time exploring the Rook Islands, but none were louder than one of the only other Americans I ran into: Hurk Drubman Jr. I often found him in two places—living on a barge called *Big Sally*, and at the top of PETA's most wanted list for strapping C-4 vests to monkeys. (For more on this high explosive, see item 076.) Needless to say, the Islands' primates are distrustful towards humans for this and many other reasons, so catching them is a challenge. Still, you can trade them with locals as pets and net some quick cash, maybe even swap a few for a weapon.

READY THE TRAP

Cut a hole in a coconut shell just big enough for a tiny, curious monkey paw to reach in. Pour out the fluid and fill it with nuts, fruits, or sweets—monkeys go crazy for that stuff. Tightly secure the coconut to the base of a tree.

SET IT AND FORGET IT

At some point a monkey will eventually show up, unable to resist the sweet aroma of your bait. The hole is only big enough to get

a money paw in, so they won't be able to pull out a fist chock full of nuts. While the monkey stubbornly refuses to relinquish its gourmet prize, you can quietly sneak up behind it and collect your own. How's that for evolution?

NET THE GAINS

Before you capture your new friend, do some stretches, and get a sturdy crate or a basket with a lid to hold your catch as well as a fisherman's net to snag your would-be buddy. If you're lucky, you might find one at an abandoned dock around the Islands. Or if he likes you, Eddie the nice Rakyat fisherman might let you rent one.

SOFTLY SOFTLY CATCH A MONKEY

While the monkey is busy trying to figure out why its paw has doubled in size and won't come free, sneak up on it (see item **024 / Move with Stealth**) and then fling the net. Crating or basketing up the critter while you're being pelted with feces, I leave to you. Good luck out there!

018 GO CUCKOO FOR COCONUTS

Much like many other places in the South Pacific, the Rook Islands are absolutely covered in palm trees—especially coconut palms. If you find yourself out of food, drink, or even some of your travel and safety accessories after betting one time too many at a card game (see item **030 / Play Poker with Locals**), take advantage of the endless coconut supply on the Rook Islands to survive in a pinch. You can eat them, drink them, make lotion from the oil, play the role of Patsy the coconut-clacking squire from *Monty Python and the Holy Grail*, or make a nice tapir curry. The possibilities are absolutely endless in this tropical wonderland!

SAFETY FIRST!

Make sure a coconut is safe to consume. Shake it—if it's heavy and you hear the water splashing around inside, it's good. If the shell is grey or the meat inside is yellow in color, it's bad.

CRACK IT OPEN

Rip away the fibrous husk by handfuls; once you have the round inner nut in hand, carefully crack it open with a machete or a sharp rock. Coconuts evolved to withstand a long drop from a treetop, so don't try to break it by flinging it at the ground; you just might see it bounce and then smash through a nearby window. (Yes, personal experience is talking here.)

DRINK ME

Green coconuts are a good source of drinkable water and electrolytes. But don't overdo it! Too much consumption can lead to diarrhea—one of the surefire fastest routes to dehydration.

EAT ME

The brown fuzzy spheres are the rib roast of fruits. The meat is high in potassium and lauric acid, which supports the immune system. But humans aren't the only Island dwellers that like to eat coconuts. Try using some as trap bait; maybe you'll catch a tapir or monkey with one. Circle of life, man! (See items **013** and **017 / Take Out a Tapir with a Knife** and **Catch Monkeys with Coconuts** for more on those animals.)

SLATHER ME

Martinize your skin suit! Crush the coconut meat to extract the oil and apply liberally over the parts where the sun gets in. Coconut oil helps protect against sunburns by blocking roughly twenty percent of the sun's UV rays.

BURN ME

The fibers in the dead husks of coconut shells are great tinder for a fire—or to use as a beard while belting Kenny Rogers songs at a karaoke bar in a hollowed-out tree stump.

KNIT ME

Fibers from certain species of coconuts' outer almond-shaped shell can be woven in cordage and fabrics, including sturdy rope. If you have some time to kill, making coconut-fur socks is a great opportunity to get a jump on that Christmas shopping.

019 CLIMB A RADIO TOWER

Those giant metal spires I saw scattered across the Islands turned out to be radio towers—critical communication hubs that are the Rook Islands' equivalent of skyscrapers. If a tower goes offline, the outage can disrupt trade and prevent critical supplies from getting to those who need them, most notably the Rakyat. From time to time they might want assistance in activating out-of-commission towers (and may offer a reward in the bargain), so here are a few traversal tips.

PLAN YOUR ASCENT

Scope out the entire structure from top to bottom and make a brain map of viable climbing routes. If you make it halfway up and run out of real estate, you could find yourself quickly losing grip and arm strength.

OUT ON THREE LIMBS

You have four functional limbs (ideally), and all four should be to maintain stability when climbing like the gravity-defying, half-octopus that you are. Maintain three points of contact at all times, using the fourth to reach for your next contact point.

RAZOR YOUR EXPECTATIONS

Razor wire can be a real pain, so throw a jacket, towel, or any piece of heavy clothing over it to protect against razor burn; an infection from rusted razor wire is bound to be a nasty one, tetanus or not.

BE A STEEL MOUNTAINEER

Climbing tools such as ropes and grappling hooks (see items **063** and **064** / **Hurl a Grappling Hook** and **Rappel on the Fly**) can make climbing much easier and can sometimes be scavenged on the Rook Islands. Plenty of professional spelunkers have come to the Rook Islands to explore the labyrinthine systems of underground caves and left some of their climbing gear behind to be used by pirates stashing caches of guns and drugs. If you're short on coconut husk rope, these will come in especially handy.

020 GET A GOOD VANTAGE POINT

As a journalist, it's important for me to make sure that I always have a solid point of view—and this definitely rings true for surviving on the Rook Islands. When it comes to both, the higher you get, the better the view. Whether surveilling a pirate camp to find the best ways into, out of, or around it, or to just enjoy the stunning view, here's how to get high on Rook Islands without all the drugs.

BE A WALL CRAWLER

Need to clear a wall? Look for any viable point to grab or step on. Holes in rock or concrete, extruding or bent pipes or rebar, rough edges—anything that can successfully support your weight is fair game. Gradually add your weight to test the strength of a grab point before committing yourself fully.

GO UP THE CHIMNEY

Scaling a narrow rocky fissure or even a pair of close neighboring walls is all about the shimmy: Find the narrowest part (also called a "chimney" in climbing terms) and put your back against one wall and your foot against the wall in front of you. Place the other foot on the wall behind you, knees bent, and push up with your legs and arms. Repeat by alternating legs until you reach the top.

BE BARBED WIRE WALKER

If you're climbing a fence with barbed wire strung across the top, take the middle route—it's where the wire is the loosest and is therefore the easiest place to cross. Just as with climbing a radio tower, use a shirt or blanket as protective padding on rusted metal or razor wire.

021 BREAK INTO PRISON

Prison can be a subjective term: It can be a dead-end job, a loveless marriage, or an actual prison! I should know: I've been locked inside all three! The question is, "Why would anyone want to break *into* a prison?" If you're asking yourself that question, you've never had friends or loved ones held hostage by sadistic pirates on the Rook Islands. One of Eddie's friends, meanwhile, did—his story gave plenty of insight on ins and outs (see the next item) of a camp. So if you're reading this to prep for a daring suicide-rescue mission, take a dead man's dose of liquid courage, a sidearm, and the tips outlined below.

KNOW BEFORE YOU GO

Assess the layout of the camp you're breaking into. Know all exits, guard posts, and patrol routes (see item **020 / Get a Good Vantage Point** to learn how to scout a location). Make sure you bring all the tools you'll need (see below).

CONSUME A STEALTHY DIET

The best feature of jungles is the dense plant life. Move within foliage for extra cover and stay low to the ground when you move to limit sound output. (See item **024 / Move with Stealth** for more help—before you head in.)

USE NATURE'S DISTRACTION

Lots of things grow on a formerly volcanic tropical isle: wildflowers, crops (both the food and "medicinal" type), and rocks. They're everywhere! Pick one up, find a spot away from your route, and throw it that way to play a little Rook Island rock music! With any luck they'll go investigate; make your move then.

PICK A LOCK, ANY LOCK

If you've made it all the way up to a cage, you're halfway there! Unless you stole a pirate jailer's keys, you'll need a hairpin, a paper clip, a steady hand, and a prayer to pick a pirate cage lock. (If you're unfamiliar with picking locks, see item **113 / Pick Locks like a Pro**.)

IN CASE OF EMERGENCY

Not everything will go according to plan during your break-in: You can have a bad rock toss happen, or step on a brittle twig, or even open the wrong door on accident and walk straight into a pirate drug lab. Whatever the case may be, if you should happen to find yourself in a life-and-death situation and you don't know what else to do, try using the Swiss Army knife of survival tips: RUN!

022 ESCAPE A PIRATE CAMP

The idea of pirate camp sounds like a dream summer outing when you're a kid, but it's honestly a nightmarish hellscape as an adult. First, the bad news: You'll face bloodthirsty, drug-smuggling pirates who delight in torturing people. The good news? Chains are heavy and a pain in the ass to lug around, so there's a high probability rope or electrical tape will be used to bind wrists—and can be cut! Use this glimmer of hope as your inspirational cat poster to motivate your pirate camp escape. Now get to work!

TIME IT RIGHT

Before you can begin to free yourself or others, check for guards. Wait for a lull to begin your escape. (There's always a lull, especially during the hottest parts of the day.)

USE NATURE'S DISTRACTION

Once again, thrown rocks make for a simple attention-getters. Choose your moment wisely and make a break for an exit. (Just don't break anything. See below.)

BECOME A CROUCH POTATO

Take one false step while making your way through a pirate camp and you likely won't get another one. Stay low and slow when moving to minimize your sound output while remaining in the shadows.

MAKE LIKE A TREE AND LEAVE

The best feature of jungles is the dense plant life, and there's plenty of it. Use it to your advantage and move stealthily within foliage for cover. (See item **024 / Move with Stealth** for more on staying stealthy.)

UPGRADE TO GRENADES

Rocks are good for distractions but won't help you in a grenade-throwing contest, so add to your arsenal: Take any knives, firearms, or explosives that may be lying around within reach . . . quietly.

023 FLEE A BURNING BUILDING

From "gun-" to "bon-," the Rook Islands' pirates really love fire. One lurid tale I picked up involved pirates holding relay races by dousing victims in gasoline and lighting them on fire, just to bet on which one made it farthest before collapsing. They tend to do this in places like out behind the old Island Port Hotel—and I just know one day that place is going up and taking any occupants with it. Should you need to egress from a burning building (or that hotel in particular), here's some useful advice.

STAY LOW

Heat rises, so get on your hands and knees to stay low as you look for an exit, and be sure to cover your mouth with a damp cloth so you don't choke on smoke or burn your lungs.

BE A KNOB SNOB

Despite what your childhood cartoons may have taught you, a superheated doorknob doesn't always glow comically red, but it can still burn you badly, so you should always feel the door for heat instead using the back of your hand. Also, look under the door for any visible indicators of fire and consider those "Do Not Enter" signs. If you see anything, look for another exit.

USE ELEMENTAL POWERS

If you need to deal with a small fire in your way to safety or if your clothing catches flame, take the air from a fire's lungs by smothering it. Throw a heavy blanket or jacket over the flame, covering it completely.

DON'T BE A HERO

Stay focused on your main objective: survival. Never linger in a burning building to fight a fire or search for others. On average, you have about two minutes before heat and smoke overwhelm you so get out as fast as you can. Once you're out safely, your best bet is to stay that way.

024 MOVE WITH STEALTH

A good journalist has to know when to tread lightly, and between round-the-clock gunfire and bloodthirsty wildlife, I often slept with one eye open during my stay on the Rook Islands. Staying alive is a great reason to learn to move with a light foot, whether you're skirting a sleeping pirate on a midday siesta or edging around a drowsing panther's nap spot. Here are a few notes I took on how to stealthily try not to wake someone (or something) that would kill you just for ruining its nap.

WEIGH YOUR OPTIONS

Carrying anything heavy (like a rucksack full of scavenged relics) will throw off your center of balance. Load the weighty stuff lowest in your pack, and if need be, ditch the gear to move naturally.

STAY SILENT

A jingle in the jungle can spell the end of the line; stealth means silence, so secure or drop anything on your person that may make a noise when you move: keys, rodent skull necklaces, syringes, fuzzy pink handcuffs, and so on.

WALK WITH YOUR EYES

Never move blindly; always know the best route to take so you can avoid any land mines—and by "land mines," I mean any object that can give you away if stepped on: broken glass, twigs, dry leaves, or actual land mines.

TAKE YOUR TIME

Keep your footfalls as quiet as possible. Put one foot down slowly, walking heel to toe and testing the ground as you tread; gradually transfer your weight fully onto that foot before taking another step.

RUN THROUGH THE JUNGLE

When things go wrong, make sure you run in the right direction. Be mindful of your surroundings as you move and plot an escape route in case nap time is cut short.

025 CREATE DISTRACTIONS

Rocks may be great for distractions, but they can only get you so far: I once tried to draw attention by throwing a stone, only to botch my throw and tag the shoulder of a pirate who came over to investigate the disturbance and brought three more pirates with him. Luckily, I slipped away in time. If you need to up your misdirection game, use these Rook Island sleight-of-hand tricks to help you disappear from dumb and dangerous situations.

LOSE A TAIL

The pirates here love drugs and money almost as much as they love torture and violence. If you think you're being tracked, try leaving a trail of loot in the opposite direction you're moving in. Anything that has trade value on the Island will do just fine—like money, jewelry, weapons, cocaine, hapless tourists . . .

BE A ROCK SHOW PYRO

Sure, a rock is good for getting a single pirate to leave a guard post, but you'll need something with a bigger bang if you're dealing with a patrol squad. Since throwing a boulder is on the impractical side, explosives can replicate the effect while saving your back and groin. Some well-placed C-4 (see item **077 / Set a C-4 Charge**) or an accurate grenade toss should do the trick. (Bonus distraction points if your explosion starts a rockslide!)

OFF TO THE RACES

Sometimes you must become the distraction, and nothing will get a pirate distracted more than stealing their drugs or vehicles. Try to stick to jeeps or four wheelers—they're the easiest to drive, as I discovered as part of my egress, but pirates tend to keep their stashes aboard; stay frosty behind that wheel!

026 LEARN TO DEAL WITH LAND MINES

While I enjoy a good nature hike as much as the next person, when I asked Eddie about the idea, he kinda paled under his Rakyat Islander tan, then shook his head at me. In the aftermath of World War II, a whole lot of unexploded land mines were left all over the South Pacific. The Rook Islands are now the stadium where pirates make hostages play sadistic games of flag football. But danger lurks under your feet at most every step; land mines are hidden almost anywhere on the Islands. Here's how to improve your chances of not bombing in the big game.

GET THE INSIDE SCOOP

The Rakyat know this Island better than anyone, so ask around for any hot spots to avoid. This is also beneficial as overgrowth can conceal any visible warning signs over time. (Also, pirates are dicks and get a kick out of removing actual warning signs.

USE YOUR MINE'S EYE

Most land mines are hidden, but the occasional telltale sign can be visible and if you know what to look for,

you'll have a leg up in preventing your leg from being blown up: Gopher hole-like mounds of earth, old trip wires, suspicious objects in trees, and wires leading away from a road are just some of the more common indicators. Also look for dead animals—they often detonate land mines accidentally.

MOVE BACK DOWNFIELD

If you suspect you've walked into a minefield, either because you've spotted a telltale sign or your running back just exploded, slowly back out the way you came, stepping carefully in the footsteps you walked in on.

BE A DIVE-BOMBER

There are no guaranteed ways to survive a land mine step. Factors such as the age and condition of the mine as well as its construction all vary, but no matter what, a mine's explosive force goes up and out. Your best bet is to hit the ground on your stomach to avoid as much of that cone of damage as possible. Unless you're an explosive ordinance disposal specialist, the only disarming will be when your arms are blown off your body.

027 REPEL BOAT BOARDERS

When the Raykat go fishing, they bring friends—and armed ones at that. Boating safety is critical as you set sail for tranquility on the Rook Island waterways. There is a high population of sharks in the choppy waters, and also the occasional heavily armed and bored pirate patrol hopped up on cocaine and hallucinating on mescaline who looks at a tiny boat and sees a yacht instead. (Always take one or the other, never both, unless you want to deal with an overdose—see item **124 / Recover from an Overdose** for more on that.) Remember when pirates just drank rum and made you walk a plank? Simpler times, man.

FORM A FLOTILLA

If at all possible, travel in a convoy with other boats if you have to sail near pirate-occupied waters. If traveling at night, keep the lights off.

BATTEN THE HATCHES

Secure all hatches and doors on your vessel with inner-locking iron bars when anchored, so no one unwelcome can find a way in.

CHOOSE TO FIGHT

Every pirate you encounter has a 100 percent chance of being armed, so you may want to think about defending yourself. If you don't have a gun or knife and your back is to the wall, most sea vessels have emergency flare guns. Grab one (or two) and a few reloads, Christopher Cross your heart, and be ready for a tooth-and-nail confrontation.

MAKE YOUR ESCAPE

If your vessel is boarded, retreat to the inner cabin and lock yourself in. Try to call for a mayday on the radio; at least one Raykat fishing trawler is almost always out on the waters around the Islands. Also, try to alert other boats in the vicinity using any available means, including your vessel's bullhorn or loudhailer: use the lights, sirens, foghorn, Foghat, Gino Vannelli, Toto, anything from the Michael McDonald Doobie Brothers era . . . seriously, do not be afraid to bring out those big guns!

028 SURVIVE A SINKING SHIP

If you find yourself on a ship sinking in the Rook Island soup, survival tip number one is to try not to think about the sharks too much. (I had a hard time with that myself, considering how many I saw in the shallows there.) But even though ships sometimes go under, you don't have to. Use these handy tips to safely abandon ship and keep your chances of survival afloat. And remember, whatever you do, try not to think about any sharks.

JUMP THE SHARK

Assess your situation before jumping in and chumming the waters. Abandon ship from the high side if the ship is rolling to avoid getting crushed if it capsizes. Anything higher than 15 feet (5 m) and you'll be shark pizza; find a lower position. Aim for a spot in the water free of debris. Cross your feet at the ankles as you leave the rail to prevent impact injuries. Inhale a big gulp of air before touchdown!

STAY OUT OF HOT WATER

Cross your arms on your chest and grab your lapels. This will protect your neck and shoulders from breaking when you hit the water like a bloody bag of shark chamomile tea.

AVOID A SHARP-NADO

Depending on its size, getting rained on by falling debris is the number one danger of being close to a sinking ship. Swim away from the wreckage and try to get to a distance of at least 100 feet (30 m). Use a sidestroke or backstroke to conserve energy but try not to thrash or splash too much—doing so can attract sharks.

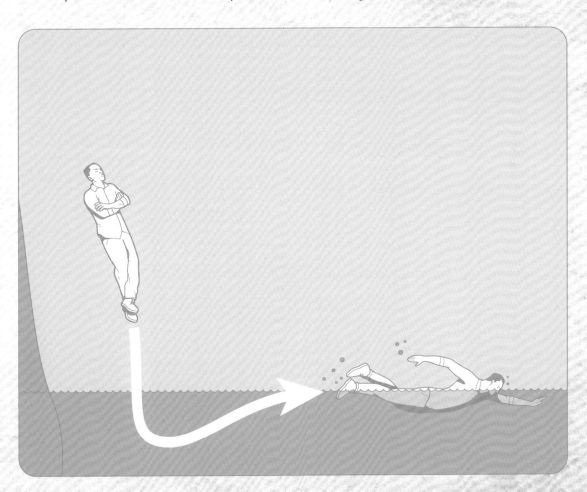

029   TAIL A TARGET

There are countless reasons I wanted to discreetly tail someone on the Rook Islands: Along with dodging pirates and mercenaries, I had a story to follow. Maybe they're heading to a secret hideout or loot cache. Maybe a pirate kidnapped your friends and is holding them in a hidden bunker somewhere. Maybe you took too many mushrooms from Doctor Earnhardt (see item 038 on how to brew a cup of mushroom tea), and you realized you had to follow ancient Rakyat spirits on a journey through old ruins in search of treasure. Whatever your target, use these tips to silently stalk like a Rook Island creep.

STAY A STEP AHEAD

Some people going about their daily routines can be as predictable as video game AI patterns—the same could be said for pirate vehicle patrol patterns. Scouting your target ahead of time will give you a good idea of paths they may take.

STEER CLEAR

Keep your distance to avoid drawing suspicion, especially if you're in a vehicle, and avoid mimicking your mark's movements.

If they make four left turns in a row, they're on to you. If you have to park your ride, face away from your surveillance target and use rearview and side mirrors to keep an eye on them.

GET A SPOT OF TAIL

Traveling the Rook Islands can be a solitary endeavor at times. But if you have a traveling partner, consider using them as a spotter on your next tail.

DO A QUICK CHANGE

If you suspect your target entered a secure location to throw off your tail, casually break away and return with a change of clothing (and identity): You may also want to have a backstory ready to go in the event inquiring pirate minds want to know who you are. Try telling them something like you're location scouting the Island for a swimsuit calendar photoshoot; that worked for me!

030 PLAY POKER WITH THE LOCALS

From the Rakyat to Hoyt Volker and his pirates to that creepy Dr. Earnhardt, it seemed everyone I met or heard of on the Rook Islands loved a good game of cards. I played more than a few rounds and even won a hand now and then, but I'll admit there were times I thought I was about to be cashed out. Luckily for me, it always ended in drinks and not drawn guns; others haven't been so fortunate. Here are a few tips to help you win a hand in poker—and help you keep your actual hand in a game of pirate poker.

KNOW WHEN TO HOLD 'EM

Everybody has a tell—a reflexive glitch in our programming that always seems to give us away when we're trying to conceal the truth for financial gain. Everyone's is different, but one example of a tell for a good hand is lots of small talk or a small smile. Bad hands set off a tell just as much as a good one; look for a slouching, bored posture, avoidance of eye contact, maybe a shaky trigger finger. Also, learn your own tell, and suppress it as best you can.

KNOW WHEN TO FOLD 'EM

If players are working together, they will sometimes use subtle hand gestures to signal each other. Keep an eye on your opponent's table hand and watch for the number of fingers extended. One finger may mean they have a pair; two fingers, two pair; three fingers for three of a kind; an open palm for a full house. Someone with no fingers probably got caught signaling in a pirate poker game.

KNOW WHEN TO WALK AWAY

The Rakyat and other friendly Island inhabitants are often happy to play a game for fun, but the pirate types play for keeps and can be really sore losers. Bring protection with you—a boot knife, a revolver, or a few heavily armed spectators—if you join their table, and don't gloat if you clean them out. In fact, cut your winnings early to cut your losses later, and depart quickly before your opponents become less than magnanimous.

I didn't come to the Rook Islands to hunt *per se*, but hunting is definitely a storied tradition for the Rakyat. (Just ask Eddie the fisherman.) As I learned in my time here, the legendary fauna can turn the tables on even a seasoned hunter—especially true for the bigger dangerous animals imported in the illegal exotic animal trade. If the Rakyat choose to invite you on a hunt, listen to the lore they've collected over the years about the animals they hunt, and know what you're facing, because those faces have rows of sharp teeth and heightened senses.

NAME: Black Panther
(*Panthera pardus*)
LOCATION: Tracked near Orphan Point
LEATHER QUALITY: Rugged but supple; good for fashioning belts and bandoliers.
HUNTING TIPS: Like all big and small cats, black panthers are extremely fast and quiet; pack something that fires faster and louder. Anything fully automatic is recommended; if you're feeling up to a Rakyat hunting challenge, try a well-placed arrow.

NAME: Albino Crocodile
(*Crocodylus porosus*)
LOCATION: Found in swamplands on the South Island
LEATHER QUALITY: This legendary beast's hide will net you a healthy return from a local taxidermist.(Or ask if they can make boots.)
HUNTING TIPS: The armored scutes on a saltwater croc's back are difficult to penetrate with ranged weapons, so a shot to the soft underbelly is the method preferred by Rakyat hunters. (If you go the machete-wielding route, be prepared to wrestle!)

NAME: Undying Bear
(*Ursus thibetanus*)
LOCATION: In the vicinity of Cradle Gas outpost
LEATHER QUALITY: Large, durable; great for sewing into big bags.
HUNTING TIPS: Asian black bears are tough as any bear; you'll need a lead punch to Yogi's pic-a-nic basket to bring this beast down. A shotgun at close range will do the trick—be warned, it may take several shots. But if you survive, the pelts can be used to upgrade your survival gear and with the right seasoning and spices, the rest is an exotic culinary delight.

NAME: Blood Komodo
(*Varanus komodoensis*)
LOCATION: Spotted near Amanaki Outpost
LEATHER QUALITY: Sturdy, pebbly; good for pouches or small bags.
HUNTING TIPS: The bloodstains on the face of a Komodo are a dead giveaway to its predatory nature—and a warning not to trifle with one. High caliber ammo can damage the hide; the Rakyat prefer bows or knives.

NAME: Golden Tiger
(*Panthera tigris*)
LOCATION: Near Mosquito Yard on the North Island
LEATHER QUALITY: Flexible yet tough; great for stowing heavy ammo boxes for the next hunt.
HUNTING TIPS: In the Rakyat tradition, a golden tiger is meant to be hunted using a bow and arrows—but if surviving a tiger attack happens to be part of your own tradition, then you should use a fully automatic rifle. (If you don't have a bow or a rifle, then see item **069 / Stand Up to a Tiger**.)

NAME: Maneater Shark (*Carcharhinus leucas*)
LOCATION: Frequenting a cove near Kell's Boat Repairs, North Island
LEATHER QUALITY: Sturdy, rough, but abrasive; could make a good quiver if you don't mind the texture.
HUNTING TIPS: I'm serious about "maneater"; skip the Jet Ski, get a bigger boat, chum the waters for a bull shark, then perform a lead lobotomy with a high-powered rifle.

NAME: White Belly Tapir (*Tapirus indicus*)
LOCATION: Often seen near Rust Yard Outpost, North Island
LEATHER QUALITY: Smooth, lightweight, resilient; good for small bags for rocks, coconuts, grenades, or other dense objects.
HUNTING TIPS: If you can take one with a knife (see item 015 for more on that), you'll deeply impress the Rakyat, but otherwise, go low caliber. A well-placed arrow will preserve the hide better than a round from a rifle.

NAME: Yellow Neck Cassowary (*Casuarius unappendiculatus*)
LOCATION: Wandering the North Island
LEATHER QUALITY: Durable, stretchy, and highly valuable; useful for slings or straps.
HUNTING TIPS: Don't underestimate this goofy-looking avian species. Cassowaries' beaks and talons make them modern-day velociraptors; they attack in packs and are nasty if provoked. I recommend a long-range sniping option.

NAME: One Horn Buffalo (*Bubalus bubalis*)
LOCATION: In the Badtown region (a great neighborhood!), North Island
LEATHER QUALITY: Tough, highly cut- and abrasion-resistant. Makes a great wallet; add a feather or tooth for a little extra Rook Islands flair!
HUNTING TIPS: Water buffalo are an obvious, but deadly, rarity on the Islands. They charge when threatened, and the thick, horned skull can take a good wallop. Pack a shotgun with solid slug ammo.

032 STICK AND POKE A TATTOO (THE RAKYAT WAY)

When a Rakyat ascends in warrior status, they earn the sacred *tatau* body ink. The more elaborate the *tatau*, the more skilled and experienced the warrior. I was fortunate to have observed the hands of a Rakyat body ink master at work during my time on the Rook Islands and picked up a few basic techniques. It will take years of dedication and practice to master the craft, but if you're feeling brave and want a give yourself a permanent Rooks Islands souvenir, here's how to DIY your own body art with a homebrew stick-and-poke tattoo.

GATHER TATTOO TOOLS

Needle and ink are the two main ingredients in a stick-and-poke tattoo. You can take the needle from a syringe, but make sure it's clean and brand-new; or, you can take the Rakyat example and use bamboo needles or bone splinters! If you're short on pigment, your best bet is to forage a firepit for charcoal ash and mix it with water in a one-to-one ratio to make a carbon-based ink. You'll also need a lighter, a canteen of water, and a rag.

PREPARE YOURSELF

You've got your needle, you've got your ink, and now you need an idea for your design as well as a bit of nerve. Clean your skin with soap and water, or alcohol—use rubbing alcohol if possible, or the highest proof hooch you can find if not. (This option means you can also boost your pain tolerance with a few swigs.) Sterilize the tip of the needle with alcohol as well, or use a lighter. Make it glow!

GET TO POKING

Dip the sterilized needle in the ink and poke it into your skin to leave a small dot. Wipe away any blood as you go and keep filling the lines of your sweet tattoo design one tiny puncture at a time. To fill bigger areas, line up a row of needles and then tape, tie, or glue them to a stick; when it's ready, dip and jab away!

INDULGE IN AFTERCARE

Your body art masterpiece is now complete! Dispose of the used needles and ink—but save the whiskey. Clean the tattoo gently but thoroughly and cover it with petroleum jelly and a bandage for the first day. Uncover it after that and keep it clean, applying antibiotic ointment or more petroleum jelly daily. If you notice any heat, redness, swelling, or pain, seek medical attention; skin infections froma tattoo (or *tatau*) are rare, but need to be taken seriously.

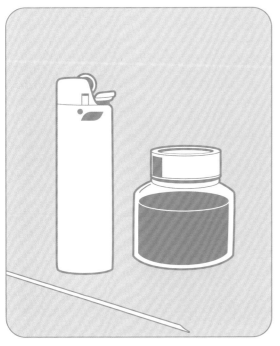
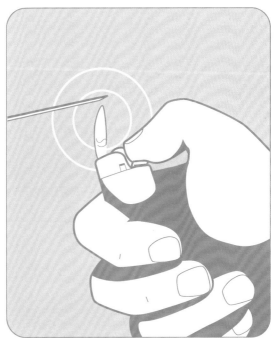
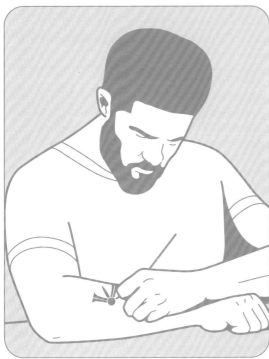
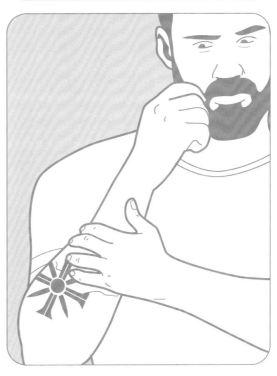

033 IMPROVISE SOME ARMOR

I once read about a soldier in Vietnam saved from a Viet Cong sniper's bullet by a dictionary in his rucksack for writing letters home. The tome turned a shot to his back from "spine-severing" to "rib-cracking." (Yet another reason to carry one of my guides at all times!) Adapt that story to life on the Rook Islands, because a bullet shattering bones and piercing vital organs will end your vacation real quick—maybe your life! It's dangerous out there, and armor does a body good, but Kevlar doesn't grow on trees. The homebrew methods I learned below may not stop everything that flies your way, but these thrift store options can armor an aspiring Rook Island knight on a scrap budget!

THE DECADENT METHOD

Ceramic floor tiles and denim can easily be scavenged on the Rook Islands; get your hands on construction adhesive, and you'll be all set. Cut a swatch of denim to about 18 by 18 inches (45 x 45 cm) to fit a 6-by-6-inch (15 x 15 cm) tile. Using the construction adhesive, glue the tile to the center of the denim,

adding a new layer of adhesive for each fold; reinforce it with a little sheet metal scavenged from a tin roof for the best armor no money can buy. Strap a set of these to your torso for serious protection—keep in mind, getting shot still hurts even without traumatic injury.

THE DECENT METHOD

If the pen is mightier than the sword, then the book is mightier than the bullet . . . if it has enough pages. Take a couple of thick, wordy books (maybe not the one you're currently reading) and tape them together for some cheap bullet wound insurance. If you can find ceramic tiles, slip one or two in for added shielding.

THE DESPERATE METHOD

If you're low on denim, metal, and ceramic supplies, don't despair; desperate times call for desperate measures. If all else fails, tape a few thick magazines around your shins and forearms, stack a few sturdy, good quality books over your abdomen, and hope the pirates are using squirt guns that day.

034 SHOOT FROM THE HIP

As an intrepid—some might say roguish—world traveling gonzo-journalist-poet with a complete disregard for his safety and liver, I have two things on me at all times: something to write the story with, and something to defend myself from the story should that survival page need to be turned. That's why I always travel with a pistol in my typewriter case and why I've had to practice extensively. On the Rook Islands, there are the quick and the dead; if you want to be the former and not the latter, here's how to outdraw your opponents like an M1911 Rembrandt.

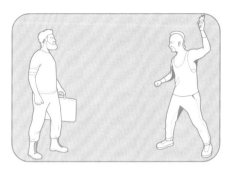

STEP 1

Get close. Hip-firing sacrifices accuracy, but at 10 feet (3 m) you won't have time to fully draw before your opponent is on top of you, so it's in your best survival interests to get the first shot. Stay in a 10- to 20-foot (3 to 6 m) range. If a pirate corners you at the local cantina to collect your bounty, this method works great for shooting under tables.

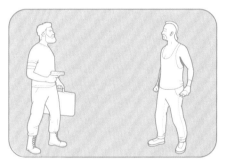

STEP 2

As you're slowly reaching into your typewriter case at the cantina—or wherever you keep your firearm holstered on your person—raise your arm at the elbow to draw, keeping the elbow socketed firmly in your side. This will help align your body with the gun barrel and stabilize your shot.

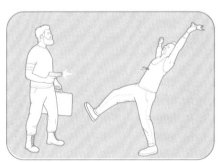

STEP 3

Take your shot! You probably have less than a second to go from holster to bolster, so try to make sure you stick your hip-fire landing with your forearm and gun parallel to the ground, keeping your wrist stiff, then fire.

STEP 4

Pay the nice Rakyat barkeeper for his trouble and apologize for the impromptu Jackson Pollock painting you just splattered across his wall.

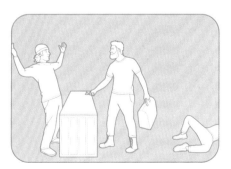

I like to take breaks while I write to let my thoughts percolate. One day after just such a break, I returned to my shack only to see someone making off on a battered motorcycle with my beloved typewriter, case and all—but I'd thought to keep my pistol with me. (Target practice sometimes helps me clear my head.) He didn't get far before my "warning" shot killed his ride. Shooting from the hip requires close quarters, speed, and very little thought. But for moving targets at a distance, you'll need a level head and a steady aim! Give your pistol and rifle game some range with these tips to help you accurately shoot—whether target-plinking out back of Amanaki market, or shooting the tire on a motorcycle ridden by a pirate with your stolen typewriter case.

KNOW YOUR PISTOL GEOMETRY

It doesn't take an expert in ballistics to know targets are harder to hit when they're moving or far away, but to accurately hit them you do need to know a little gun math. The most effective handgun firing stance is called the "Power Isosceles." Get square with your target and stand with your feet shoulder-width apart. Aim your gun with both hands while leaning slightly forward, and then slide your strong foot to the rear for increased stabilization while you're firing.

STAND ATOP THE RIFLE TOWER

Good footwork is the strong, sturdy foundation that rifle accuracy is built upon. Stand with your feet about shoulder-width apart and bend your knees slightly to take a boxer's stance. This posture will allow you to pivot quickly if you're engaging multiple targets. Lean forward slightly when aiming your rifle in order to better absorb the recoil. Dig your elbows into your sides firmly, too, so you don't chicken-wing your firing arm and end up throwing off your shot.

036 CHAR CROPS WITH A FLAMETHROWER

I initially got into flamethrowers back in 'Nam: I was in my hotel in Saigon on a layover from Malaysia last year, watching *The Thing*. As I beheld Kurt Russell lighting aliens on fire, I just knew I had to find and master a flamethrower myself. As I found from both trying one out myself (and later finding a blackened field on the North Island where someone went scorched-earth on a cannabis farm) they're great at their one task: burning everything to ashes. But they can be just as dangerous to the wielder as they are for the target—such as a hostage covered in chocolate syrup and marshmallow fluff in a pirate camp. (If their name was actually Graham, Vaas deserves creativity points on that one.) Pirates and victims aside, flamethrowers are used for controlled prescribed burns and destroying military equipment. Whatever the reason you're picking one up, here's how to wield one safely and effectively.

INSPECT YOUR GEAR

A broken flamethrower valve can spell a very hot end to your day (and to everyone within a 50-foot radius!) so check to ensure the seals, tank, and chassis are in proper working order, with no dings, knocks, scratches, or leaks.

HEAT IT UP

Open the feed valve to the fuel tank and check the gauge to see the pressure reading, then start the pilot jet. If your face hasn't melted, proceed to the next step.

PLAY WITH FIRE

As you prepare to spit fire like a dragon, remember that the longer you hold the trigger down, the quicker you deplete fuel. Test-fire with short, controlled bursts. If your entire body hasn't been engulfed in flames, you can proceed to the next step.

SPRAY AND PRAY

Using a flamethrower is a lot like putting a fire out. In fact, you can use the fire extinguisher's PASS method: Pull out your flamethrower, Aim it at the base of your target, Squeeze the handle, and Sweep the target area like the devil's fire extinguisher to watch the flames rise!

037   SPROUT KILLER 'SHROOMS

I had the somewhat dubious pleasure of meeting the Rook Islands' resident doctor, Alec Earnhardt. He doesn't really do a great deal of doctoring around here, but he does make good money off the sick—and sometimes by manufacturing and selling drugs to pirates and privateers. I was lucky enough to sit down with the good doctor, and he gave me these tips for growing and cultivating the perfect mushrooms, which I would later use for an article in *Good Appetite* magazine. Doctor Earnhardt assured me you can still grow any mushroom this way . . . not just the more entertaining varieties.

STEP 1

Get yourself some mushroom spawn—that's sawdust saturated in mushroom mycelia to you and me. Think of it as "mushroom fairy dust." (If you're on the Islands, don't worry; Doctor Earnhardt will have you covered.)

STEP 2

Prepare your substrate; mushrooms need a sterile medium to grow on, so toss some straw in boiling water to kill off those microorganisms that always ruin a good time.

STEP 3

Inoculate the now sterilized substrate with your mushroom spawn, and place the whole thing in a warm, humid area; about 70°F (21°C) will be the ideal temperature for growth. Mushrooms need darkness to grow, so toss the inoculated substrate into a cabinet or field locker and give it about three weeks for the mushroom magic show.

STEP 4

Be a good mushroom roommate: Periodically check on your fungi friends and mist with water from a spray bottle daily to keep everything damp and cool. (It's almost like making sure a friend stays hydrated during a bad trip—see item **040 / Handle Hallucinations** for more information.)

STEP 5

When the mushroom cap has fully bloomed from the stem, it's time for you to harvest away. Carefully cut each mushroom at the base of the stem to preserve any new fungi that may be developing beneath the surface.

038 TAKE A SPORE PRINT

You may be reading this, and asking yourself: "Why would I want to take a spore print?" Well, one time I searched the Islands for weeks looking for a certain species of wild mushroom, only to stumble over them growing on an unidentifiable carcass in the jungle. (By the ragged gear and shreds of T-shirt on the bones, it might have been a dead pirate; who knows who he pissed off.) Thankfully after that, Doctor Earnhardt taught me about spore printing—the science of mushroom DNA collecting—so I didn't have to revisit it later. Here's how to get your own prints, and hopefully avoid wandering the wilds in search of fungi—whether harvesting them for dinner or other purposes.

CHOOSE YOUR 'SHROOM

Pick a mature mushroom that isn't bruised or shriveled. The flatter the mushroom cap, the better the print will be.

GET INTO STEM WORK

Remove the stem from the cap with a sharp knife—not too dissimilar from widening a cracked rib cage with a stick to harvest psychedelic mushrooms growing within.

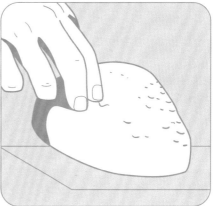

MAKE A PHOTOCOPY

Place the mushroom cap gill-side down on a piece of paper and cover it. A glass bowl is ideal so you can watch while your print is developed. This process usually takes a few hours, but the longer you leave it, the deeper the texture of your final print.

DEVELOP YOUR PRINTS

Now that you have a proud print, you can either preserve it as a piece of art suitable for sticking on a mycologist's lab refrigerator, or use it for further spawning: Sterilize a shot glass and a scalpel and scrape the dust making up the spore print into the glass. Add distilled water and draw the mixture up into a sterile syringe; use the hydrated spores to inoculate another substrate for a new round of growing.

039 BREW MUSHROOM TEA

On one of my visits with the good Doctor Earnhardt, we sat and had a lovely conversation about life on the Rook Islands, sipping tea in a gazebo overlooking the ocean at his cliffside estate. The conversation was moving along swimmingly as golden sunlight spilled between clouds following a tropical shower, leaving brilliant rainbows everywhere. Then an elf rode up on a unicorn, waving a sword and accusing me of stealing his treasures. I managed to convince him I didn't have them, and eventually the ravenous wood sprite removed his blade from my throat and rode off. It took me a while to process what had happened as Doctor Earnhardt shared with me how to make his simple but very heady signature mushroom libation. When my head fully cleared later, the rainbows had faded (and Earnhardt assured me the killer sprite wouldn't return), but I kept the recipe.

DRINK ME

Use five grams of crushed or chopped mushrooms for every cup of water (you can reduce the amount of mushrooms for a lower dose). Place the mushrooms in a teapot and add boiling water. Steep for about ten to fifteen minutes while stirring occasionally.

STRAIN ME

Pour the tea into your mug, using a strainer to catch the mushroom chunks, but don't throw these out yet! (See below.) The tea will taste bitter on its own, kind of like a really watery cream of mushroom soup without the cream, so I recommend a sweetener like honey or sugar.

HAVE ANOTHER CUP

Toss those strained 'shrooms back into the teapot for another round and repeat the process. (It pairs well with a nice shortbread cookie!)

040 HANDLE HALLUCINATIONS

Taking Doctor Earnhardt's special fungal remedy for your brain will send you down a bright and twisted rabbit hole and into Lewis Carroll's version of *The Jungle Book*. In this version, however, white rabbits were replaced by albino crocodiles, the doctor was of course the Hatter, and a lawless Rakyat woman was the Queen of Hearts. If you've just had some kind of mushroom and you can feel its hallucinogenic grip pulling you further from reality, don't panic, delirious traveler! Here are some tips to help you hang on for dear reality until you come down from your bad trip.

JUST RELAX

Remember, hallucinations can't hurt you—mostly. If you see a leopard in the form of Garfield, don't walk over to ask him which Italian place on the Island has the best lasagna. Mistaking one thing for another can happen, but generally speaking, what you see isn't really there. Try to stay as relaxed as possible: Breathe slowly and steadily and remind yourself it's just a symptom. Make it your mushroom mantra.

STAY ENGAGED

Keep your mind focused on reality by doing something you're familiar with, like listening to relaxing music, talking to someone, or reading this book.

HAVE A TALK SHOW

Don't let the hallucination win the argument. Sometimes having a verbal conversation with a hallucination can make them seem less scary. Give them silly names! Take away their power! The ghost of the dead pirate standing in my hotel room corner demanding I share the mushrooms held no sway once I dubbed him Bobbo.

GO TO YOUR SAFE PLACE

If your brain has turned into magic mushroom soup, head to a familiar, comfortable space. Go to your home, draw the shades, and occupy yourself with a favorite calming distraction. Less sensory input and more comfort will help ease your mind; a dim room and a warm blanket may be the perfect answer.

SEE A DOCTOR

If you've taken too much to easily tell a hallucination from reality, your body might also "think" it's been poisoned; symptoms will include nausea, dizziness, vomiting, and rapid heartbeat. A medical professional—and that includes Doctor Earnhardt—will know how to treat it with antianxiety meds, antipsychotics, or sedatives. (Earnhardt won't take insurance, though.)

041 HANG ON TO A HANG GLIDER

The sky above the Rook Islands can be a dangerous place. It's far from the ground and if you're leisurely descending with a parachute, you're an easy, slow-moving target to shoot at. But parachuting isn't the only way to fly the unfriendly skies: Hang gliders are a great option for short distance traveling, a quick mountaintop escape, surveying hard-to-reach locations, or just enjoying flying like a bird . . . far away from privateers. You don't need a license to fly one (not that it matters on the Islands), but every hour of practice helps. I'm no professional pilot but after having taken a couple of tandem flights, I can at least give you a crash course in not crashing your own hang glider.

PREFLIGHT

Much like a parachute, your glider is your lifeline between air and ground, so make sure to inspect the hardware and harness. If anything fails, so could your attempt at flight, and you just know birds will make fun of your mangled corpse on bird Twitter if you crash.

LAUNCH

Lift the glider by the control bar and run fast downslope. (This part is easy if you're being shot at.) The sail will fill, giving you enough lift to leave the ground and send you soaring like a majestic aluminum and polyester eagle.

SOAR

Place your feet in the harness behind you and pilot the glider using countersteering: Push the bar opposite your desired turn direction to shift your weight. Be careful not to lean forward too far or you'll nosedive. The wind is your engine here, so you'll need to hit an updraft if you want to gain altitude.

LAND!

You'll want smooth, level ground to land, and plenty of it. Push the bar forward when you're a few feet from the ground to stall. If everything goes well, you'll have a smooth touchdown on the landing wheels, or if you're really lucky, your landing legs.

042 PULL ON A PARACHUTE

Other visitors on the Rook Islands told me about how breathtaking it was to go skydiving over the Island. I think it was the high altitude (especially after my trip to Kyrat—see item **050 / Equip Yourself for High Altitude**), and besides, I'd also heard about a few jumpers ending up as kidnapping victims when they landed in the wrongest spot possible. I'll pass; the only way things could get worse was if they had jumped without chutes. No matter how cool Keanu made it look in *Point Break*, don't do that: Whether you're skydiving or BASE jumping off a cliff or radio tower, make sure to pack some nylon the next time you decide to go sky-skiing down the triple black diamond gravity trail. Parachutes are also mandatory if you're flying a wingsuit (see item **087 / Wing It (with a Wingsuit)**) and can be a great life insurance policy if you're hang gliding and have to deal with an abrupt emergency descent.

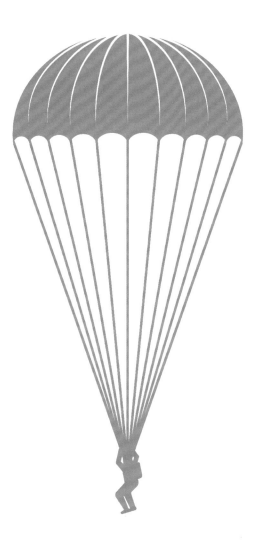

BE A SMART CHUTE SHOPPER

The parachute you choose will depend on the height of your jump. Skydiving rigs have a main and reserve chute, but BASE jumps are too short to deploy a reserve so that rig will have just the one. (You can use the extra free space and weight to easily stash your last will and testament.)

DO A PREFLIGHT CHECK

Proper fit of a parachute rig is essential to ensure a safe landing. Make sure the shoulder straps' ring system is tightened high on your chest and the hip attachments are, well, on your hips. If it's all on right, you'll land safely. If anything on your harness isn't where it should be, you'll still land—well ahead of your parachute's touchdown.

TEST YOUR FLEXIBILITY

You'll want to ensure your harness is firmly strapped to you, but make sure you have free range of motion so you can arch your back during freefall (see the next item) and reach your deployment chute at the bottom of the container (BOC). If your rig is equipped with one, make sure to turn on your automatic activation device (AAD).

043 FLING YOURSELF FROM A PLANE

I've traveled on more than a few puddle jumpers held together with electrical tape on my journalistic adventures around the world, so I do know a thing or two about jumping out of an airplane. It just so happens, considering the Rook Islands' remoteness and rocky reefs, skydiving is also one of the safest ways onto the Island (barring a pirate reception upon landing, that is). Whether you find yourself needing to exit a rickety, flying coffin flown by a CIA spook, or you're planning on dropping in for your first Rook Island visit, here's how to throw yourself out of plane and not become ground meat.

BE ASTUTE, CHECK YOUR CHUTE!

Make sure to double-check to ensure all the straps and connection points on your harness are nice and snug—especially to compensate for added weight if you're exiting the plane with, say, a duffel bag full of money—and that you can reach the deploy handle on the BOC.

GET SOME FRESH AIR

Jumping is the hard part; gravity will take care of the rest. Face the exit and jump out, arching your back, keeping your legs apart and your knees bent. When in free fall, make like a pirate hostage at gunpoint: Extend your arms up and out to an angle and reach for the sky!

SPREAD YOUR WING

If your chute lacks an AAD, pull the BOC deployment handle to deploy your canopy. Much like a run-in with Hurk, be prepared for a jerk: You'll go from terminal velocity to a glide, but the sudden deceleration will feel about three times the pull of gravity for a moment. (If you find you're still plummeting, see item **044 / Survive a Chute Failure** on the next page.)

STICK THE LANDING

Parachutes form a gliding wing that lets you control descent speed and steering using the handles hanging just above your shoulders. Pulling the left handle makes you glide left; pulling the right handle makes you go right. Pulling both makes you spin in circles. Kidding! Pull both handles for a hard stall as you're about to land. Tuck your knees into your body; you'll either land on your feet and have to jog to a stop or skid along on your rear. (Kissing the earth afterward is up to you.)

044 SURVIVE CHUTE FAILURE

There's a reason I don't make skydiving a regular hobby of mine: Whether you're dealing with twisted suspension lines, becoming tangled with another jumper, or a blown-out panel in the canopy from a swarm of lead mosquitoes, parachute failures can and do happen from time to time. Here's how to make an emergency landing if flapping your arms wildly during a rapid descent doesn't do the trick.

CUT LOOSE

Sometimes you have to cut your losses, and that means pulling the handle to cut away the main canopy if you're high enough. (You should make sure you have a reserve chute available for this option; otherwise, flap your arms harder and see below.) Much like life, the ground can come at you pretty fast when parachuting, so try not to spend too much time debating the pros and cons of this particular option.

RESERVE GOOD JUDGMENT

If you're not at a high enough altitude to waste precious time cutting your busted chute loose, then skip that step and just pull the D-handle to deploy your reserve. The opening velocity should be enough to fill the reserve canopy and avoid getting tangled with the main.

PREPARE FOR A CRASH LANDING

If all else fails, try and stick a PLF—short for "Parachute Landing Fall." Keep your feet and knees together slightly bent and relaxed. Tuck your chin into your chest, cross those flapping arms across your chest, and grab onto your pack's shoulder straps. Tuck and roll when you hit the ground.

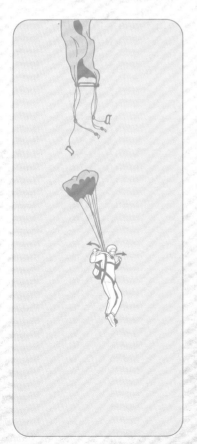

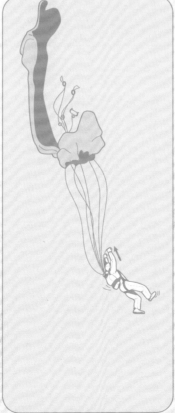

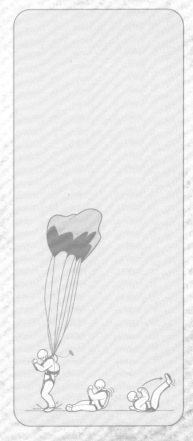

045 PATCH A LEAKY BOAT

Out on the waters with Eddie the Rakyat fisherman, we ran into minor trouble one day when we got a major scrape on his boat's hull. Luckily, we had duct tape and we were in only thigh-deep water. Still, I owed him for the repairs since I was piloting. Staying afloat is crucial on the Rook Island waterways to ensure a safe arrival by boat—or a speedy escape from pirates or marauders, and to avoid all the dangers that lurk beneath the surface: sharks, jellyfish, and drowning. Here's how to keep your watercraft shipshape in an emergency and avoid a watery grave.

PLUG THE LEAK

Locating any leaks are your top priority; if you're unable, locate dry land instead. Check the drain plug; if it's open, go ahead and close the case of the mystery leak. If a fracture is the culprit, secure a plastic bag across the leak on the outside of the hull with ropes. Water pressure will keep it in place as you head for land. If the crack is small enough, make a repair with good old reliable duct tape and a prayer to Poseidon.

GET YOUR MOTOR RUNNING

An outboard motor is the heart of watercraft and fuel is its lifeblood, but it can easily flood and stall. If your boat has flatlined, give it a little CPR: Remove and dry the spark plugs, crank the motor to clear excess fuel, and reinstall the plugs. Raise the warm-up or fast-idle lever and crank the starter for about eight to ten seconds; if the motor doesn't come back from the dead, crank it again. On a successful revive, keep the fast-idle lever raised until the engine runs smoothly again.

046 JUMP ON A JET SKI

Personal watercraft are often called by more exciting names—think a "jet on a ski"—but whatever name they have, riding motorized watercraft is always a blast—even more so on the Rook Islands, on account of any undetonated WWII-era naval mines. But speed and explosives aside, jet skis are the fast, reliable watercraft option for quick jaunts across the water. They're surprisingly accessible, especially if you find one left on the beach by kidnapped thrill seekers.

KNOW THE CONTROLS

Typically, Jet Skis have a throttle, handlebars, and emergency shutoff; some also have a braking system. It's hard to think straight when being shot at by pirates, so get familiar ahead of time because it could save your life in a pinch. Tie the jet ski's kill switch tag firmly to yourself; in case of a sudden dismount you'll want it close by for a quick retrieval . . . which you will need if you're being pursued.

KNOW HOW TO CONTROL

Head away from the shore at a cruising speed of about ten to fifteen miles per hour. Increase your speed once you reach a safe distance. Jet skis don't have a rudder, so much like with a motorcycle, you have to lean in the direction you want to turn. First-time jet ski riders tend to keep their focus on the water just in front of the handlebars, but keep your eyes on the horizon to help you steer straight.

STAY WOKE FOR WAKES

The ocean can get choppy so be prepared for some wave jumping. Against your natural instincts or your need to escape from a pirate patrol boat, don't go too fast when you hit the wave or you'll push through it.

PUNCH IT

Speaking of natural instincts, don't slow down when turning. The slower you go, the more your ability to turn is diminished, so maintain an itchy throttle finger and lean hard into those turns, especially if you're trying to avoid danger.

FAR CRY 4

THE KINGDOM
OF KYRAT

THE KINGDOM OF KYRAT

Welcome to the Himalayan mountain Kingdom of Kyrat!

Or should I say, congratulations on surviving a border crossing *into* the Himalayan mountain Kingdom of Kyrat! I quit serious journalism after my near-death experiences on the Rook Islands, but it did inspire me to become a food journalist after stress-eating my way through the Path of the Hunter gastronomy tour while I was there. While on the lookout for my next big story, I heard that people come to this heavenly realm seeking adventure, to see nature at its most beautiful and pristine, achieve enlightenment from its mystical and spiritual peaks, then end up never leaving because they didn't know how to survive. It was one of the most isolated and dangerous borders I had ever risked my life trying to cross, but this was *Good Appetite* magazine, and I was writing an article about the best crab rangoon in Asia. Kyrat is under the control of a tyrannical monarchy ruled by the mad King Pagan Min. No need to pad my word count giving you all the details about this guy; you'll be hearing all about him in the propaganda being blasted by the loudspeakers that keep me up ALL DAY. His face is even on the Kyrati rupees you may have in your pocket. He's dangerous and fanatical and makes Vaas Montenegro look like a pirate in a theme park attraction by comparison. But credit where credit is due, Pagan Min is one hell of a snappy dresser. (Kyrat survival tip number one: Don't be within arm's reach of him if he gets blood on his shoes!)

But once you get used to the distant (and not-so-distant) hails of gunfire from the ongoing civil war being waged—and accustomed to being light-headed from the thin mountain air—you start to relax and appreciate Kyrat for its rich mythological history, and get inspired by the passion burning within the Kyrati freedom fighters combating oppression. But dodging bullets in the frigid cold of an avalanche-prone Himalayan mountain is a far cry from dodging bullets in the warm Rook Islands sun. You can stay out of the water to avoid getting shredded by the local Demon Fish (instead of sharks), but the wildlife can come at you from any direction, whether it's screaming golden eagles, territorial Indian elephants, or hungry Himalayan brown bears . . . and that's to say nothing of honey badgers. There's even been a sharp increase in both missing mountain climbers and yeti sightings in the region. Simply put, the wildlife is hungrier and meaner in the cold.

One final note of caution as you begin your survival journey in Kyrat: Lines that appear black and white may actually be different shades of grey in certain casts of the mountain light. Choose your alliances wisely.

Ready to take your survival skills to new heights? Welcome to Kyrat!

If you're traveling off the grid to a dangerous location, you should invest in a trustworthy survival guide. Might I recommend the *Far Cry Survival Manual*? Great, now that you've done that, you can skip to step two. But before you can start surviving the ravenous wildlife, gunfire, frigid weather, and avalanches of Kyrat, you need to cross the border first. Pagan Min's brutal regime isn't exactly the most welcoming to outsiders, and passing through safely or getting killed will depend entirely on Pagan Min's mood. Here's how to increase your chances of safely crossing the fortified Kyrat border.

BRING BRIBE MONEY

Any international travel advisory will suggest you not travel to Kyrat. But since you're going anyway, bring a valid passport and a concealed envelope of emergency money. Don't bother with a money belt or a bra; those tricks are worn out. A leg pouch hidden under your pants or skirt is a better option and can buy your way out of a gunfight (if you're lucky).

DRESS THE PART

Don't advertise where you're from by sticking out like a sore thumb. Avoid hats or clothing with brand names or local sports teams, fanny packs, or anything that makes you an easy pickpocket target.

BRING A BUDDY

If you're traveling to unfriendly territory, the best thing you can bring is a friend. As the saying goes, two heads are better than one, and that gives you four eyes to keep peeled when traveling through dangerous and unknown territory. It also never hurts to have someone covering your six in a gunfight, which brings me to the next tip.

WATCH YOUR SURROUNDINGS

Maintain situational awareness at all times without looking obvious or nervous. Staying calm is key. Have your buddy keep an eye out for anything suspicious as you haggle a bribe with the border guards.

048 GET TO KNOW LOCAL CUSTOMS

Familiarizing yourself with the local Kyrati culture will not only help you maintain a lower profile as you travel, it will also win you some local respect—and maybe a favor redeemable with the heavily armed Kyrati freedom fighters who call themselves the "Golden Path."

DO YOUR HOMEWORK, SAVE YOUR HEAD

Learn the local body language, as hand gestures common in your hometown can be considered rude, and that's enough to get you shot in Kyrat. (That includes Ol' Faithful, of course. Flipping the bird pretty much means the same thing everywhere.)

BE A CULINARY ADVENTURER

The best way to get to know a culture is to eat the local cuisine. Eat what the locals eat the way the locals eat it. If you're offered a toothpick whittled from the penis bone of a honey badger after your meal, just use it. Check out the Crazy Cock Bar; they pour a mean drab of Raksi. And

in case you haven't heard, the crab rangoon in Kyrat is excellent. (I even found a winning recipe; check item **085 / Cook Up Crab Rangoon**.)

LISTEN TO THE BELL TOWERS

Min's messages go out nonstop, but don't ignore the droning too much. Curfews could be put in place in a moment's notice, so keep your ears tuned to the Bell Tower broadcasts for updates—and adhere to them.

IMMERSE YOURSELF

Don't be a tourist. Break your regular travel habits, and be an active participant in the local culture to learn its customs firsthand. Avoid pulling out your camera every thirty seconds to take a picture of the breathtaking scenery Kyrat has to offer. Stow your camera in a bag, and I recommend only using the lens to scope guard positions at outposts or identify hunting targets.

From bullets to brown bears, trouble is unavoidable when exploring the mountainous Kingdom of Kyrat. But getting there isn't exactly a picnic either; the more prepared you are to face the dangers that come with traveling to an isolated country ruled by an authoritarian regime, the better your chances of surviving them. Here are some tips on avoiding trouble as you travel from Point A to Point B and hopefully out of Point B in an emergency.

TRAVEL LIGHT

On trips to dangerous locations, take only what you need with you, carrying one small bag or EDC kit if you can. Before you disembark, check to make sure the host country allows the items you plan on bringing. You'll have plenty of opportunities to arm yourself once you're in-country (or score some recreational drugs if that's your scene). So, unless you have a typewriter case with a concealed pistol compartment, don't risk trying to smuggle weapons or illegal narcotics across the border. If you'd like to experience a hard labor sentence at Durgesh Prison camp, then by all means go right ahead.

EMERGENCY EVAC

The location of the nearest airport is one of the most important things you need to know in case things go south. The only problem is, Pagan Min can shut down the airport anytime he wants, so you should also know the locations of the nearest gun shops and Sherpa routes in case you're stuck here and need to arm yourself. Bring some emergency cash to buy yourself out of danger—whether a plane ticket at an inflated "emergency" price, extra ammo, or a well-placed bribe to get you to safety.

050 EQUIP YOURSELF FOR HIGH ALTITUDE

As a traveling journalist, I have to pack as light as possible at all times, typewriter notwithstanding. Choosing the right gear means striking a balance between having all you need and avoiding overload—this is key in the mountains of Kyrat, where the air is thin and fatigue sneaks up on you easily. Consider adding the following for extreme survival conditions.

■ MOUNTAINEER'S HARNESS, ROPES, AND CARABINERS

Even if you don't plan on technical climbs, the gear could save your life.

■ ICE AXES

You might not expect ice where you're going, but weather may force you to change course (and an axe in the hand is worth two in the shop when it comes to fending off hungry honey badgers).

■ CRAMPONS

Like an ice axe, these might spell the difference between being stuck and able to get to safety.

■ COLLAPSIBLE SNOW SHOVEL

If you end up in a white-out blizzard, digging a shelter in the snow may be all that separates you from freezing to death; you'll be glad to have this on hand.

■ PERSONAL LOCATOR BEACON (PLB)

There's no reason to go up into this mountainous terrain without one: They're eminently affordable, and as long as you have a clear line of sight, rescuers can locate you (or at least your body) on the most remote slopes with a PLB signal.

■ INSULATED PAD AND SLEEPING BAG

Get one rated for arctic temperatures, and made for sleeping on snow; you can freeze without it.

■ HELMET

You only have one head. A single misstep could mean a concussion or worse, so going bareheaded is a no-brainer. (And that's to say nothing of the eagles.)

051 TRAIN FOR THE MOUNTAINS

When I told my doctor I was headed for Kyrat, he made the same face as when I told him about my plans to visit the Rook Islands—even though I came back in one piece plus-tattoo. Then he suggested an aggressive cardio regimen, and after weeks up in the high Kingdom of Kyrat, I'm glad he did: Sprinting from pirates at sea level in an oxygen-rich jungle is one thing; hiking steadily up a mountainside around 10,000 feet (about 3,000 m) in thin air and potentially on a yeti's menu is another. You don't need to be young, or be a marathon runner or bodybuilder to be fit for the heights. But, you do have to be able to hike long-distance with a full-size pack on your back.

PREPARE EARLY

Get physically ready months before your trip. Walk, run, or ride a bike. Then carry a pack while you walk or run. You'll curse every step now, but you'll curse every step later a little more gratefully.

TEST YOURSELF

Evaluate your performance honestly: Do you feel healthy and strong? Got any joint or tendon issues? If you have to, modify your adventure plans accordingly. (You'll be glad you did, especially when you find yourself NOT running from a Royal Army patrol . . . or a honey badger.)

ENDURE ALTITUDE

The way my Sherpa buddy Lobsang put it: If you can run a mile (1.6 km) at low elevation, you can walk the same distance at 10,000 feet (3,000 m). It's a fact, Jack: The air is plenty thin way up here, and just walking briskly can leave you panting. Plan on arriving early close to your ascent destination, and spend several days acclimating to the elevation. The body has an amazing ability to adjust, and three days will make a huge difference. As a bonus, you'll also be less likely to develop any of the more severe forms of altitude illness (see the next item).

052 CONQUER ALTITUDE SICKNESS

In spite of having done a lot of cardio before I boarded my flight to India and my rickety bus ride into Kyrat afterwards, I'm not too proud to admit the thin air took my breath away faster than the vistas. The cause of altitude sickness is simple: going too high too fast. The higher your altitude, the longer it takes to acclimate. When you're climbing in the mountains, slow down. Ascents beyond 8,000 feet (2,400 m) should go no more than 1,000 feet (300 m) per day. Avoid overdoing it for at least twenty-four hours after reaching a new height, and keep hydrated.

What happens if you don't take these instructions seriously? Watch for two forms of serious altitude illness: The first is high-altitude pulmonary edema (HAPE), characterized by shortness of breath, fatigue, dry cough, and blue lips and nails. The second is high-altitude cerebral edema (HACE) which typically features severe headache, loss of coordination, and increasing confusion. Both HAPE and HACE are potentially deadly; victims must immediately get down to at least 2,000 feet (600 m) to save their lives and must evacuate to a medical facility soon as possible.

You'd be hard-pressed to find a doctor or hospital in Kyrat. Even if you did, they're likely on Pagan Min's payroll, so improvised field medicine should become your specialty if you want to improve your chances of survival. You may have to get creative with the items available to you, as medical supplies are scarce. (Don't be so quick to discard that box of tampons you find when scavenging.)

DON'T BE A HERO

Stitching a wound with a needle and thread like a crochet commando may make you look like a badass action movie star, but if you're not using sterile sutures you'll soon feel more like infected death bed patient number four on a second-rate medical TV drama. Save the sewing for socks: it's cold in the Himalayas and you'll definitely need them.

BE A SUPERGLUE HERO

Named for its super-adhesive properties, and because it's made from only the finest quality racehorses, superglue can be used to hold your wound closed in a pinch. Coat only the outside, and avoid getting it in the cut itself. You can also use duct tape if you need to patch yourself up quickly after a gunfight or surprise honey badger attack.

A BUTTERFLY WITH BANDAGED WINGS

Adhesive strips are the best way to hold a wound together. After disinfecting (see item 119), line up the edges of the cut and apply the bandages in a crisscross pattern while pushing the wound together. Dress with a sterile wrap, and in about seventy-two hours your wound cocoon will reveal a beautifully healing injury.

054 DEAL WITH BLOOD LOSS

Whether it's jagged rocks, tiger claws, whizzing bullets—and don't get me started on those honey badgers again—all of Kyrat wants to spill your blood in some form or another. But your survival depends on making sure you keep as much of it inside you as possible. Take these tips to help keep your blood from spilling on the ground.

CLOSE THE BLOODGATES

Elevate the wound over your head if you can, and after you've bandaged the injury, if blood is soaking through, don't remove the bandages; add more on top of the existing ones and apply direct pressure firmly. This constricts blood vessels manually, helping to stem excessive bleeding. In situations where pressure isn't effective at stopping the bleeding, find the appropriate pressure point to constrict the major artery which feeds the injury. This is usually done where a pulse is found. If using a pressure point is ineffective, it's time to apply a tourniquet (see item **144 / Rig a Tourniquet**). And much like when smuggling a Caesar salad across the Kyrati border, use duct tape to secure the dressing.

DON'T GET DISARMED

For a bleeder on your favorite shooting arm, you'll stop it by compressing the brachial artery. Look for it in your inner arm, between the shoulder and elbow.

GIVE ME A HAND

If you've opened an artery in your hand and it's spurting blood like you're a vampiric web-slinging comic-book hero, apply pressure to the radial artery. Just like the end of the bone it's named for, it's at the inside of your wrist.

GET A LEG UP

You won't get anywhere if you're slipping on your own spilled blood underfoot. Seek out the femoral artery—found in the groin area just below the "bikini line"—and squeeze it hard.

MAINTAIN YOUR FOOTING

If there's blood soaking the inside of your boots from a lower-leg injury, avoid wet squelching and dizziness from blood loss by pressing on the popliteal artery, located just behind your knee.

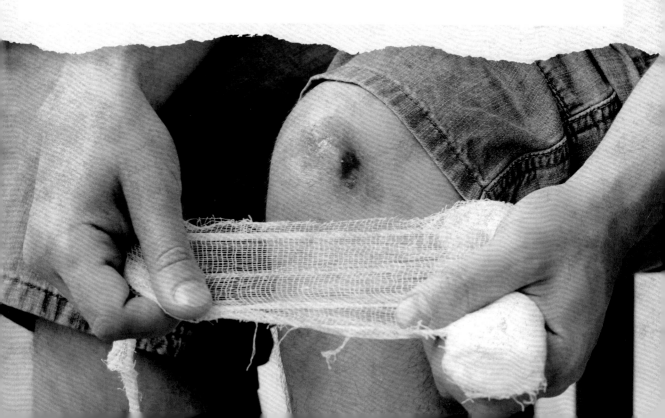

You have to maintain a thick skin during your adventures. Even if you do, you still may find yourself needing to perform some skin knitting work after a bad cut from one of Kyrat's many sharp edges. That's suturing a wound, to you and me. So, if that sliced-open bloodbag in need of a sewing lesson just so happens to be you, you're in luck: A nice Kyrati farmer once taught me how to suture a pig after a C-section! Here's what I learned about stitching a cut.

PREPARE THE WOUND

Remove any debris, such as hay or dirt, from the wound, then clean it thoroughly (see item **120 / Disinfect Wounds** for more) and apply antibiotic ointment. You may also want to administer a few sips of your preferred proof of internal anesthesia. (If you're also the surgeon, take a moment to steady yourself after doing so.) If the person you're suturing begins to fight or struggle, consider hog-tying them.

STITCH AWAY

It may feel weird at first running a needle and thread through flesh, whether yours or another's, but it'll pass. Pierce through the skin on one side of the wound using a curved suture needle, then up through the opposite side to make the first stitch. Tie the stitch off with a surgeon's knot (which is just a double-wrapped overhand knot with a medical degree), and follow that up with three or four overhand knots. Trim both ends of the stitch to roughly ¾ inch (2 cm).

DRESS AND REPEAT

Continue the suture with a stitch every ¼ inch (6 mm) until the wound is nicely closed, then tie off the last stitch with a surgeon's knot again. Gently but thoroughly wash the site in warm water, then dry and dress it. Now have all the butter tea and dumplings you can eat along with the leftover medicinal whiskey; you've earned it.

056 HANDLE A CONCUSSION

In Kyrat, what doesn't cut you will usually concuss you. (Sometimes it can even be both!) Concussions are caused by your head moving back and forth rapidly enough to bounce your brain around—whether that happens by blunt force trauma from a falling rock, an auto accident, being struck by a weapon, or thinking too fast. (Well, okay, maybe not so much that last one.) A concussion can be a dangerous injury if it is not identified quickly and treated properly, so it's important to know the signs of a concussion, because you won't find very many signs pointing the way to a hospital in Kyrat.

WATCH YOUR WORDS

If you're reading and you suddenly notice the text becoming blurred or appearing jublmed, tops dreaing nad seke emdicla natetnio. Just kidding! But in all seriousness, take note of blurred or double vision, uneven pupils, light sensitivity, and seeing spots—all of these are concussion signs.

GET A BIG MOOD

Look for abrupt changes in mood or personality, like unusual irritability or inappropriate, angry outbursts—you know, acting just like a Kyrat Royal Army Charger.

HANDLE A HEADACHE

Watch for headaches, nausea, drowsiness, or unconsciousness; they either have a concussion or they read my novel. (Watch your step for vomit.)

TAKE CARE OF TREATMENT

If you've followed all the signs and arrived at a concussion conclusion, carefully check for a spinal cord injury, and apply a cold compress to that egg on their head. Keep the victim still for about twenty-four hours and assess their condition every three hours or so. You can administer a pain medication that doesn't contain aspirin. Do not apply pressure to a head wound if you suspect there's a skull fracture. If there's any spine or head trauma, seek medical attention immediately.

057 RESET A DISLOCATION

In Kyrat, what doesn't cut you or concuss you will probably still dislocate a joint or two (and sometimes it'll do all four)! You don't need a joint GPS to find a dislocation. When the ends of the bones in a joint don't line up, you'll know that you have one from the stiffness, pain, and numbness—not to mention the fact that it just plain looks wrong. Here are a few tricks to use if you decide to go out on a limb to press reset on that dislocated joint.

DIGITS

The most common (and easiest to reset) dislocations will be found on your toes and fingers. Bend and pull the end of the digit while gently pressing in place. Use gauze or bandages to splint the recently dislocated joint loosely with the finger or toe beside it.

WRISTS AND ANKLES

Resetting a dislocated wrist or ankle is relatively easy but it can definitely become a lot more tricky if any fractures are present. Wrap the wrists and splint well, then seek medical attention. Keep the injured appendage immobilized to keep pressure off of the affected joint.

LEGS AND KNEES

Resetting a leg dislocation is easy: Gently pull the leg straight and splint securely. For knees, straighten the leg and massage the kneecap into place. Carrying the victim because they're not able to walk is the hard part.

SHOULDERS

Dislocated shoulders are a common injury in Kyrat, often associated with carrying heavy objects (like helping people with leg injuries or hiding a dead body in a bush—see item **083 / Hide a Body**). Lay the victim down, grab their arm by the elbow, and apply inward traction towards their body, then away.

HIP

This one is painful and difficult to reset; seek medical attention immediately if they've fallen and can't get up from a hip injury.

JAW

Who has two thumbs and is ready to reset a jaw? This Kyrat survivalist! Place clean, gauzed thumbs in the victim's mouth, pressing down and forward on the back of the molars.

058 SET A BROKEN BONE

A Stryus is a common vehicle to get you from point A to point B on Kyrat and is notorious for having bad brakes, but the worst breaks you'll experience in Kyrat will usually involve your bones. Breaks can range from incomplete hairline cracks to open fractures protruding from flesh, but regardless of severity, they have one thing in common: They all hurt like hell. Here's how to deal with a fractured bone because unfortunately on Kyrat, those are the breaks.

LIV, LAF, LUV

If no bones are protruding from the flesh, you can assess the injury using the "LAF" system. LOOK: Remove clothing to assess the injured area. Check for discoloration or swelling. ASK: "Do you think it's broken?" "What is the pain level?" "If I have to find a hospital, do I have to drive a Stryus?" FEEL: Gently probe the injured area for point tenderness.

GO FOR BROKE

For simple or slightly misaligned breaks, try to straighten the injured appendage by applying gentle traction. This method helps the muscles on the limb to relax, allowing you to realign and thus reset the injury. Never use force, and stop applying any traction immediately if the pain increases while pulling.

LOVE, FRACTUALLY

If you have bone protruding from skin, you should seek medical assistance immediately. But in Kyrat, that means you could be hours or days away from help; if it'll be a while, gently clean the bone and wound to the best of your ability and carefully apply traction until the bone recedes back into the skin. Bandage, splint, and finish with painkillers. Elevate the injury, apply ice, and hope you don't have to climb down a mountainside.

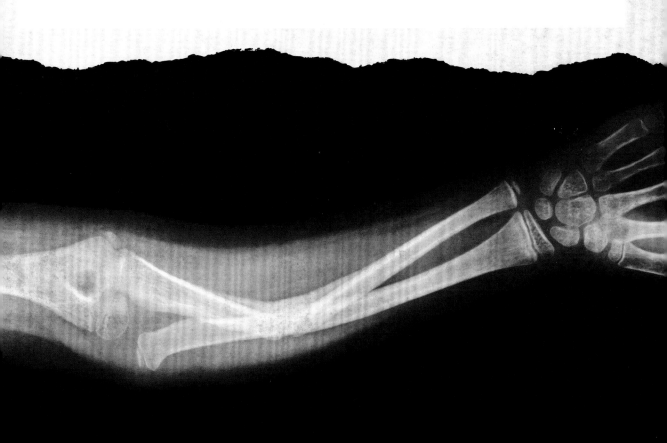

When you travel to dangerous locales all over the world, you learn to remain on high alert and keep your typewriter and trigger fingers frosty. But it's hard to stay alert in Kyrat when your senses—and hands—are always numb from the chill. Dressing properly for the cold is an essential part of surviving in Kyrat, so if you're going to try smuggling anything across the border, make it cold weather gear. Bundle up with these tips to take a bite out the Kyrat cold before the frost bites you.

GET THE SEASON'S COLD LOOKS

For the light traveler, triple up on medium and heavyweight socks, wear weatherproof or insulated boots, bring two pairs of pants (one medium, one heavy), and consider a pair of heavy gloves—or even better, see my next suggestion.

GO TO THE SNOWBALL GAME

Leave your gloves at home when you play in the Kyrat snow and bring catcher's mitts instead. They'll make your hands stay warmer and can be quickly slipped in and out of when you need a trigger finger. But if it's -40 °F (-40 °C) below outside and you have a clear shot at your target, I advise you to fire quickly.

HEAD THE WINTER GEAR CLASS

One of the most essential pieces of winter gear goes on your head. You know it as a beanie. Warm and comfortable, it keeps your body's brain engine warm so you can concentrate on important things like surviving the freezing temperatures.

GET YOUR SHOES ON

Insulated boots will help you keep your legs warm as you're tramping through snow. Calf-high "pack" boots are the best suited for deeper snowfall and extreme cold. Aside from traversing any number of slippery and dangerous cliff sides, you may also need to run from wild animals and gunfire, so go with an air-bob sole for traction.

060 HOLD OFF HYPOTHERMIA

Once, while traversing through one of Kyrat's dangerous and frigid mountain passages, a rogue blizzard struck. The icy wind howled so loud and lashed so hard I knew I couldn't go on. I had to make the heartbreaking decision to bludgeon the yak I was riding to death with my typewriter so I could sleep inside its carcass for warmth (I thanked the yak in my award acceptance speech for the crab rangoon article—see item **085 / Cook Up Crab Rangoon**). Here are some 100 percent yak-carcass-free ways to keep your body temperature up when the freezing temperatures start to get you down.

GET OUT OF THE COLD

Your first step is getting warm and out of danger. Get somewhere as warm and dry as possible, and remove any wet clothing you may have on—like one might after jumping into a freezing lake to loot a drowned footlocker only to risk hypothermia and Demon Fish bites for an old mobile phone. (Congratulations.)

GETTING WARMER

Now that you're out of the cold, wrap yourself in blankets or coats; if you have any chemical warmers, now is the time to use them. Place in the armpits, stomach, and groin area. Warm water bottles will also work. Have none of the above? Use your travel buddy to warm up to. (Skin contact is best and now is no time to be shy.) Have a warm, sweet drink, but avoid alcohol; despite what you may have heard about liquor keeping you warm, that bottle of Kyrati lager giving you the doe-eyes is not your friend right now.

GET TO A HOSPITAL

Once stabilized, seek medical attention as soon as possible, especially if you have any signs of frostbite. Milder cases of cold, pain, and numbness are relieved with warmth and time; more serious cases involve continued numbness or severe pain after warming, discolored skin, or hardened or blistered areas.

061 SURVIVE AN AVALANCHE

One time, I and a group of Golden Path fighters were tracking a Kyrat Royal Army convoy through the mountains, and a gunfight ensued. Someone had the bright idea to throw a grenade—to make a long story short, I ended up becoming a Kyrat snow-surfing champion as the only one in the group to survive the avalanche. Here's how I did it.

RIDE IT OUT

Try to ride the top of the avalanche using skiing (or swimming or body surfing) moves and attempt to maneuver towards the edge of the slide. Try to catch hold of a nearby tree if the snow in the avalanche is moving slowly, but also try to avoid getting a face full of tree trunk.

WIPE OUT

It happens even to the best champion skiers and surfers. But you need to react quickly if you find yourself stuck in the snow. As the snow making up the avalanche stops moving, it hardens from a fluid-like consistency to something closer to cement, so try to work your way out as the slide slows.

REMEMBER TO BREATHE

If you end up buried in the snow, shove an arm towards the surface to create an air shaft for the purpose of breathing. Conserve your energy to avoid exhaustion. Conserve your breath as well, and avoid unnecessarily screaming for help. Wait until you hear rescuers above you—and hope they aren't Royal Army soldiers.

GO TOWARD THE LIGHT

No, not that one! If you took a tumble down a mountain in an avalanche and are lucky to have survived the experience, you may not know which direction you've ended up in. Light can shine through thin snow layers so you should direct your digging efforts in that direction. If it's too dark and deep for light to guide you to the surface, clear a space near your mouth and do a spit take. Dig in the opposite direction gravity pulls your loogie luge.

062 GET YOUR BEARINGS

Even in a small realm like the Kingdom of Kyrat, it's easy to get turned around or lost, especially in the dark or a freezing blizzard—or if you've just emerged from an avalanche (see previous items 059–061). Turning a corner on the wrong mountain road and running face-first into a Royal Army patrol convoy tends to be an awkward experience, so here are a few ways to keep in mind to get your bearings and travel Kyrat in safety!

GO STARGAZING

In the northern hemisphere, one star faithfully maintains position in the night sky—the North Star. How do you pick out one star from the millions shining above? It's simple: The North Star is the bright one pointed to by the front edge of the Big Dipper. (In the southern hemisphere, such as on the Rook Islands, look for the Southern Cross instead and draw an imaginary line down its length to about a finger width above the horizon to find south.)

SALUTE THE SUN

The sun and moon always rise in the east and set in the west. Unless the world begins turning backward on its axis in an apocalyptic flip, they'll keep rising and setting that way, so you can count on them to help find your direction.

STUDY YOUR SURROUNDINGS

Look around yourself to find clues pointing the way. In some environments, moss grows heavily on northern-facing tree trunks. What about the winds? Do they mainly prevail from the southwest? You'll notice that the trees and grass will all lean to the northeast, bent and fatigued by wind. In plenty of places, the south and west slopes are relatively open and grassy, while north and east slopes are covered in dense timber or brush.

REMEMBER LANDMARKS

Try to memorize the position of a few distant landmarks. What about that easily recognizable peak to the north? Or that small lake to the southwest? Check out that long, northeast-to-southwest valley run—it must stretch at least fifty miles (eighty kilometers) or more. Commit various geographical features to memory, and getting just one glimpse will help orient you.

Faced with a sheer cliff or gaping canyon? When they say, "Watch that first step!" in Kyrat, they really mean it. A grappling hook, though, is the perfect solution for these and other situations where the alternative involves plummeting to an ignominious demise! This tool was invented centuries ago for boarding enemy ships and breaking into castles. Now, castles are mostly obsolete (and reminding Pagan Min of this may land you in an old Kyrati fortress's dungeon), but the grappling hook hasn't changed much: It's a sturdy handle and a few hooks attached to a long rope. Whatever the size or configuration, it should hold at least twice your weight. Here's how to be like Batman.

STEP 1

Stand as close to the cliff or drop-off as possible to minimize the amount of rope needed. Pick your grappling point such as a tree, ledge, or statue, and loosely coil enough rope to reach it; hold the rope lightly in your free hand.

STEP 2

Throw the hook underhanded if the point is within a story or two; If it's farther away, try overhand or spin it for momentum. Once the hook catches the object or wraps around it and grabs the rope, pull steadily to test your weight.

STEP 3

Tie the rope to yourself in case you lose your grip, and climb. To swing across a gap, get a good grip on the rope or tie it on, then jump! (Tarzan yell for style points—your screams echo for a good long time up here!)

STEP 4

Once you've traversed, unhook the grapple or shake the rope to dislodge it from the hook. Coil your rope and bring the hook with you—you'll probably need to use it again sooner than you think!

064 RAPPEL ON
THE FLY

On a hike one day in the hills outside Banapur, I found myself on the run from a territorial honey badger. As I stopped to catch my breath, my trusty typewriter case slipped out of my pack and skidded down a sheer slope to the bottom of a ravine. Finding a safe, easy way down to retrieve it would have taken hours and miles of travel, and I wasn't about to leave my favorite typewriter—and favorite handgun!—behind while I did that. With no specialized climbing gear and only a coil of rope, I came up with a quick method.

SET YOUR ANCHOR

First, loop, the center of your rope around a tree or rock, and let both ends dangle over the cliffside. Make sure both ends reach the ground below. Test your anchor, then straddle the double rope, facing uphill.

GET ROPED IN

Bring the rope around your right thigh to the front and diagonally across your chest. Lead the rope over your left shoulder and diagonally across your back to your right hip. Grab the double rope ahead of you with your left hand and the double rope behind your hip with your right hand.

WALK IT OFF

Now for the fun part: Walk backward over the cliff, leaning back on the rope and feeding it over your body to overcome friction. Keep stepping back and feeding the rope until you reach the bottom. If you don't intend on making a return climb, pull on one end of the rope to retrieve it. (If you do intend on climbing, watch for badgers.)

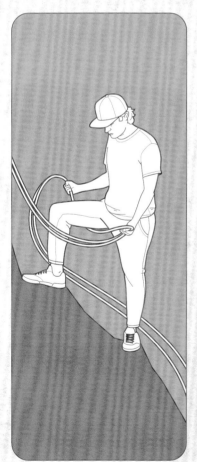
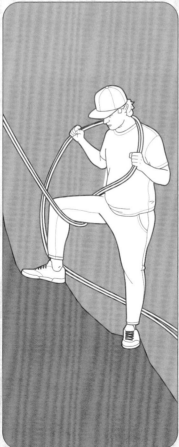
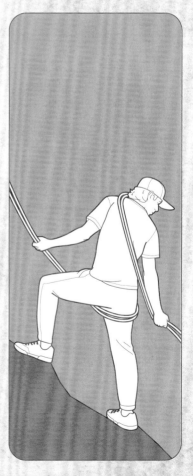

065 BE A MODERN CAVEMAN

On a trek to get a good view of the village I was staying in during much of my time in Kyrat, I took the time to explore a few caves—not as many as I liked, since I'd heard of a few ancient treasures lost in old caves . . . but then again, I also didn't find myself in a Himalayan bear's home. And there's a good reason that bears and other animals often hole up in caves: They're ready-made shelters, protecting the inhabitant from driving rain, freezing snow, biting cold wind, and brutally bright sun. No need to erect a hut or tent; just move in and set up housekeeping.

DON'T GET STUCK

A cave should be a haven, not a tomb, so be sure your would-be shelter is out of the way of flash floods or tides at lower altitudes, and higher up, out of the way of potential avalanches or rockslides.

MAKE A FENCE

Erect a low stone wall at the opening, to help keep dirt from blowing around, and block the worst of the cold drafts.

START A FIRE

Stone makes a good reflector for a campfire—plus, no worries about fire spreading to nearby vegetation and getting out of control. Build the fire near the entrance to keep smoke from becoming a problem!

BEAT THE DRAFT

Remember, you're in a cave, not a palace; caves generally retain cold. They're good for escaping desert heat, but less desirable in cold weather. Unless you have a good fire going, or you partition a section of the cavern into a small room, cold air will always surround you.

066 STAY SAFE IN A CAVE

Just like any neighborhood, especially in the Kingdom of Kyrat, a cave has both advantages and drawbacks. Before you take up residence in one yourself, first make sure that it's not already occupied. Depending on where you are, caves might be favored dwellings for any number of dangerous creatures: venomous snakes, honey badgers, wolf packs, hungry bears, big cats, deranged mask-loving serial killers—you get the idea. Even if your only cavern roommates are rodents, hantavirus might be in their urine or feces, so be sure to look for a clean cave floor before you bed down.

Another note of caution: Some caves exist because the ceiling "caved" in from erosion. If you see evidence of instability like cracks overhead, fresh rockfalls on the floor, or water flowing through the cave, it's probably unsound. Best to move on in this case.

I've avoided talking about honey badgers in detail until now, and for good reason: Those nasty, crazy, fierce critters haunted my dreams long after I fired my last shot at them. Another name for the honey badger is "ratel," which is what they call an armored fighting vehicle in these parts. It's an apt comparison: Honey badgers are tough for their size, and just like that one viral video says, they don't care at all. But their insouciance manifests in snarling, slavering, clawing, and biting; I've seen a pissed honey badger actively pursue a full-size Himalayan bear and send it packing just because it was within eyeshot.

What does this have to do with anything? The Prabhakar family farm in southwest Kyrat, where they were kind enough to put me up for a night, has been harassed by wild animals seemingly since their forebears hitched a yak to plow their first field. Most anything from wild dogs to, well, honey badgers have cropped up in this area, and so to repay the Prabhakarses' kindness, I got to see the antisocial animals up close by joining in a cull—a hunting drive to keep down their numbers. Here's how we put the badgers to bed.

TEAM UP

Along with myself, hunters from neighboring farms drew lots for "push" and "stand" positions. And we needed the numbers: "None of us say, 'I've got to kill a badger,'" one farmer told me. "It's all about 'us.'"

TAKE POSITIONS

Everyone climbed the hillsides in total silence. I and the rest of the standers dropped off first, forming a straight line down a hill's steep flank. Pushers continued on a half-mile (1.6 km), then did the same. Then we closed the vise.

HOLD THE LINE

If a pusher got bogged down, the shout rang out: "Hold the line!" The line of pushers driving out any badgers had to remain straight no matter what.

BE SMART

Standers had to watch even the smallest openings. We killed one badger when I looked under the brush and saw four quick, sharp-clawed paws. That one got to within 12 feet (3.7 m) of us, snarling and spitting, before two shots brought it down.

KEEP MOVING

After the first push, we left a small group to deal with any downed badgers, then moved quickly for a second round to catch more driven out from nearby thickets.

068 SET A BAIT PILE FOR PREDATORS

Occasionally, a hunt in Kyrat—whether it's held for food, or sport, or a cull (see previous item), or the legendary Fashion Week hunts sponsored by Mumu Chiffon (see item **073 / Go on a Fashion Hunt in Kyrat**)—means nothing more than sitting and waiting: Set out a baited trap or just bait, hide somewhere nearby, and take down the prey when it arrives. My guide, a friendly Sherpa named Lobsang, explained the local wildlife's dietary preferences; turns out it's a bit more complex than a little piece of cheese on a snap trap.

OFFER UN-BEAR-ABLE FLAVOR

A good bear bait could be honey, used cooking oil, sweets, or even a Demon Fish carcass hung from a tree, but the greatest ones use bacon. Smoked pork belly from a local farm, fried upwind of a bait site, will make a hungry Himalayan bear weak in all four knees.

BADGER THE SUBJECT

Honey badgers are the garbage disposal animal of Kyrat: They're generally carnivorous but with a very wide palate. If you set out almost anything that's odiferous enough—meat (whether fresh or off) including that from lizards, rodents, and birds; insects including scorpions, beetles, and larvae; or honeycombs (or just the whole hive)—and you'll have badgers in record time.

GO EAGLE SCOUTING

They're majestic and beautiful swooping through the sky, at least until they come shrieking down on your head, talons first, like steroidal Australian magpies with rage issues. Fish, rabbits, carrion, and even spilled garbage draw Kyrati eagles like filings to a magnet . . . but so will your uncovered head.

SEND THEM PACKING

Dholes, wolves, and other pack animals can be lured with deer carcasses or those of downed farm animals. The trouble is the entire pack shows up; bring armed friends to even the odds.

GET A TIGER BY THE TAIL

Big cats mean big game hunting, for both the tiger and the bait. An animal this large and dangerous will take down anything its size or smaller, sometimes even something larger like water buffalo. Set out a big bait pile and prepare to deal with any smaller prey that comes to investigate—until a tiger (or a honey badger) comes along.

069   STAND UP TO A TIGER

Famed across all of Kyrat, the tiger is regarded as a symbol of royalty and divine blessing—at least, that's what the propaganda broadcasts kept saying—and I also learned that they make for good entertainment in Shanath Arena, where Pagan Min runs blood sports involving political prisoners (see item **084 / Survive in the Arena** if you end up there yourself). The people of Kyrat deal with them in the wild too, whether they're protecting their farms or just themselves. Here are a few tips I learned on my hunting day at the Prabhakar farm.

STEER CLEAR

Unless you're loaded for bear (or tiger), stay well away from any tiger you see; this kitty has claws and fangs, and outweighs you by a lot. Even if you think it's escaped captivity, whether from a farm cage or one of Min's Royal Army outposts, you shouldn't assume it's friendly at all.

USE DISTRACTIONS

If you can leave a personal item behind and sneak away (see item **024 / Move with Stealth**), you might temporarily distract a curious killer cat. Throwing a rock might direct them to the noise, but they're cunning: Be careful not to draw attention to your hiding spot instead.

BE TWO-FACED

Tigers have been known to sneak up on unsuspecting farmers facing away from them . . . and they've also been known to shy away from anyone wearing a mask on the back of their head. I wore a mask on the back of my head the rest of the hunting day, and I wasn't attacked by a single tiger—that's proof enough for me that it works!

GET BIG AND LOUD

Predatory animals will respect a target they can't take down, or one that's not worth the effort. If you're out of options, stand as tall as you can, flap your jacket wide open, raise your arms, and make as much noise as possible. That part might be really easy if you're already screaming in terror. If you have to fight off a tiger hand-to-claw, use every means at your disposal (see item **105 / Fight Off a Cougar** for a few useful tips).

070 RIDE AN ELEPHANT

Transport in Kyrat is mostly by foot, followed by vehicles and sometimes by mount, if you count the occasional Indian elephant. But don't go thinking of those beasts as docile, friendly animals from *The Jungle Book*. In a Royal Army camp recently liberated by the Golden Path, I got close to an elephant's cage to take a few photos; the bull's displeased huff at my camera shutter's noise was followed by angry trumpeting and infuriated cage-slamming. If not for heavy steel mesh I'd have been crushed, and I learned elephants are not domesticated, only tamed—sometimes brutally so, especially by Min's regime. I did get a few tips on riding the elephant once I put away my camera and the bull calmed down, so here they are. (Leave taming to the professionals unless you've got really good medical—and life—insurance.)

UNDERSTAND THE ELEPHANT

These are not pets, but intelligent wild animals often starved or beaten into compliance. Be polite and calm with them, and there's more of a chance they'll do the same. Make sure the elephant is healthy and friendly, as their condition says a lot about who's caring for them. Approach from the right side, and let the elephant see you; they may use their trunk to examine or sniff at you.

An elephant staring silently at you, huffing, or holding their trunk in their mouth signals anxiety or hostility. A set of flapping ears or a swaying tail or trunk means a happy pachyderm.

MOUNT UP SAFELY

It's best to ride an elephant bareback; a howdah or saddle is often painful or chafing. Let the elephant kneel on their own or by command, and step onto their bent knee and grasp the right ear, then bend your knee and bring your other leg over the elephant. Sit up straight but relaxed, and forward on the neck as much as possible with your toes behind the ears. Dismount later by doing these steps in reverse.

RIDE LIKE A KING

Much like when you're on horseback, you steer an elephant with your feet, but be polite or risk getting swatted by a trunk at the least. Press with your toes to walk forward, and push with your heels to back up. Turn left by nudging with your left heel and right toes; turn right by using your right heel and left toes. To ask the elephant to sit down again, press with just one heel.

While watching an old movie about jungle explorers on an equally old black-and-white TV in Banapur, I was struck by a scene where someone ended up in a river teeming with famished piranha. The end of the scene was predictable: The carnivorous fish stripped the poor bastard to the bone in a thrashing, bloody horror. But my Sherpa friend watching over my shoulder merely laughed at the sight. "Go find Demon Fish," Lobsang said, "and tell them about piranha. Then tell me what the Demon Fish did."

I didn't take him up on his offer, especially once he explained further: Demon Fish are cousins to the African Goliath Tigerfish, and both are constantly violently angry, ravenously hungry, and possessed of barbed fins and a mouthful of fangs. These killer fish are the wolves of the water in Kyrat, like their African cousins, sometimes even working in small "packs" to clean a victim of soft tissue so fast it would make Pagan Min wish his arena was aquatic.

If you need to wade a high mountain stream inhabited by these fish, wait until night to cross, as they tend to be more active by day—but don't treat that as an absolute; a hungry Demon Fish can be upon you faster than my editor hounding me about my last deadline. Stay out of the water entirely if you're bleeding from an injury, as they will attack anything they think is wounded; the same goes if you've been handling meat. Do not wash your hands off in any deep streams unless you don't like your hands anymore.

Be as calm and quiet as possible when you cross the water, swim or walk smoothly, and douse lanterns or flashlights. As a last resort, a chunk of bloody meat thrown into the water downstream may help distract the Demon Fish . . . but this will work for only a precious few seconds, so make them count before they decide they want a second helping and spot you on the menu.

072 SKIN A DEMON FISH LIKE A PRO

Along with his advice on avoiding Demon Fish, my Sherpa buddy also gave some fishing tips—namely, "Don't use a pole or net. The Demon Fish will break it, and you will be sad." I asked about noodling (and then carefully explained what noodling was); his look of horror told me all I needed to know. "Use this instead," he advised, and handed me a grenade.

One pulled pin and a tossed handheld explosive later, the crack-blam and spray of water let me know it was working . . . as did the ringing ears and a Demon Fish bobbing to the surface of the lake. It turned out these water-breathing monsters make good eating, similar to catfish or gar—provided you skin them first, because just like catfish or gar, demon fish have a thick tough skin under their scales. Lobsang showed me his time-tested skinning method, and so I pass it onto you. It's simple, too: All you need are a broad wooden plank, a knife, pliers, nail, and a hammer . . . and a Demon Fish.

STEP 1

Use your knife to scrape off the scales, then score the skin around the fish's head in front of the gill plates, making another slit down to the back of the tail. Then drive a nail through the skull and into the board, and cut away the dorsal fin.

STEP 2

Brace the board against your waist with the fish tail near your body. Grasp the skin with pliers and peel it back toward the tail. You don't want your grip to slip while peeling, since that results in punching yourself in the face, so consider using locking pliers.

STEP 3

Pull the nail out of the board to remove the fish, grab the head in one hand and the body in the other, and bend sharply to break the spine. Bend the body up and twist to separate the head; most of the guts will come out with it, but split the belly open and clean the cavity thoroughly.

STEP 4

Prepare the fish to your tastes. I recommend deep-frying in a hot skillet of peanut oil after dredging in flour, egg wash, and a curry-spices-and-breadcrumb blend. Two fingers of scotch to settle the nerves and eardrums post-grenade is optional but encouraged.

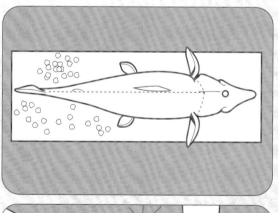

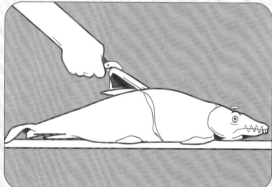

I still can't decide whether that shocking-pink satin suit of Pagan Min's is a fashion triumph or tragedy, but it's possible that it came from the fashion house of Min's former royal tailor, a man who goes by the name Mumu Chiffon. This Kyrati fashion maven had some crazy concepts, especially when it came to incorporating the local wildlife in his Fashion Week designs—which might have had something to do, I later learned, with his sudden fall from Min's favor and subsequent disappearance: The theme of his final Fashion Week event involved arming and armoring the Golden Path rebels as a take-that for being dismissed by Min.

I tend to prefer cuisine over couture (as my food-writing award would attest, if it could talk), but I did a little digging, asked around, and ran from more honey badgers yet again until I had the full scoop. Turns out Fashion Week involved doing the hunting for Mumu, as his strabismus made aiming a firearm damn near impossible, but I can't lie: Mumu Chiffon was inspired indeed—by what, though, I still can't say. Wherever he is now (perhaps he's in exile in Paris, designing gowns from goat hide?) I wish him well, and in his honor I present his notes on the variety of Kyrati animals last targeted for his haute couture creations.

NAME: Sky Tiger (*Panthera tigris*)
LOCATION: Last seen near Barnali's Textiles.
LEATHER QUALITY: Durable and flexible; useful for a medical kit bag.
HUNTING TIPS: Like their Rook Islands cousins, the tigers of Kyrat are not to be trifled with. High stopping power is needed, and lots of it; pack the biggest hunting rifle you can get.

NAME: Tenzin (*Cuon alpinus*)
LOCATION: A pack of dholes often rove around the Kyra Tea Terraces.
LEATHER QUALITY: Smooth, sturdy, a little stretchy; modest hide size makes for useful archery accessories.
HUNTING TIPS: These wild dogs travel in packs, so find high ground, and bring plenty of ammo and arrows.

NAME: Black Water Dragon (*Hydrocynus goliath*)
LOCATION: Swimming in waterways near the Kyra Tea Weigh Station.
LEATHER QUALITY: Tough, rubbery, and solid; good for belts and bandoliers.
HUNTING TIPS: Named for the dark turbulent waters they swim in, so if you're seeking this albino breed of Demon Fish, employ explosives to make your trip a quick one—no bite marks needed!

NAME: Gulo (*Mellivora capensis*)
LOCATION: Spotted close to Pranjjagat School
LEATHER QUALITY: Soft and stretchy, but tough; stow bait for luring or distracting animals in a bag of badger hide and they'll be chewing on it all day.
HUNTING TIPS: After a cull (see item **067 / Take Part in a Cull**) I'd had enough of honey badgers to last a lifetime. Bring an SMG, and as much ammo as you can carry.

NAME: Thick Skin (*Elephas maximus indicus*)
LOCATION: Last seen traveling near Rajgad Gulag, one of Min's old fortresses-turned-prison.
LEATHER QUALITY: Coarse, thick, and very durable. Good for safely carrying heavy munitions.
HUNTING TIPS: You don't ride a Pagan-Min-maddened monstrosity like this; bring serious stopping power to deal with its namesake instead—or to challenge yourself, use fire. (See item **036 / Char Crops with a Flamethrower** for more info on how to bring the heat.)

NAME: The Mad Devil
(*Canis lupus chanco*)
LOCATION: Packs of Himalayan wolves have been seen near KEO Gold Storage.
LEATHER QUALITY: Mildly stretchy and thin but sturdy. Strut your stuff with an ebon-pelted wallet and money clip like a Kyrati king!
HUNTING TIPS: Melanistic Himalayan wolves are often seen leading packs. As when hunting dholes, stay high and bring enough ammo and arrows for the whole class.

NAME: Shadow Leopard
(*Neofelis nebulosa*)
LOCATION: Bronze-pelted clouded leopards spotted close to the KEO Logging Camp.
LEATHER QUALITY: Lightweight, flexible, and resilient. Pack handgun ammo into a pouch made of this hide.
HUNTING TIPS: Like all cats, these darker-tinted clouded leopard offshoots are stealthy and swift. Get the drop on one with explosives.

NAME: Karkadann
(*Rhinoceros unicornis*)
LOCATION: Last seen grazing near Shanath Breeders.
LEATHER QUALITY: Dense, heavy, incredibly tough; useful as a big case for heavy loads of ammo.
HUNTING TIPS: Load up on guns, bring your friends, and pack a box or three of 12-gauge solid slug ammo—you'll need it to pierce rhino hide.

NAME: Ghost Bear
(*Ursus thibetanus*)
LOCATION: Bears have been sheltering in the old KEO Pradhana Mine of late.
LEATHER QUALITY: Dense, mildly stretchy, tough; a pelt this size makes a voluminous bag.
HUNTING TIPS: Get loaded for bear—for real. Pack a shotgun for close encounters in those mine tunnels along with plenty of shells, and remember: "Check those corners."

074 BECOME AN ALLY TO LOCALS

As a traveler, your responsibility is to be a good guest: Don't be the archetypal obnoxious tourist with the Hawaiian shirt, huge camera, and excessively boorish *bonhomie*. (Some exceptions apply; see below.) Be polite and grateful, and cause minimal fuss wherever you go—unless you're looking to aid a nascent rebellion against a local dictator. The journal I carried in Kyrat was water-stained and fire-scorched after my journey, but I still saved a few notes on how to conduct oneself if you're looking to join the local scuffle.

THIS IS THE REAL DEAL

Joining up with a rebellion means risking consequences up to and including prison, injury, or worse, so read your ticket fully before signing your mental death-and-dismemberment waiver. Commit yourself, and keep any badass boasts to a minimum: They'll sound like chicken noises in your rebel friends' memories if it turns out you'd rather hightail it at the first sign of real trouble!

IT'S NOT ABOUT YOU

Surrounded by heroically garbed folks with big guns talking big ideas about freedom and liberation, it's easy to get lost in revolutionary fervor—but remember that you're the outsider here, so don't make it about you. If this were *Dungeons &*

Dragons, they'd be the heroic warrior, and you'd be the henchman. Even if you share an ethnic background, there will always be things you'll never be privy to.

A FAMILY SQUABBLE

This is likely an all-out fight for your new friends, so be willing to help out wherever you can—but don't overdo it. To those new to the Kyrati dialect, "indispensable" sounds a lot like "pawn," and revolutions mean internal power struggles. (Trust me: There are ALWAYS power struggles.) If you see two freedom fighters butting heads, don't get between them. Try being everyone's best friend, and you're likely to become the most popular corpse in the street.

WHERE'S THE GIFT SHOP?!

If you're good at improv, now is your time to shine. Be the bumbling backpacker or entitled foreigner the regime expects you to be! Ask for an autograph from Pagan Min. Beg for a selfie with the local Royal Army commandant, and snap a few extra photos for your DIY recon slideshow. Distract a guard by asking for bathroom directions extra loudly, extra slowly. Complete a stolen uniform by bribing a soldier for their hat as a "souvenir." Your imagination (and insurance payout) is the limit!

075 PROVIDE HELPFUL SUPPLIES

The troops of Kyrat's Royal Army were bandits with aggressive PR management, so I saw firsthand how wealth was given back to the people they took it from, as well as what to bring with you if you (wisely) decide not to be on the front lines of a local conflict. Napoleon has been quoted as saying, "An army marches on its stomach," but even if you're in a peaceful part of the world, you can still lend aid. Just keep in mind that extra supplies can slow you down and may even possibly raise suspicion in authorities. (Plan ahead accordingly, with extra bribe money at the least.)

DON'T DO IT FOR THE 'GRAM

By showing respect, you can be a true friend, not a faux savior. Give meaningful and thoughtful gifts and offer them with the right hand. Skip the alcohol, flashy jewelry or makeup, or cheap plastic toys, and don't hand out candy to every kid you see; dentistry is a Pagan Min–level luxury here. Pairs of new shoes, though, especially for kids, defend dozens of li'l piggies from frostbite.

BE A MINISTER FOR HEALTH

Developing nations mean the locals could use a visit from some NGO humanitarian aid doctors—but there's a waiting list. Bring medical supplies, toiletries (especially floss and toothbrushes), tampons and pads (which can also be retasked as bullet hole patches), painkillers and antibiotics, even birth control or prophylactics of any and all kinds, from pills to condoms.

ADD SOME EDUCATION

I didn't see one school my whole time in Kyrat; I was often distracted by gunfire a lot so I wasn't paying attention as much as I should. Learn from my fail: Sponsor local education with simple math books, notebooks, journals, pens, pencils, and crayons; photo calendars, puzzles, and posters; and durable games and toys such as soccer balls.

RUN POWER AND WATER

Lighting and sanitation are big challenges in much of Kyrat. Water treatment tools such as tablets or UV-sterilizing lights will take care of microbes in that oh-so-clear-looking lake when local pipes run dry for the day. Finding an outhouse in the frigid Kyrati evenings gives terror a new dimension, for the night is dark and full of honey badgers: Bring candles, hand-crank flashlights and radios, and solar battery packs—and your favorite pistol—for when power is cut for the evening.

GIVE 'TIL IT HURTS

Buying local gifts helps stimulate the economy (and makes you some new friends), and the practice of microfinance and microloans through reputable agencies go to virtually anything from cleft palate surgeries to women-owned businesses to local infrastructure.

Day in, day out, propaganda broadcasts droned out from the tannoys mounted on local crumbling towers with the same messages over and over, until I barely noticed changes in curfews or other news. After a while, "May Pagan's light shine on you all" got to be a bad in-joke between myself and Lobsang about the sun shining out King Min's ass instead. Disabling broadcasts, tearing down posters, and even setting them on fire now and then for dramatic effect will only get you so far. Here's what I learned about waging a propaganda war, because it does come down to winning hearts and minds—from more of Pagan's "shining" if nothing else.

KNOW YOUR OPPONENT

"Those who forget their history . . ." might end up in Pagan Min's dungeons. Study history, along with psychology and philosophy, especially as they apply to ideologies such as fascism, nationalism, and totalitarianism.

SEARCH YOUR FEELINGS

When you're exposed to propaganda, notice how you react and how your emotions respond. Propaganda is meant to manipulate your feelings and thoughts; being aware of your reflexive reactions puts you one step closer to reacting rationally instead.

DON'T DOOM SURF

It's tempting to look for every bit of data and propaganda you can (especially in Kyrat where it's as if the Royal Army pastes up new posters to rip down daily), but it'll fatigue you. Take a break. Put down your social media fidget-widget and unwind.

SUBVERT THE MESSAGE

Propaganda overwhelms reason with rhetoric, so undermine and counter it. Be your own local Banksy and put your artistic talents to work inverting the message or making fun of it—at the least you might just get a good laugh out of drawing a huge handlebar mustache on Pagan Min's face.

CLEAR A CHANNEL

Find or create alternative means for people to communicate. Secluded from any propaganda machinery, you'll have a much quieter time with an unmonitored radio frequency, internet chat room, or even physical meeting space well away from the endless announcements.

077 SET A C-4 CHARGE

Sound carries easily in the clear, thin air of Kyrat: the staccato crackling of gunfire, the crisp crack-boom of grenades in firefights (and fishing trips, too; see item **072 / Skin a Demon Fish Like a Pro**), and, every once in a while, the heavy thunder of plastic explosive—sometimes followed by the even heavier thunder of an avalanche. I discovered the wonders of C-4, everyone's favorite plastic explosive, up close and personal: It's malleable, portable, very hard to accidentally detonate, and it's a universal solvent good for clearing away both rockslides and Royal Army roadblocks alike. Here's what I learned about handling the stuff.

STEP 1

Unwrap and shape your spicy play-dough to the job at hand. You can press it into a crack in a wall to blast an opening, mash it into a lump, or sculpt it into a tiny elephant statue for a bit of wartime whimsy. Bricks even come equipped with a peel-and-stick backing for fast and easy deployment!

STEP 2

Insert the detonator. C-4 doesn't explode if you burn, throw, microwave, or even shoot it with conventional bullets, but combine heat and shock from a blasting cap (or a stray tracer round . . .) and your new toy gets very loud, hot, and upset.

STEP 3

Connect the trigger. Attach a timer or, better yet, a remote radio trigger for best results. Timed explosives are great for dramatic movie scenes; not so much if a random farmer and their herd wander too close by.

STEP 4

Get clear and detonate the charge. You don't want to be anywhere near C-4 when it's set off unless you'd like to become part of the scenery—or rather spread across it. A minimum of 300 feet (100 m) plus a solid barrier is a good bet against shockwave and debris. (If you set off an avalanche, see item **061 / Survive an Avalanche**.)

Sometimes, instead of blowing something up, you need to stop something from going boom in the night instead—for example, when I found a charge the Royal Army had set on a small bridge used by local farmers to force them to take a patrolled route. There are lots of options to make a bomb more disarming, depending on your circumstances.

CUT SOME WIRES

Explosive ordnance disposal jobs mean dressing in blast armor like you're in *The Hurt Locker*. They're hard to come by in Kyrat (and in the Royal Army's possession), so protect yourself with your eyes and reflexes: If you see a trip wire leading to a bomb, cut the wire and take it back to the charge. If you spot a remote trigger attached to a C-4 charge, you have an easy task: Pull the trigger out or turn it off. (Just do it quickly before someone out there pushes the big red button.)

MAKE A BIGGER BOOM

Counter-explosives (or a precisely targeted artillery shell) are sometimes used to detonate and destroy a planted bomb—but in the wrong situation, this method can also mean doing the explosive's job for it.

RISE OF THE ROBOTS

If Pagan Min had any bomb robots in his Royal Army arsenal, he'd probably outfit them with explosives for an ironic arena fight instead—but in places where they do exist, they're used by a trained operator to remote-manipulate a bomb, safely blow it up, or cut it apart with a high-pressure water jet.

079 CHOOSE YOUR BLADE

Knives have been with us since early humans first looked at predatory animals' claws and teeth, and said, "Oh, $#!+, we need an upgrade." They're one of our simplest and best tools next to a loaded .45 and a typewriter, and I carried at least one knife on my person in Kyrat . . . and the Rook Islands, and pretty much anywhere else I travel. A good knife is a tool, weapon, utensil, and if need be, surgical instrument; having used one for most any good reason you can imagine, I can still attest to the near-magical properties of a blade wielded by a skilled owner. And there are a lot of choices.

KNOW YOUR ROLE

Your choice of task defines what kind of knife you need, as well as its design. A fishing knife is suited for gutting and cleaning fish and other marine tasks. A kukri is good for gutting and slicing humans and water buffalo. A surgeon's scalpel helps get out shrapnel and put humans back together. (Ultimately, though, the best knife is the one you have on you.)

BE A POINT-TO-EDGE LORD

When deciding on a blade, look at the shape of the point and edge. Straight and convex-backed blades are generally heavier and suited to cutting and stabbing; curved blades are usually lighter, thinner, and better for slicing, skinning, and filleting.

KEEP IT SHARP, KEEP IT SAFE

Stow your knife in a sturdy quick-draw sheath if it's a fixed blade (especially for throwing; see item **080 / Learn to Throw a Knife**); folding blades can go on your belt or into a hip pocket for quick retrieval. Keep your knife sharp, clean, and oiled, and carry a sharpening tool or stone with you if you can. (Some sheaths even have pockets for them.)

Threats come at you fast sometimes—like when that yeti lunged at me from behind a tree while I was trying to make a quiet midnight trip to the outhouse. My knife flashed out of its sheath and stuck the yeti's leg . . . which turned out to be a foraging wild boar, but a follow-up shot with my pistol made sure it didn't run off with my knife in its flank (and we had pork for weeks after). At least it wasn't another honey badger.

Throwing a knife keeps a healthy distance between you and an assailant; otherwise you have to learn to get cozy and fight up close. But you should be damned good at slinging the blade or all you'll do is irritate—and potentially arm—your opponent. Practice is imperative.

Start by holding your knife by the spine of the blade if it's a single-edged knife or a pointed knife made for throwing. (If it's double-edged, have a hand surgeon on speed-dial.) Keep your wrist rigid during the throw to control the blade's rotation. Raise your throwing arm up and over your shoulder. Then lunge forward and throw the knife like pitching a baseball straight-arm (or beaning a Royal Army gunner's helmet with the grenade they just hurled in your direction). Learn to adjust your distance and rotation speed to accommodate for each other, so your throw always lands point-first.

Like I said: Practice is key. Lots, and lots, and lots of practice.

081 SHOOT FROM A MOVING VEHICLE

Traffic in Kyrat is virtually nonexistent, but it does crop up now and then—okay, okay, trading paint with a Royal Army truck while trading lead with the occupants crops up now and then. I was hitching a ride across the central valley in the shotgun seat of a Golden Path technical, enjoying the pleasant breeze and scenic view, before we reached a new Royal Army checkpoint. Our ride became a reenactment of a heist movie car chase, but we eventually made it to safety after picking up a few new bullet holes in the fenders—and learning to improve my aim on the go.

GIVE IT THE GAS

Your options are to fight or escape, and in a vehicle you can do both! Don't give them a free shot by trying to reverse gear or duck down; get this bullet party started by being bold and mashing on the gas pedal like our driver, a charmer named Sejun. If you run your opponents down, you even save ammo, and if you're recording your drive for posterity (like in item **086 / Record a Race, Kyrati Film Style**), then your home movie just became a home action movie.

CRACK (OR SHATTER) A WINDOW

Overpressure is the earsplitting shockwave of gunfire in a closed vehicle—and you thought guns were loud already! Mid-firefight, it's one more distraction from good aim and

your ears will ring later, so roll down the windows (or just sweep away any broken glass with your gun barrel), but don't try shooting through the windshield unless it's already been knocked clear; the steep angle of the glass might deflect your shot into the dashboard or skew it above the target.

THE SUSPENSE IS KILLING THEM

If your combat ride has all-wheel drive, traction control, and premium suspension, you're in luck! Ours was "gently used," however, so I had to account for every loose rock, crack, pothole, and water buffalo carcass Sejun drove over. Be your own shock absorber: Keep your wrists and arms tense (similar to item **117 / Shoot in the Right Stance**), but relax just a bit so your firearm floats a little more serenely while you judder and bounce harshly along.

PRAY AND SPRAY

Once you're in a focused Zen-like state, calmly exhale and squeeze the trigger. Do it again a lot. In a firefight like this, it's tough to remember all the basics, but with enough practice—and moving shootouts—your accuracy will improve. (Or just be like Lobsang, who rode in the back and dumped a light machine gun turret's worth of rounds at the target instead.)

Pagan Min is one paranoid individual. Even though he's living in high castles and hardened compounds, gets escorted in armored vehicles, and is guarded around the clock by morally deficient people with guns, I've heard stories of Min hiring paid actors and giving them cosmetic surgery to create "political decoys," as they're known in the trade. I never met King Min myself, but I think I saw him at a distance once—or it was one of his body doubles, and a good one is hard to tell from the genuine article. The first challenge is getting close enough to tell the difference without being riddled with bullet holes, but there's more to it than just asking for them to show their SAG card.

GET A GOOD BODY

To start, a decoy must be as close a match to the original as possible: Age, skin color, height, weight, and build are all important. If you only ever see him from a distance at a rare public appearance, it might just be a similarly framed person in a similarly eye-watering pink satin suit instead.

SPEAK TO POWER

Pagan Min's voice is a distinctive one: He has a British accent by way of Hong Kong. Decoys have to learn to mimic speech patterns, but when you rattle a double's composure or challenge them by asking them to solve complex math out loud, you just might hear a very different voice.

FACE THE TRUTH

His cheekbones may be highly distinctive, but with the millions in Kyrati gold and other resources in his vaults and accounts, Min could pay for a whole squad of body doubles with plastic surgery, blonde wigs, and colored contacts. If you suspect a decoy, look closely for thin telltale scars and taut skin at the jawline or hairline, under the chin and nose, and so on.

WALK THE WALK

Making a doppelganger dictator means bodily movements, habitual gestures, facial tics, even a stride to imitate. A trained actor can learn the moves (and wear custom shoes to help their gait), but you might see their real behavior emerge in a lull or when they're alone—or when they're fleeing in absolute terror after Pagan Min finds that they've borrowed his favorite fountain pen and is calling the double's minders to have his decoy summarily shot.

083 HIDE A BODY

If you end up in situations like I do as an award-winning combat journalist and poet, you'll see plenty of bodies. And whether it's a fallen companion, a dead guard, a defeated head honcho like Pagan Min himself—or maybe just a body double (really? Did you read the previous item?)—at some point, you're going to need to do something about a body. Burial is for ones you *care about*; you'll just want to tidy up the one in front of you before someone else spots it. If they were friends with the corpse's previous occupant, they'll have pointed questions to ask . . . and axes to grind, so pay attention.

FIND A RESTING PLACE

Once you've satisfied your curiosity about any spare change and spare condoms in its pockets, find the closest possible location to stash this meat rag doll. You need it to both fit a body and be out of the way—don't shove the rapidly cooling corpse into the camping cooler on the front porch. Think "in the woodbin," "under a dense thicket of brush," "behind the outhouse," or "over a nearby cliffside above a lake teeming with ever-hungry Demon Fish."

COLD STORAGE TIME

Now you need to move the dead body to your dead-drop location. If you have help, it's easy: Pick up one end each and walk away. Most likely, though, you'll be on your own, so your job just got harder. When this happens, remember my words of advice: "You should have brought someone with you."

GET CARRIED AWAY

One way to lift a body is the fireman's carry: Squat in front of a face-down body, lift it by the armpits, and drape one arm, then the torso, around your shoulders. Alternatively, try sitting the body up, knees to the chest, then squat down in front of it, pull the torso and arms over your shoulder, and stand up while holding the legs to your chest.

A REAL DRAG

Unless you're a bodybuilder or lumberjack, you won't hoist a carcass like cordwood. Time to drag it! Don't be shy; they're beyond all suffering—but you'll be found guilty over Exhibit A in your upcoming murder trial-by-gunfire if you leave drag marks or blood trails. Grab the shirt collar or pack straps if you're really lucky; if you're unlucky, grab the legs or shoulders, and get pulling. (If you can't drag a body, see item **051 / Train for the Mountains** for helpful fitness tips.)

Blood sports combine terror, excitement, and luck—and I'm just talking about the crowd. Since Shanath Arena was first built in 1759, hundreds of gallons have spilled to entertain the Kyrati people (read: distract them from revolting). I got to see a few matches after bribing my way in since they don't exactly sell tickets, and it was standing room only: a sea of spectators roaring as loudly as the combatants. I left soon after, especially once I noticed an elegantly dressed Kyrati woman overseeing the fights—apparently named Noore—looking my way a little too often for comfort. The screams faded behind me, as did the hot-iron tang of blood, but I'd seen enough to take notes on how to survive as a gladiator in Kyrat . . . if only for a few minutes.

NO MERCY, NO RETREAT

Living means becoming the biggest, baddest, deadliest sonofabitch on the sand. If you end up on Pagan Min's "naughty" list and he has you thrown to the wolves (or tigers, or honey badgers), it's time to choose between humanity and survival. Maybe you can rediscover your humanity after scrubbing off all the gore.

ARE YOU NOT ENTERTAINED?!

In ancient Rome, gladiators were like pro wrestling stars; so too with longtime fighters here. Use dirty, flashy tactics: Spit the blood running down your face at your opponent! The sand under your feet? Kick it in their eyes! Be flashy with your blade, work the crowd, make them love you, and you just might survive to do it all over again later.

I HAVE THE HIGH GROUND

Use the terrain any way you can. A stone block can be cover from stray rounds. Use a fallen column as concealment to sneak up on an enemy. Scale a ledge to leap onto an elephant's back (see item **070 / Ride an Elephant** for a few tips) . . . and hope you're not thrown and trampled instead.

A FRIEND ON THE INSIDE

Amid the snarling of beasts and screams of human contestants, I saw one combatant facing a surprisingly sluggish bear—then I spotted the handler discarding an empty syringe. If you can beg, bribe, or steal an extra blade or gun for yourself, or sedative for your opponent, do it. You'll be really glad you did.

085 COOK UP CRAB RANGOON

Several hundred miles southeast of Kyrat lies the nation of Myanmar, home of the province and city of Yangon—better known to most westerners as Rangoon, as in "crab rangoon." Cream cheese didn't come from southeast Asia, but since this appetizer debuted on the menu at Trader Vic's back in the '50s, it's taken off at Asian-style restaurants worldwide. I'm mildly allergic to shellfish, but King Min is reputedly a big fan. (I'm guessing he imports the main ingredient; goat or yak cream cheese would be . . . let's say pungent.) I considered offering an award-winning preparation to get into his graces, but when I heard he executed his last chef and their family in a fit of pique, I chose to play it safe, but his loss is your gain. Enjoy the crab rangoon!

INGREDIENTS

8 ounces (240 g) crab meat, well drained
8 ounces (240 g) cream cheese, softened
2 medium green onions, thinly sliced
1 large clove garlic, minced
1 tablespoon (15 ml) Worcestershire sauce
1 teaspoon (5 ml) soy sauce
½ teaspoon (2.5 ml) fish sauce
½ teaspoon (2.5 ml) sesame oil
Salt and pepper to taste
48 wonton skins
Oil for frying
Sweet and sour sauce

STEP 1

Combine the first nine ingredients in a bowl, stirring with a fork until blended thoroughly. Cover the bowl and refrigerate 1 or 2 hours until chilled. If you've no fridge, set it outside in the cold Kyrati night.

STEP 2

Set a small bowl of water next to your workstation. Add ½ tablespoon (7 g) of the filling to the center of a wonton skin wrapper. Dip your finger in the water bowl then dab the water along the edge of the wonton skin to moisten the edge. Fold the wonton skins into pyramid shapes and pinch the seams together, squeezing out any air trapped inside.

STEP 3

Heat the frying oil in a heavy-bottomed pot to 350°F (220°C); for high altitude cooking in Kyrat, drop the heat by 3°F (about 1.5 °C) for every 1,000 feet (300 m) elevation to avoid overcooking the outside and leaving the filling underdone. Fry in batches, being sure not to crowd the pot, for about 3 minutes until crispy and golden. Remove from the oil and place wontons on a paper-towel-lined plate. Continue frying until all wontons have been cooked. Serve with sweet and sour sauce; this recipe makes 8 servings of six wontons each. (If you end up presenting the dish to Pagan Min, get your will in order and your family somewhere safe first just in case.)

086 RECORD A RACE, KYRATI FILMS STYLE

While in Kyrat, I met Sharma Salsa, a former Kyrati adult film performer bitten by the directing bug, and our backgrounds (mine in gonzo journalism, hers in gonzo porn) led to some bonding. Amidst some fulsome flirting, I learned she diversified her portfolio after her co-star Riti died some years ago; Sharma now produces action and stunt films. We traded a few tips on camera work . . . including a how-to on extreme closeups, but mostly about

mounting cameras on vehicles to film wild rides on the narrow mountain roads of Kyrat. The Royal Army's heavy trucks crawl on these trails, but light vehicles (except tuk tuks; see item 089) can much more easily handle the twists and turns of a high-speed action-filled ride. Don't believe me? Do a search for Kyrati Films sometime—or grab a car and a camera, and try it yourself!

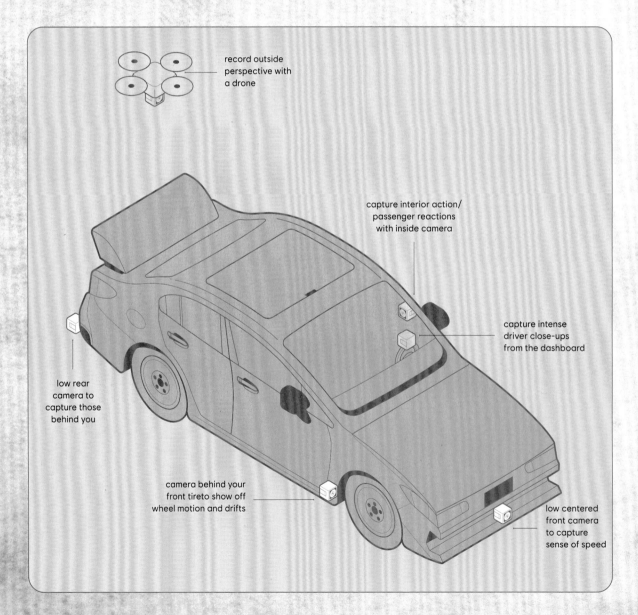

record outside perspective with a drone

capture interior action/ passenger reactions with inside camera

capture intense driver close-ups from the dashboard

low rear camera to capture those behind you

camera behind your front tireto show off wheel motion and drifts

low centered front camera to capture sense of speed

087 WING IT (WITH A WINGSUIT)

If you're familiar with skydiving (see item **042 / Pull On a Parachute**), you might have heard of wingsuiting. Not content with just plummeting out of the sky, some use a suit equipped with airfoils similar to parachutes and fall with style. Kyrat's spectacular heights mean cliffs aplenty for BASE jumpers, as well as wingsuit flyers—and they're often both. It takes around two hundred jumps before a skydiving instructor will offer wingsuit training, so I have plenty to go, but here's what I've learned in my own experience, and after meeting a few extreme sports enthusiasts gearing up to leap off King's Bridge. (Hopefully they landed safely somewhere.)

GET FIT FOR FLIGHT

Wingsuit flight demands peak physical ability; you're fighting a wind blowing in your face the whole time, which means you need to be strong enough to control your flight. Prepare for cardio, calisthenics, core exercises, and doing push-ups using handles hanging from ropes while your feet are similarly suspended.

SOAR LIKE AN EAGLE

You might waddle like a duck on the ground, but at altitude you'll be a rocket: the record is 250 mph (400 kph), set in 2017, and on average you can easily reach 120 mph (225 kph) or more. Mostly you'll glide downward, but with enough airspace between you and the ground and a little luck finding thermal updrafts, some flyers have gained up to 250 feet (80 m).

KNOW THE DANGER

Flying nap-of-earth after a BASE jump gives an amazing sense of speed—but maybe don't do that. Multiple jumpers die yearly in accidents; plenty are wingsuit flyers who misjudge the terrain and—like a fly meeting a windshield—find the last thing going through their mind is their own ass.

088 HOP IN A HOVERCRAFT

When I was a kid, I had a beloved RC hovercraft toy, and I dreamed about driving a real one someday. On one of my last days visiting the Kingdom of Kyrat, my dream came true when Sharma Salsa asked me to meet her on the lakeshore near Banapur. I know, it sounds like the opening to a salacious story, and I anticipated helping her apply sunscreen; instead, she gestured to a watercraft parked by her sunning spot and handed me the keys. Unlike the giant seagoing vessels, this tiny version is ridden by one or two people—more akin to an airboat in the Florida Everglades, only with fewer alligators and less cocaine smuggling (replaced by crocodiles and opium smuggling). The best part, aside from the sheer awesomeness of fulfilling my childhood dream? The taste of hovercraft is entirely unappetizing to Demon Fish.

START OFF SLOWLY

A parked hovercraft looks like a dead jellyfish washed up on a beach, but once you fire it up, the skirts inflate and

your ride slips and slides around loosely unless you're in control . . . just like the RC toy from my childhood. Baby this beastie until you're very competent.

GET WET GRADUALLY

Just like I was, you'll be tempted to scream "Banzaaai!" then twist the throttle and zip across the water. I'm glad Sharma tied the thing to a post by the water or I might have sunk it. Begin on relatively level ground where the friction helps you learn control . . . and where you won't sink if your engine stalls and the skirts deflate.

LEAN IN AND HANG ON

A hovercraft has about as many controls as the RC version: steering and propulsion. It helps if you lean into the steer like you're on a motorcycle (or a tuk tuk on a cliffside road). It's open-topped, so if you don't lean into a hard sudden turn you just might end up under the hovercraft—once again, just like a motorcycle.

089 BUZZ OFF

The rocky peaks and windswept hills of this land don't afford many options for air travel, and the one tiny airport is perilously short on visitors or aircraft. A good helicopter with a skilled pilot at the stick can handle the windy skies over Kyrat, but both are usually in the hire of King Min. Still, some folks here have options in the form of the autogyro: a tiny helicopter-ish aircraft with a whirling blade of doom just above the pilot's head. My buddy Lobsang introduced me to a friend who uses one to ferry supplies for the Golden Path and others, for a price; his friend showed me his brightly painted autogyro he dubbed the "buzzer" for the angry giant insect noise it makes, then gave me a ground-level training course. I might even fly one someday. (Maybe not.)

SPIN IT UP

To get up in the air, you need your blades spinning. Once the engine starts, engage the clutch to wind up the blades, then twist the throttle smoothly to lift off and accelerate. Just don't ascend too high or too fast; you'll soar like an eagle until you reach your flight ceiling and begin an "unscheduled landing"— again, while screaming like an eagle, only in terror.

TWIST IN THE WIND

You steer this contraption with your feet on rudder pedals to rotate left or right, instead of speeding up or braking; imagine curling your toes around a second steering wheel and you'll be close. Kinda.

ADD SOME JOY(STICK)

The big joystick in front of the pilot's seat won't have any fire controls, but it still tilts the rotor back, forward, and sideways. Use it to guide your flight, but exercise caution—rotary-wing aircraft need their blades overhead to maintain lift, not to the side, and most definitely not underneath.

STICK THE LANDING

To return safely to Terra Firma, find yourself a clear area large enough to land with space to spare, then throttle back to descend. Be very careful upon landing and climbing out of the seat, or you'll find out how a dandelion feels when it meets a weed whacker. Hunker down when you exit, or wait for the blades to stop spinning, and you'll save anyone nearby from seeing your impression of Vic Morrow.

090

TRY A TUK TUK

The tuk tuk is Asia's answer to the age-old question: "What would happen if a Shriner's scooter and a motor tricycle had a lovechild in a glitter factory?" These vehicles are like a microcosm of Kyrat or King Min himself: They're colorful, inherently unstable, and will kill you if you don't take them seriously. But much like Kyrat itself, my Sherpa companion Lobsang absolutely loves the things . . . and to be honest, so do I; they got us from one end of Kyrat to the other, in between roadside repairs—and once, fending off an amorous elephant who mistook our shiny ride for his mate-to-be. (If this happens to you, see item **070 / Ride an Elephant** to turn the tables.)

MOTOR IT

Driving a tuk tuk is very simple: Turn the key to start the engine, and rev the throttle on the right handlebar. Disengage the parking brake, and manage the footbrake below. Squeeze the clutch on the left handlebar and shift gears, then throttle up and let out the clutch. Motorcycling experience helps here, and it's a forgiving machine—mostly!

DON'T GET COCKY, KID

Three wheels give a tuk tuk plenty of agility; these things turn on a rupee and give you change! But when I said "inherently unstable," I meant it. Think of it like the three-wheeled ATV your cousin rode on the farm and nearly got himself crushed under that one time you visited on summer vacation, and treat the tuk tuk accordingly: less recklessly than your cousin and his ATV. (You'll thank me when you're driving at speed along a 6-foot- (2-meter) wide cliffside "road" in a gradually building white-out.)

MAGIC CARPET RIDE

Taking a ride in a tuk tuk is very much like a county-fair carnival ride: It's full of whimsy and music, hard plastic and metal surfaces, and lots of things whirling by just outside the chassis. And just like the carnie barking out safety warnings told you before he engaged the Tilt-A-Hurl 9000, secure your belongings and keep your arms and legs inside the vehicle at all times!

SOULS DO NOT
HARVEST THEMSELVES

HOPE COUNTY, MONTANA

"Was this the face that launched a thousand RPGs, and blew up the towers of Ilium?"
—Paraphrase of pastoral poet Christopher Marlowe, 1592

After spending enough time dodging bullets on the Rook Islands and in Kyrat, I desperately needed a vacation. I returned to the US and traveled to Hope County, Montana, to take a much-needed break from insanity and enjoy some local flavor—experiencing the world-famous testy festy, ample fishing opportunities and beautiful landscapes stretching farther than the eye can see. It's enough to ignite a poetic pilot light inside the heart of anyone. Its beauty is a warm and cleansing bath for the soul, offering endless hours and countless broken limbs' worth of extreme outdoor enjoyment for you to say "yes!" to. A great place to visit for adventure seekers, aspiring poets, and sinners alike in search of verticality, inspiration from God's green thumb, or salvation. There's plenty of all three in Hope County for anyone who wants it. But the bucolic splendor can be hard to take in over gunfire echoing off the mountains, cult propaganda on the radio, and the occasional hallucinogenic high from crawling through crops of Bliss. All that aside though, it really is just a beautiful place to visit. It wasn't long before my vacation devolved into my third tour of insanity.

Hope County is cut off from the rest of the country, run by a doomsday cult that calls themselves the "Project at Eden's Gate." (The locals refer to the members as "Peggies.") They've completely taken control of the region and don't take too kindly to outsiders . . . but then again, when are these places ever kind to outsiders? The father figure of this "family" is a deranged preacher named Joseph Seed. He, along with his holy trinity of heralds—his sadistic brothers John and Jacob, and a mysterious woman named Faith—command a cult of fanatical devotees armed to the teeth and willing to bullet-spread the word of Joseph's gospel into sinners with a baptism by bloodbath. When they're not trying to kill you, they like to spend their time outdoors kidnapping and brainwashing locals, exposing them to extreme doses of a hallucinogenic drug, Bliss, and rendering them into brainless, zombie-like drones. But really, all that aside, Hope County does have a robust and dedicated doomsday prepper community that reminded me of my father and I've never felt more at home because of it.

This chapter will give you the basic, essential survival knowledge you would expect for a place like this, including the standards: how to make your own fishing pole, how to ride a zip line, and how to deprogram after brainwashing. And if you ever get lost, just walk the path. It's a pilgrimage that will lead you to salvation.

Grab your guns and a tinfoil hat; it's time to survive Hope County!

091 STOCK A BUG OUT BAG

Survivalism and self-sufficiency are major things for most people I met in Montana. Nearly everyone I met was proud to admit they had their own personal stash of "prepper" gear. My dad would have appreciated the ingenuity locals put into hiding their prepper stashes. He would have flourished here. Knowing the importance of traveling light in an emergency, the locals usually disagreed with me adding a typewriter to a bug out bag (BOB)—but everyone approved of the pistol that went with it. If the world is caving in and you have to run, you'll need a go-bag of your own. Keep it close at hand or in your car trunk, along with some crucial road safety gear. Long after leaving Hope County, I've kept my own BOB stocked (with a backup typewriter and pistol) just in case.

- Energy bars, trail mix, and a few ready-to-eat packaged meals

- Bottles of water, a filter, and purifying tablets

- Reflective emergency blanket, tent, and sleeping bag

- Lighter, fire striker, and tinder cubes

- A change of clothes (pants, shirt, socks, underwear, gloves, hat, windbreaker, and poncho)

- Flashlight with extra batteries

- Knife, spork, and can opener

- Paracord, snare wire, and fishing line, hooks, and weights

- Battery-powered radio, and solar panel battery

- Sanitation and hygiene items (toilet paper, soap, small towel)

- First aid kit and manual (see item **001 / Build Your First Aid Kit**)

- Any special needs items (medication, eyeglasses, contact solution, typewriter, handgun)

- Car safety items (spare tire, tire iron, jumper cables, windshield scraper, flares, extra oil and coolant, a small shovel, tire chains, and a bag of kitty litter)

092

FIND WATER IN THE WILDERNESS

Following a story is often thirsty work for me—and sometimes that even means water. For those in the Whitetail Militia, staying a step ahead of religious maniacs sometimes means no convenient faucets or water coolers. In the wild, drinking water has to be found and collected and purified as well. We're all mostly water, and we all need the clear wet stuff, so take note even if you're not dodging the armed and dangerous yourself.

PLAN AHEAD

Look for reliable water sources in the area. Check topography maps and Google Earth; local Bureau of Land Management and National Forest Service offices can also provide valuable info.

GET THE LAY OF THE LAND

The backcountry often has plentiful water sources, but sometimes they're few and far between and hard to find.

One water source in the hills of Montana was at the base of a high cliff atop a tall escarpment, and I reached it from above by a narrow game trail. If I hadn't been shown it, I'd never have known it was there.

SEEK THE SIGNS

Out in dry country, you need to know how to find small seeps and tanks. The most obvious clues are vegetation: Tamarack, willows, and cottonwoods all indicate water. Following game or livestock trails along with wild honeybees point to potential water sources. Sometimes you can find one at the bottom of a ravine, wash, or cliff base, like a "hanging garden" where water seeps under the cliff, creating a small marshy area.

093 PURIFY WATER SAFELY

Before you go face-planting in a creek you happened across on a hot, dry, dusty trek, remember: Drinking tainted water is always a bad idea, even if you have a bottle of Pepto and a hospital close by. In the backcountry, with no hospital and medicine in short supply, it can be a real disaster. Sometimes you can tell if the water is potable, but after one mercifully short case of bubble guts, I chose to purify any source that was even the slightest bit suspect. Luckily, there are plenty of proven tools for the job.

BOIL IT

If there's one thing I've learned (especially from handling a flamethrower; see item **036 / Char Crops with a Flamethrower**), it's that fire kills everything. As long as you have fire and a container, water can go from "pukeable" to potable: Five minutes of a rolling boil, and 99.99 percent of evil water buggies are eliminated.

ADD IODINE

It doesn't taste great, but then again, vomit is much worse. Iodine kits usually have two tiny bottles: one with iodine tablets, the other full of neutralizing tablets. Drop in the directed amount of iodine, wait thirty minutes, then add neutralizer and wait three minutes more. Drink up!

CLEAN WITH CHLORINE

It's not just for your relatives' swimming pool! Much like iodine, chlorine kits can quickly kill bacteria and parasites in thirty minutes. It won't taste as unpleasant, either: Most folks are used to the taste from home water filtration systems.

PUMP AND PURIFY

Using a dedicated purifier is still the most effective method, as it even removes heavy metals and other toxins that boiling or tablets won't take care of. The ceramic filters in a hand pump mean sparkling clean spring water, but keep in mind a pump is heavier and bulkier than drops or tablets.

094 PREVENT A FOREST FIRE

In the wildlands of rural Montana, fire was (and still is) a major concern, whether sparked by dry hot weather, a stray coal from a campfire, or a cult "angel" who just fumbled a Molotov Hail Mary and is now auditioning for the role of Human Torch. No matter the source, a certain bear would have you remember that only you can prevent wildfires—don't let your fire get away with you as it could torch fields and forests. I prefer my fires in a controllable size, so I picked up a few fire safety tips to share.

INSTANT CAMP, JUST ADD FIRE

The safest spot to build your fire will be in an existing fire pit, since surrounding flammable material is already burned away. If you happen across one, you're in luck! If you haven't, well then . . .

START FROM SCRATCH

If you need to build a fresh fire base, find a site at least 15 feet (5 m) from brush, dry grass, overhead branches, Eden's Gate members, and other flammables. Clear a 10-foot-wide (3 m) spot of anything that can burn and dig a pit 1 foot (30 cm) deep into the soil. Circle the pit with rocks.

DROWN OR BURY IT

Much like people, fires don't last long underwater or in the ground. When you're done with the fire, ensure it won't rise again like Rasputin: Smother it with plenty of water, or if you're short on water, bury the embers deep under the dirt.

Despite the stereotypes you might have seen in *Deliverance*, most people I met who self-identify as rednecks aren't into banjos or terrifying city folks. They are definitely into hunting, though—including Darnell, a resident of the town of Fall's End who befriended me. Aside from his favorite camo-painted shotgun, he advised me that the best hunting companion was man's best friend. "Don't take just any old hound and jump in your truck," Darnell cautioned. "You've gotta train 'em up first." It's not a common skill, but with a little work, you too can turn Fido into a sniffing machine.

BUST SOME CAPS

After general obedience training, the first thing you need to do is to train the fear of gunfire out of the dog. Absent any shootouts with cultists, your best bet is to start by shooting a cap gun near them until they learn to settle down. Trade up to a real firearm loaded with blanks after that; once your hunting-hound-in-training is used to the louder sound, keep them nearby and leashed during target practice. Offer reassurance along the way, and your dog will learn in time that gunfire = time for them to go to work.

DRAG OUT THE HUNT

Run 10 feet (3 m) of paracord through a 5-foot (1.5-m) length of PVC pipe, and attach the cord to a training dummy bird or bundle of cloth and scrap of deer hide. Add an appropriate animal scent or blood as needed, and lay down a trail by holding the pipe away from your body. Start with short straight line retrievals; up the difficulty with twists and turns, tall grasses, and short gaps in the scent trail.

TREAT SUCCESS RIGHT

Use treats sparingly and only to keep your dog interested. The point is to reach the deer or bird payoff at the trail's end; don't hand out Vienna sausages the whole way!

096

BUILD A MAKESHIFT FISHING POLE

Next to hunting, fishing is one of the favored activities defining a rural lifestyle. Even though I was carrying a stocked BOB (see item **091 / Stock a Bug Out Bag**), I didn't have a pole with me, but Darnell had a solution that would have pleased even Eddie the Rakyat fisherman. To help feed a handful of militia folks we met up with one day, he simply whipped out a Swiss Army knife and went to work making his own fishing gear. If you have hooks, line, and weights, the pole is the next obvious part. Here's how we made ours, in three easy steps.

STEP 1

Find a flexible hardwood sapling, about thumb thickness at the base and 2 or 3 yards (1.8-2.7 m) long. Look for a slender young tree growing in a thick tangle of brush. The tree will be skinny but strong from competing with other plants—and you'll even do them a service by removing it.

STEP 2

Cut the tree with any tool you have. An axe, a saw, or even a pocketknife will work; just make sure the cut end is smooth and free of cracks or splinters.

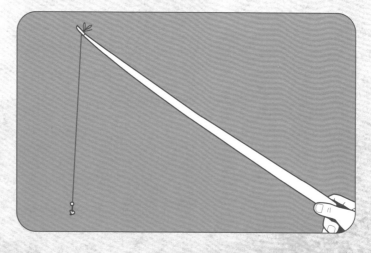

STEP 3

Trim off any branches and tie your fishing line to the slender end of the pole. Add hooks and bait, or if you're short on lures, see the next item.

To catch a good fish, you need a good fishing pole and a good set of lures. If you have an alright fishing pole made from a local stick (see previous item), you at least need an alright set of lures. Luckily, the fish won't really know the difference, especially once the hook is set and you've landed your aquatic opponent. Along with the pole-making skills I witnessed, I got to see Darnell's work embellishing his tackle with a few quick and easy methods.

GET THE HOOKUP

If you can't find a hook, go low-tech and pop the top off a beer or soda can. Cut part of the tab free to make a hook shape, then tie it on!

PLUG THE LINE

For a brightly colored floating option, stick a foam earplug on a hook or tie a line around it to the hook, then cast away. Just be sure to retrieve it later if you think you'll want hearing protection during a shootout.

CAP IT OFF

All those fishing beers can even draw the fish to you, if you prefer bottles over cans like Darnell does: Grab a bottle cap and toss a few tiny pebbles into it, then crimp it shut. Pierce a hole in each end and attach a split ring to each one. Add a swivel and hook to the rings, and you're set.

CLIP AWAY

My journalistic background let me in on the DIY action, thanks to some pocket litter: Find a paper clip, wrap it with electrical tape, then slide the rubber sleeve from the barrel of a pen over it. Add a hook and line. Voilà! A redneck-approved lure resembling a squashed leech is now yours.

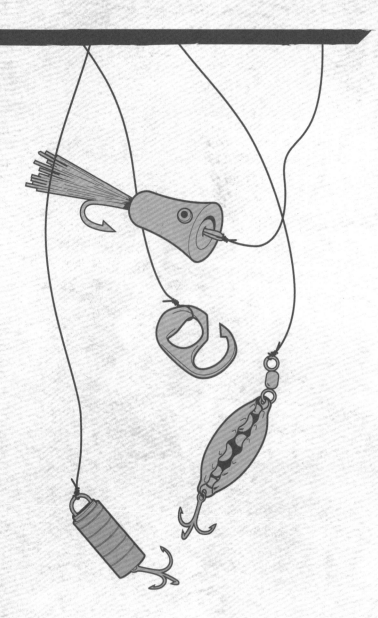

098 REEL IN A BIG FISH (WITHOUT GETTING TIRED)

Unlike my visits to the Rook Islands or Kyrat, where I saw firsthand how to fish with nets and grenades respectively (see item **072 / Skin a Demon Fish Like a Pro**), fishing in Montana was confined solely to poles. (The latter would have drawn too much attention from cultists.) While casting and retrieving with the pole I'd made (see previous items **096 / Build a Makeshift Fishing Pole** and **097 / Make Your Own Lures**), I suddenly felt the branch dip down hard when a sizable fish took the bait. A hard fight ensued, with Darnell a little too enthusiastically offering creekside tips, and amazingly my pole survived the retrieval—before snapping just as I landed a trout. A fish in the hand is worth two in the creek, though; after a few more casts (with another hand-cut fishing pole) we all dined on freshly caught fish cooked by the stream.

SPARE THE ROD, SPOIL THE FISH

Once you know the fish is hooked, let the rod's elasticity and the friction of the line in the water help do the work of tiring the fish out. With a simple hand-cut pole, tire the fish out by going easy at first, then gradually bend the pole backward while letting it curve down toward the water. If you're using a reel, set the drag to about a quarter of the line's weight and wind it in steadily.

DON'T BE A SLACKER

Both a non-reel and a reel-equipped pole can use a variant of this technique. Start by raising the pole to take up some slack and draw the fish closer. Reel in the line as you lower the pole again; with a stick pole, take a half step or two backward from the water.

TAKE IT FOR A WALK

Unlike your opponent, you have the whole land to work with, so show this fish who's boss: Move along the creekside, pulling the pole low and steady in the opposite way the fish is facing, and you'll keep the fish hooked while it tries to swim away. Combined with the rest of these tactics, you'll soon have a fish on the riverbank.

099 BEFRIEND A WILD ANIMAL

In a place like Montana, you'd think most animals would be in either the "food" or "trophy" category—or both. But animal sanctuaries do exist, like the Friends of the Animals Nursing Grounds, home to Cheeseburger, the famed grizzly bear. I learned the F.A.N.G. Center had become home to other animals—namely Peggies, as I heard some in the Resistance dubbed members of the Project at Eden's Gate—and the bear was missing, but I found a few handy brochures scattered around. The most important fact I read in them: Cheeseburger is unusually friendly for a bear. Most other wild animals are, well, wild. Trying to tame them can mean they lose their fear of humans and need to be put down—or in larger numbers, culled. (See item **067 / Take Part in a Cull**.)

PICK YOUR PREY

To become a real-life fairytale princess, try befriending prey or scavengers: squirrels, rodents, small birds, even some larger ones like crows or ravens. The animal will be skittish; sit as still and quietly as possible. Improve your odds vastly by offering treats: A handful of trail mix is a buffet to tiny beasties. (Bonus points if you have a dead mouse or bait fish to offer up to a corvid.) Set down the treats or offer them at arm's length, and don't expect to pet or grab the animal. Once again, be patient.

PASS ON PREDATORS

Remember, these are wild animals. Your options are limited unless your definition of "friendship" involves letting a mountain lion pick your bones clean. Larger animals such as big cats can be bribed with enough food—as in "raw meat tossed from a good distance." Hand-feeding is likely to be extremely literal if you try it up close. As for Cheeseburger . . . processed foods are unhealthy for wild animals. (If you run into a bear that isn't Cheeseburger, see item **104 / Survive Grizzlies**.)

100 CHOW DOWN ON SQUIRREL

Along with an inexhaustible stream of hunting and fishing tips, Darnell also demonstrated his favorite method of varminting for me. Squirrels may be full of "aww" factor (especially if you want to befriend one; see previous item), but they're also pests. Keeping their numbers down can keep you from going hungry if you can't hunt down or fish up something more sizeable. All you need is a stick and some electrical wire.

STEP 1

Find a sturdy branch at least 3 inches (7.5 cm) wide. Prop it on the trunk of a tree, where the lower branches grow.

STEP 2

Cut electrical wire into 1- to 2-foot (30-60-cm) lengths. No wire? Follow Darnell's example and strip wire from a spare coaxial cable or phone line. Add a loop 2 to 3 inches (5-7.5 cm) wide to each length. Twist the wire around itself so the noose tightens easily.

STEP 3

Tie the other end of each noose to the pole. Make sure each loop is no higher than 1 inch (2.5 cm) above the pole's surface. At least a dozen total loops on your rodent hanging tree means squirrels have to pass through at least one.

STEP 4

Sit and wait. Squirrels are naturally curious, and they'll eventually explore the pole. When one runs through a noose, it will fall off the pole and strangle.

STEP 5

Much like what happens after knocking out a cultist with a too-accurately-thrown rock, others will come to investigate—and unlike with cultists, you'll have a squirrel feast.

STEP 6

After skinning and cleaning, Darnell recommended frying: Dredge squirrels in a mix of flour, garlic powder, cayenne, salt, and black pepper, then sauté away! (I say skip the PBR, though.)

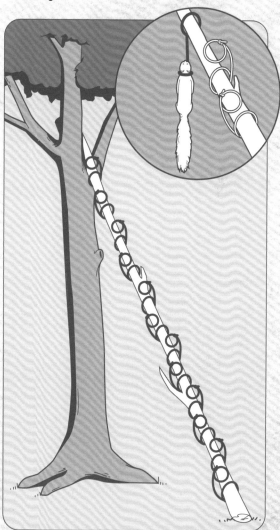

101 ENJOY ROADKILL

The roads through Hope County are dominated by trucks: everything from light pickups to dualies to eighteen-wheelers for logging and farming. That means roadkill—lots of it. I can't think of a single food award given out for "best highway pizza," but my avowed redneck companion told me not to turn my nose up too quickly. In worst-case scenarios such as evading religious nuts who've taken over your hometown, food can be scarce, so how can you tell if that rigor mortis raccoon is still within its best-scraped-up-by date?

MARK THE CALENDAR

Rigor mortis isn't necessarily bad. In rigor, a carcass is good for at least a day in warm weather, and up to three in cold.

CHECK FOR FRESHNESS

If your critter caprese wasn't on the roadside yesterday, it's fresh. And the nose really does know (as I learned when I passed by something too flat to recognize); if it smells bad, it is.

LOOK FOR PESTS

Flies are usually the first guests to the road-pizza party, so seeing them is a good sign. If you see eggs or maggots on the carcass, though, you'll want to skip the buggy buffet.

DON'T FORGET TO EYEBALL THE ORGANS

Swelling means internal decay and gas buildup. If roadkill resembles the world's worst birthday balloon or if you see ruptured organs, don't poke this piñata, just drive on!

SKIP THE SOUS VIDE

Be extra thorough in cleaning and preparation. When it comes to cooking, the longer and hotter the better.

102 TRY A PRAIRIE OYSTER

Every year since 1971, the Spread Eagle Bar in Fall's End has been home to "Testy Festy"—the local affectionate nickname for the Testicle Festival, where the main course is, well . . . bull testicles. High in protein and vitamins, they're Hope County's own regional delicacy. At the time of my visit to Hope County, the festival was under threat thanks to the Eden's Gate Project, but I got to share recipe ideas with Casey Fixman, who runs the event yearly. They might be a bit hard for some to swallow, so I also added a few suggested beverage pairings.

FRIED

Peel the membrane from each "oyster," then slice into thin medallions. Cover in a flour and cajun spice mix, then deep-fry and serve with hot sauce. Goes well with a malty ale.

BAKED

Peel and slice into 1-inch (2.5 cm) disks; cover in salt, pepper, and flour. Sauté garlic and onions in a skillet, then add red wine, tomato paste, and testicles. Bake at 350°F (160°C) for thirty minutes, let cool for ten minutes, then serve with the remaining bottle of red wine.

GRILLED

Peel and slice testicles into halves. Soak in light beer for one hour and grill over open flame. Sprinkle with lemon juice; serve on a sandwich roll with coleslaw. Pair with a robust IPA.

BREWED

Casey also shared a taste test of his experimental festival beer, which he called Brew Ball Stout. He was cagey about the exact recipe, but admitted it uses cane sugar, roasted and flaked barley, dark malt, champagne yeast, and at least two whole testicles. Much like other stouts, it has a creamy mouthfeel and a nutty finish. As for pairing? He wants to sell it in two-packs.

VEGETARIAN

For those shy about gonad grub, try the "vegetarian" option: Crack an egg into a shot glass, add a splash each of tabasco and soy sauce, and a dash of salt and pepper. Toss the whole thing back like a shot of whiskey. Follow with a real shot of whiskey.

103 MAKE MOONSHINE

The Montana spirit of self-sufficiency is embodied perfectly in, well, spirits: the age-old practice of moonshining. Some families even keep stills they've used since before (and during) Prohibition. After a few sips of white lightning, I could see why—moonshine will put hair on your chest, scrub your brain cells clean, and even kill some of the weaker ones to boot. To make moonshine, you'll need to acquire a still from a brewing shop; you can also rig a small one with a pressure cooker and some copper tubing. I promised Darnell I wouldn't share his family recipe, but he did give me the basics. (I'll be submitting my own formula in an upcoming craft spirits award entry once I perfect it.)

INGREDIENTS

10 gallons (38 l) water
10 lb. (5.5 kg) sugar
2.5 lb. (1.1 kg) cornmeal
2 oz. (56 g) yeast

STEP 1

Fill the still with water and light a fire or burner underneath. Once the water is at a rolling boil, add the cornmeal and stir thoroughly to make a mash.

STEP 2

Let the mash cool to 80°F (26°C), then add the sugar and yeast. Mix thoroughly into the mash, then cover the kettle and let it set for four or five days to ferment.

STEP 3

Once the mash has stopped bubbling, it's called sour mash. But don't drink it yet; fill the condenser with cold water, connect the kettle to it using the still head, and fire up the burner again until the mixture reaches 173°F (78°C).

STEP 4

The heat will bring the alcohol content to the top of the sour mash, where it will vaporize and flow through the still head. Keep cold water circulating through the condenser, and it will cool the vapor inside the coil, condensing it into liquid once more.

STEP 5

Dispense the moonshine into a mason jar or clay jug of your choice. Hide it in a tree stump on the back forty to age the old-fashioned way. Enjoy responsibly!

I saw plenty of bears in this part of the world, but aside from the famous Cheeseburger (see item **099 / Befriend a Wild Animal**), most grizzlies are obviously wild. The trouble is, even up close you can't really tell it's not Cheeseburger you're greeting until you're being mauled. The grizzly probably doesn't want to eat you, but once you get in the animal's face, if you didn't come loaded for bear, it's time to bear the consequences—especially if this is a female bear protecting her cubs. Luckily, the F.A.N.G. Center brochures I found also had some ursine survival suggestions.

TAKE YOUR LUMPS

The best way to avoid injury or death is to go facedown on the ground with your backpack protecting your back (and hope you're wearing one; see item **091 / Stock a Bug Out Bag** for suggestions on how to fill it). Cover your head and neck with your hands and play dead to avoid becoming dead for real.

STAY SILENT

Curse yourself for getting into this mess, but do it quietly. You have to play dead, and corpses don't talk—or scream. It'll be tough if the bear is gnawing on you, but let's face it: You pissed off a grizzly. Expect to be batted around, bitten, maybe clawed.

WAIT IT OUT

Once the bear is tired of chewing on you, it'll probably huff and wander away. Stay still until it's long gone, or the grizzly might decide you're still a threat or annoyance and return for a second helping.

105 FIGHT OFF A COUGAR

Peaches' Taxidermy is a haven for hunters around the entire county: If you can kill it, they can preserve it. Wilhelmina Mable, the shop's owner, claims to handle everything from squirrels to salmon, brown bears to big cats—a mixed message if you ask me, since the shop is named after Wilhelmina's "pet" cougar, Peaches. Just like Cheeseburger, Peaches went missing sometime after *Inside Eden's Gate* went viral; Ms. Mable assured me that if I found Peaches, I could mollify her with enough meat or fish. But after seeing up close what big cats can do (see item **069 / Stand Up to a Tiger**), I declined, just in case Peaches had slipped her signature bright red collar. Still, if you go looking to try to befriend the wrong killer kitty, here are her tips on surviving the experience.

FACE OFF

Don't turn away; if you run, you're likely to trigger an attack. Back away slowly, facing the cougar the whole while. A cougar's roar is a chilling sound, so roar back if you have to: Stand tall, flap your coat open, wave your arms overhead, and shout back to become as unappealing a target as possible.

FEND OFF THE FANGS

A big cat's claws are dangerous, but the fangs are made for crushing skulls and snapping necks. If the feral beast closes with you, protect your neck, face, and abdomen, and use any sturdy object you can to keep those jaws away.

FACE OFF, PART TWO

If you're lacking a handgun loaded with .45 ACP rounds, take the fight out of the feline by returning the favor and going for the face—but don't use a typewriter unless you like permanently italic letters. The eyes are obvious targets; whacking a big cat hard in the nose will often stun them too.

106 SURVIVE A BULL CHARGE

All the sweetmeats that go into feeding the fans of Testy Festy (see item **103 / Try a Prairie Oyster**) have to come from somewhere. In Montana there is no shortage of cattle, including those bulls. But when it comes to bulls for breeding, their testes stay attached—which gives them a territorial attitude, even if you're not there to steal their harem. Early in my trip to Hope County, I tried crossing a field near Teller Ranch to get a closer view of Eden's Gate operations. It nearly led to being trampled; fortunately, I learned a lesson or two in how to beat the bull. Follow what I figured out, and you'll be a rodeo clown captain instead of a bull's hoof-scraper.

DON'T HORN IN

Avoid pastures, or at least stay close to the fence. Don't harass any cows or calves or make eye contact with the bull.

WATCH YOUR TAIL

They're a half ton of beef on the hoof, but cows are surprisingly quiet, and bulls sneak up to investigate sometimes. Make sure the bull isn't playing the starring role in *Ninja Cattle: Catch These Horns* with you as the target.

BEAT THE CHARGES

Beeves can indeed be sneaky, but a bull still steers like a cow. If Ferdinand decides to run headlong at you, dodge sideways, then run past him while he has to reorient.

FLIGHT BEFORE FIGHT

This is a massive animal. Choose to flee first: Drop anything heavy, throw your jacket in the bull's face, and seek barriers such as boulders, farm equipment, or female bovines giving their aggressive bull-beau the cow's eyes. If you must fight, make as much noise as possible, and whack it as hard as you can with a rock or a big stick. (They can't read, so skip threatening them with a Testy Festy brochure.)

As a globe-trotting journalist, I've been on more flights than I can count, and only one of them ever crashed. I was on a trip to Alaska to write a story about the finer points of Inuit seal and whale meat cuisine, and it turned out the bush pilot was a semifunctional alcoholic—as I discovered when he forgot to lower the landing gear on his Cessna and set the plane belly-down on the runway instead. Statistically, it's still the safest form of travel, but that rough arrival (and spotting the remnants of an air crash in the Whitetail Mountains) taught me a few things about making it through an unscheduled landing in one piece.

DRESS FOR THE CRASH

Much like the last time I got on a 1400CC superbike (and got off later by twisting the throttle too hard), you want to dress for the crash, not the ride. Skip the sandals, tank top, and Bermuda shorts; wear shoes you won't run out of and long pants to protect your legs, at the least.

BRACE FOR IMPACT

If your seat is behind another, put your head on its back with your hands between as a cushion; if not, bend over and hold your chest and head to your legs. Either way, tuck your feet as far back under your seat as possible.

DITCH THE LUGGAGE

Get anything pointy out of your pockets; your favorite pen can become your favorite implant in a crash. Once the plane has stopped, get out now and worry about your luggage later. If you try to fetch your carry-on, you just might end up as carrion instead.

After surviving a plane crash, there's a new challenge: staying alive until you're rescued. Depending on where the plane goes down, salvation could be minutes away (as it was for me in Alaska), or it could take days or weeks for rescuers to find you—if any hungry wildlife doesn't first. I didn't see any remains at the Whitetail crash site so I can't say if the occupants made it or not, but to endure a harsh landing like that yourself, you'll need to get creative.

■ If the plane's radio still works, send out a distress call.

■ Use the fuselage as shelter; if there's spilled fuel and thus a fire risk, get at least 100 feet (30 m) away.

■ Use electrical wire and cables to lash together elements of your shelter.

■ Put cabin debris to good use: Carpeting, upholstery, cushions, bulkheads, doors, windows, and fuselage panels can all be part of a temporary shelter.

■ Dig through cargo compartments and luggage bins to look for clothes, blankets, food, and water.

■ Punch a hole in the fuel tank (usually found in the wings of larger craft) and drain the fuel into a container to start a fire.

■ Use reflective material for signal mirrors.

■ Nearly all planes carry some medical supplies, including automatic defibrillators. Don't leave these behind.

109 SPOT A SOCIOPATH

With all the places I've been, I've run into a good number of less than sane people. After *Inside Eden's Gate* popped up on YouTube, I decided to investigate Hope County and get the story myself—partly because I saw a look in Joseph Seed's eyes that I've seen in the likes of Hoyt Volker and others: Utter belief in themselves, and total disregard for anyone in their way. People like these seem smart, charismatic, and competent . . . and they live to wield power over others. Here are some traits to beware before you decide to change your religion or talk to the guy on the corner who approached you with a too-perfect sob story.

LOOK AT ME!

A sociopath is often very charming, seeming like a born leader. In fact, sociopaths are con artists, using charm and wit to manipulate and control others. Ultimately, their actions are often purely for their own profit or pleasure.

IT'S ALL MINE

Sociopaths believe they are better than others and will stop at nothing to prevail, as they genuinely believe they deserve it. If you're not with the program, you're just an object in their path.

I'M (NOT) SORRY

Sociopaths can be nice and helpful when they need to, but they lack true, deep emotions, and show no remorse for their actions. An apology from a sociopath just means they want something from you.

IT'S YOUR FAULT!

Introspection isn't a sociopath's strong suit; when things go wrong, they always manage to pin the blame on someone else. Even if they're not cult leaders or crime lords, sociopaths can often be bullies, intimidating or manipulating people to get what they want—or (like Vaas Montenegro, for example) just for the sheer hellish fun of it.

With the stranglehold the Eden's Gate cult held over Hope County, it was like a war zone—especially when you factored in the random gunfire and explosions. From Yara to Yemen (or Kyrgyzstan to Kyrat, or the Rook Islands to . . . you get the idea), as a journalist who's been in many conflicted places, I can say that war also belongs to civilians; they're in fact the most affected. What can civilians do to help end a war? The solution, as I've learned in my travels, is to become involved—especially as an underground force.

THIS IS SABOTAGE

A resistance can disrupt or destroy equipment important to the enemy—such as the fields of flowers harvested by Seed's cult to create Bliss. Everything from burning the plants to spiking the formulation all went into ruining their plans.

TELL ME LIES

False info or propaganda can send enemies after nonexistent targets, and waste more time, effort, and resources.

I SPY FOR YOU AND ME

If you're willing to risk being caught, going undercover can help with spying on enemies and passing info to the good guys.

COME WITH ME AND ESCAPE

POWs—or cult victims (see following item)—can be taken to friendly locales and given a temporary hiding place, clothing, food, medicine, and so on.

FORGED IN TRUST

If you can fake any important documents, they'll be a godsend if you have an enemy checkpoint area you can use them to get through.

TURN ON THE RADIO

Alternative means of communication (such as pirate radio, and I don't mean the Rook Islands; see item **112 / Set Up a Pirate Radio Station**) can provide a source of inspiration and send messages to Resistance members.

From Vaas' pirate followers to Pagan Min's most loyal troops and beyond, every charismatic sociopath I've encountered or heard of has a cult, and a cult means cultists—that includes Peggies. They're not just there for the church buffet; a cultist's beatific smile can turn to killing fury when they're immersed in their leader's doctrine. How do you save someone from giving up all their possessions and willingly ingesting Bliss or other thought-crushing drug du jour? The free people of Hope County had their hands full liberating loved ones from Seed's clutches (see item **110 / Join a Resistance**) . . . and as I sat with Pastor Jerome Jeffries of Fall's End one day to hear him talk about what to do next, I learned it took a careful approach to free their minds.

START BY UN-KIDNAPPING

If someone is in a cult, they may already be in too deep to just ask them to leave. You might have to abduct them back. (see items **021 / Break into Prison** and **022 / Escape a Pirate Camp** for helpful tips.)

TIME FOR AN INTERVENTION

It's dangerous to deprogram alone. Your rescued buddy may be angry; after all, you've just stolen them from Paradise. Involve as many friends and family as you can and provide a familiar caring group to rival a cult's pull.

QUESTION WITH COMPASSION

It's tempting to besmirch the name of the cult and its figurehead, but inflammatory language won't help. Talk with your friend about the experience calmly, and ask questions to get them to doubt their involvement.

DE-MYTH-TIFY THE MAGIC

Cults are led by charming monsters, but even monsters make mistakes. Point out any and all errors in the cult's supposed logic. Provide solid facts in contrast to the claims. Ask the ex-cultist to think hard, but don't force it.

SEND THEM TO DETOX

Charm and purpose are a cult's chief weapons—that and real weapons, as well as drugs. If you suspect your newly freed friend has been dosed with Bliss or something similar, see item **124 / Recover from an Overdose**, and seek medical care to clear their head and their bloodstream.

Joseph Seed's control over Hope County's people was absolute enough that trusting strangers was a big risk. In fact, it's how I first met Darnell in Fall's End—I took a risk walking up to him, then he stuck his camo-painted shotgun in my favorite left nostril and demanded to know who the hell I was. We're fast friends now, but without building trust and communication, my journalistic adventure could have ended right there. Communication can take all forms—including pirate radio broadcasts, especially if most other methods are in enemy control. And after smashing a couple of King Min's broadcast radios in Kyrat, I even learned a thing or two about putting one back together. Here's how to become a pirate captain of the (air)waves.

POWER IT UP

You need a good radio transmitter to start, such as a CB; if you don't have one, then you have to make one. Start with an FM radio transmitter, preferably one you can plug into a car's 12-volt adapter for mobile broadcasts. Open it up and remove the antenna connection (usually marked with the cryptic letters "ANT"). Solder or wire in the stripped end of a coaxial cable to the antenna connection.

TOWER OF BABBLE

Hook up your transmitter to a signal amplifier. Smaller transmitters have extremely short range, and more costly ones are still not as powerful as what you'd find at a local radio station. Connect the setup to a portable, collapsible antenna that you can put up and take down in moments.

RADIO FREE HOPE

Find a UHF or VHF station clear of any traffic and keep its frequency a secret to share only with those in a resistance movement. Set your transmitter to that frequency, then set up your portable broadcast system somewhere remote but within range of friendlies.

CAN'T STOP THE SIGNAL

If your opposition triangulates your signal and finds you, your pirate radio career will be shorter than Anne Bonny's beard. Keep messages and music short and sweet, consider coded transmissions, and choose a new random location each time for maximum security.

A lock is a kind of physical social contract. If it could talk, it might say, "Don't touch this stuff, and we won't touch yours." But in times when I needed to open a door—like when I slipped into a Royal Army base in Kyrat on the search for Pagan Min's favorite crab rangoon recipe—shooting or breaking a lock was infeasible. So, too, with slipping into Dodd's Dumps in Holland Valley to see if Joseph Seed's cult had left anything enlightening in their trash. (Spoiler: They didn't; not so much as a single nudie mag. Peggies are weird, man.) Breaking and entering isn't exactly a time-honored tradition for most journalists, but if you're someday faced with a lock and you're short on keys, remember these tips. Ideally you should have a tension wrench and lockpick set, but hairpins or paper clips can do the trick.

STEP 1

Insert the wrench into the keyhole and wiggle it back and forth. The lock will give a little when turned the right way. Keep pressure on the wrench to hold the cylinder there.

STEP 2

Insert the pick just above the wrench and feel for the locking pins. Starting with the farthest pin, push up until you hear a click. Repeat with the rest of the pins until all are pushed up and out.

STEP 3

Turn the wrench to rotate the cylinder and open the lock.

As a journalist, sometimes you have to get your hands dirty. More often than not, that's a literal statement—like the time I was on assignment fresh out of journalism school, digging through Mel Gibson's trash to find what brand of hair formula he used to maintain his locks. But that sort of past experience digging for dirt on celebrities has served me well in sifting for survival, whether I was poking through a pirate camp's junk heap—a human femur makes a great billy club!—or picking over Dodd's Dumps for cult evidence. Here's how to turn trash into treasure . . . or at least recycling.

GO THE GREY WAY

The "grey man" theory is all about being seen yet ignored. Wear dark nondescript clothing or take the Method Acting route like I did: Wear dirty, greasy, and worn clothes; push a battered shopping cart (wobbly wheels give bonus points); and mumble about aliens and Elvis while you dig away.

DO IT IN THE DARK

Unless you're a bald eagle on a landfill, daylight is not your time to forage. Embark on your maiden mission to the midden under cover of late night or early morning after sunrise—right after times when trash is usually taken out.

PICK AND PULL

Some more assiduous garbage guardians tend to lock up their trash, especially if they know they're a target. If you know how to pick locks (see previous item) or at least have a set of bolt cutters, your junk-jumping job just got easier.

PILFER PROPERLY

Trash is rarely considered private property, but you run the risk of trespassing and taking a shotgun barrel of rock salt in the rear. Look up local laws if you're worried about legal penalties for prodding around a trash pile.

Fun facts: Montana has more deer, elk, and antelope than humans, and it's the continental state with the highest grizzly population. I'm also pretty sure it has the highest number of reclusive gun-toting survivalists—and that's not counting Eden's Gate cultists and Bliss-addicted "angels." Whether hunting, hiding from the world, or fighting a religious doomsday cult, it helps to have a clean firearm, because jams and misfires are always inopportune. I keep both my typewriter and .45 clean and in working order because I never know when I'll need to use either. (Also, I swear my typewriter's action is faster with gun oil.)

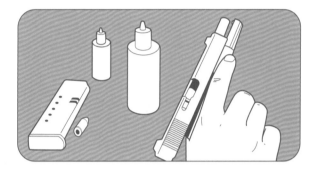

STEP 1

Get out a gun-cleaning kit—solvent, oil, and scrubbing brush and patches—and unload the firearm. Accidental discharges mean anything from plaster repair to suicide.

STEP 2

Soak a rag with gun-specific solvent, then run it down the inside of the barrel. Give it a few minutes for the solvent to loosen deposits.

STEP 3

Run a solvent-soaked brush down the barrel, scrubbing back and forth, then mop up with patches until they come out clean and dry.

STEP 4

Finish by adding a few drops of gun oil to a patch and running it down the barrel. Your firearm (and maybe your own typewriter, too) is ready for action!

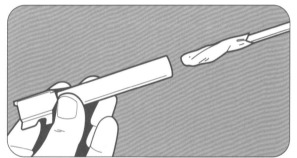

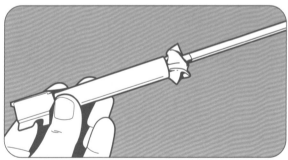

I shoot as fast as I type and I type as fast as I think, but sometimes physics catches up with me. When firing a semiautomatic weapon, a spent shell can jam in the chamber without fully ejecting. On a practice range, it's mildly embarrassing—in a shootout, whether you face pirates or Peggies, it can be downright fatal. I've learned a few simple routines for clearing jams that lets me get back into action fast, though they only work for firearms. (Jammed typewriters need a little more finesse.)

EMPTY YOUR BREECHES

With a jam in the barrel, use the "tap, rack, bang" maneuver: Slap the magazine's bottom to seat it, rack the slide back to clear the cartridge, then take aim and fire again.

BE A CHIMNEY SWEEP

If the empty is "stovepiped"—sticking up from the breech—sweep your hand hard across the top of the slide to knock it clear and resume firing.

DON'T DOUBLE UP

In the heat of the moment, some folks accidentally tap-rack-bang when they get a stovepipe jam, and double-feed the chamber. Release the magazine, rack the slide twice to clear the breech, then reload and chamber a new round.

With a clean and cleared firearm, it still helps to ensure accurate shooting no matter the context. I've lost bets with a missed practice shot, but missing the real thing might mean a lost life: yours. As I've learned from my many years carrying a gun—and from beating my brain finding *just* the perfect turn of phrase to type out—accuracy begins with a strong stance and ends with good finger control.

STAND LIKE A FIGHTER

Minimize your profile like you're Michael Biehn dodging shots from the Terminator: Stand sideways with your shoulder facing your target. Move one foot slightly forward and lean toward your aim point.

GET A GRIP

Use a two-handed grip for stability, wrapping your off-hand over the one gripping the gun. Hold firmly, don't choke it, and leave your trigger finger relaxed; position it so the crease under the first joint contacts the trigger.

TAKE AIM AND FIRE

Line up front and rear sights on the target, then squeeze the trigger smoothly. Much like my editors' deadlines, the instant of discharge should be unanticipated, keeping your shot true to the target.

Just as with handgun work, my reportage has to get close for the right impact. But after having seen Peggies and angels a little too close for comfort (and plenty of hostile animals—see items **031**, **104**, and **106 / Walk the Path of the Hunter**, **Survive Grizzlies**, and **Survive a Bull Charge**), I agree there's merit in long-range shooting, whether with camera or firearm. I'll stick with Gonzo journalism until I die or it kills me, and I'll stick with my trusty .45, as traveling means I have to pack light; I can't stash a rifle in a typewriter case. A few days of practicing with Darnell's second favorite Remington Model 700, though, refreshed me on some useful tips for long-range shooting, whether it's at bears, honey badgers, or gun-and-machete-waving maniacs.

BE ONE WITH THE GUN

The fundamental part of rifle shooting is holding it right. Socket the butt in the pocket of your shoulder and hold the fore-end lightly but firmly in your off-hand. Wrap your trigger hand around the grip high enough to let your forefinger rest lightly on the trigger and exert no pressure with your thumb.

TRIGGER WARNING

Set the pad of your forefinger on the trigger close to the first knuckle crease, and don't brush against the bolt handle. It helps to dry-fire practice a smooth pull so nothing interferes with your trigger finger. Keep your sights set on the target, and keep your finger pressed to the trigger for follow-through after firing.

BREATHE DEEP

Breath control steadies your nerves and your thumping heart, and steadies your shot no matter what gun you wield. Take three deep controlled breaths in through your nose and out of your mouth and pause after your last exhale. Squeeze the trigger before the lack of oxygen affects your vision or muscles.

From exotic sea snakes to classic rattlesnakes, I've encountered plenty of serpents in my adventures. Some bites are "dry," but if venom is delivered, neurotoxins cause seizures and paralysis before shutting off your heart while hemotoxins destroy blood cells, tissues, and organs. Venom also tastes nasty, as I discovered with the "Snakebite Challenge" at a bar in Taipei: a shot of the local snake-in-a-bottle whiskey with a floater of viper venom. (I resolved never to try that again once the hangover faded.) In the wilds of Hope County, prairie rattlers seemed to come out of nowhere thanks to natural camouflage, but at least they were honest predators, unlike the Peggies—and rattlesnake bites are much easier to treat than cult brainwashing (see item **111 / Use Cult Deprogramming**).

STEP 1

Make sure the snake can't bite anyone else—a .45-caliber round usually settles the issue quickly. Keep the victim calm and hold the bite below their heart level to slow the spread of venom. Remove constricting jewelry or clothing as swelling may occur.

STEP 2

Let the bite bleed freely for about a minute, then clean the area. If you're more than an hour from medical help, apply a suction device, but not your mouth; any cuts in your mouth or ulcers in your stomach will leak venom into your bloodstream.

STEP 3

Monitor vital signs (see item **002 / Check Vital Signs**) and prepare to treat shock (see item **005 / Treat for Shock**) if you notice the symptoms.

STEP 4

Get the victim to medical help; they can prepare treatment faster if you can identify the reptile. Photograph or bring the (dead) snake with you to determine its species if you are unsure.

120 DISINFECT WOUNDS

If you're anywhere from the rot-inducing humidity of the Rook Islands to the miasmic sewers under the streets of Yara (see item **137 / Navigate Sewers Safely**), knowing how to keep wounds clean can be critical. Hand injuries are an especial concern for me; my typing and trigger fingers must be in perfect readiness at all times. Even a tiny, dry snakebite or small cut can become infected—especially in the Montana wilderness, which, like most untamed areas, is not exactly known for sterility. The same goes for most any injury in the wrong place and time, whether it's a gunshot wound from a cultist or a cut from an angel's blade. Infections also cause your body to divert resources to fight them, leaving you weakened and vulnerable to other illness or complication.

STEP 1

Stop the bleeding (see item **003 / Stop Bleeding**) and assess the injury. If you can't stop the bleeding, seek medical attention and leave the severe wound cleaning to the pros.

STEP 2

Flush the wound with clean water. Don't use peroxide or alcohol; not only do they sting and burn like hell, they also kill healthy tissue cells.

STEP 3

Saturate the wound with antibiotic ointment, then apply a dressing to keep out dirt and debris.

121 KNOW THE SIGNS OF POISONING

In many of the places I've journeyed to around the world, clean water has been hard to come by—even in some locales in the United States. In Hope County, it turned out that the Eden's Gate cult had tainted the local water supply. The resistance was forced to purify their own water (see item **093 / Purify Water Safely**) or seek other sources to avoid poisoning or becoming a near-mindless zombie "angel" for the Project. If you need to evaluate a child for poisoning or a suicidal person who refuses to say what they ingested, you can look for some common signs.

OBVIOUS SIGNS

Check for burns or redness around a victim's mouth and lips, or burns, stains, and odors on them or nearby objects. Look for empty medication bottles or spilled or empty household chemical containers.

LATER SYMPTOMS

The victim may become nauseous or vomit, become drowsy or unconscious, have difficulty breathing, or even go into respiratory arrest. They might also be agitated, restless, or have seizures or uncontrolled spasms. Assume poisoning until proven otherwise and treat accordingly. (See next item.)

NO SIGNS OR SYMPTOMS

If you suspect poisoning, call a regional poison control center. Give the victim's age, weight, and any information you may have about the poison, such as how much they ingested, how long since exposure, and any containers found nearby.

122 TREAT A POISONING VICTIM

Poisoning can happen from a multitude of sources, whether too many shots of snake-infused whiskey or a drink from a tainted water line, so helping a victim can be tricky. As I've discovered from dealing with both, there's no one-size-fits-all solution. But in every case, determining the nature of the toxin and seeking help for the victim is vital.

STEP 1

Call your local emergency number to request help for the victim, and if there is a strong chemical odor or you see fumes, get the person into fresh air.

STEP 2

Put on gloves if you have them and check the victim's mouth for any remaining substances. If you find any, wipe them away, and if anything spilled on the victim's clothing, remove it.

STEP 3

Check vitals (see item **002 / Check Vital Signs**); if the victim isn't breathing or has no pulse, begin CPR immediately.

STEP 4

Flush any exposed bare skin or eyes with lukewarm water for twenty minutes or until help arrives.

STEP 5

If the toxin is a household product, check the label or call poison control; don't induce vomiting unless instructed. If the victim is taken to the ER, take the container with them to help doctors with proper treatment.

Of the many brave folks I met in Hope County, I was most struck by Kimiko Rye, better known as Kim to her husband Nick and friends: When I met her, she was very far along in her pregnancy. You'd think a religious cult of zombie-drug-slinging sociopaths would be reason enough for her to flee with her unborn, but she chose to stay and join the resistance—and convinced her husband to do the same. The last time I saw her, she was going into labor, and Nick, myself, and others were preparing for home delivery. A local sheriff's deputy arrived in time to get the Ryes to a hospital for the birth, but if you happen to be holed up with someone about to pop and can't get to medical professionals, here's what to do.

DON'T PANIC

Babies have been born outside hospitals ever since the first pregnant protohuman climbed out of a tree. Stay calm and call emergency services (who may be able to offer help over the phone); if the mother is having contractions two minutes apart or fewer, delivery is imminent.

MAKE ROOM

Wash your arms and hands thoroughly and cover the birthing area in sheets or towels. If you have a delivery kit, open it and prepare the gloves, drapes, suction bulb, and other tools.

GET IN POSITION

Help the mother assume a comfortable posture during labor. Reclining is traditional but not most effective; some may want to be on hands and knees, squatting, or even standing.

CATCH A BABY

Give help only if needed. When the baby's head is showing, gently cup and support it as it emerges. If the umbilical cord is around the neck or head, gently slip it off. Be ready to support the rest of the baby, too—they'll be slippery!

HELLO, KIDDO

Gently wrap the baby in a towel and clean off blood and fluids; this also stimulates the baby to breathe if that hasn't happened already. Skip the spanking; that's only for movies. You can use the suction bulb to clear the baby's mouth and nostrils. Give the baby to the mother (skin contact is good for both) and keep them warm.

CUT THE CORD

Wait for the umbilical cord to stop pulsating and apply clamps: one about 12 inches (30 cm) from the baby's abdomen, another 6 inches (15 cm) past the first clamp. Cut the umbilical between the clamps.

SPECIAL DELIVERY

The placenta will also come about fifteen to thirty minutes after the baby. You can gently encourage this by massaging the mother's lower abdomen in slow circles. Don't pull on the cord or placenta; once it's delivered, make sure it's intact (if not, the mother may bleed more and need extra medical care). Your delivery kit may include a bag to take the placenta to a doctor.

SEE A DOCTOR

Use sanitary pads or dressings if the mother is still bleeding. Take both newborn and mother to a skilled medical professional as soon as possible.

124 RECOVER FROM AN OVERDOSE

Having experienced everything from opium dreams to mushroom visions to cannabis munchies in my adventures, I've never seen anything quite like the scopolamine analog, Bliss. In hope of understanding it better, I snuck a tiny dose from a lab the cult used to make the drug. It left me stupefied for hours, filling my head with sparkling light and heavenly visions and leaving me smiling like a lobotomy victim. No wonder Joseph Seed's "angels" were so compliant and willing to kill . . . if the Bliss didn't kill them first. I'm no biochemist—just a humble psychonaut—but I've dealt with overdoses, and they're all nasty.

PACIFY THE PATIENT

From personal experience, an overdose is always uncomfortable at least. If the victim is conscious, they can be anxious, panicky, paranoid, even combative, depending on what they took and how much. Help keep them calm and comfortable, and call emergency services.

SEE THE SIGNS

Stimulant overdose signs include dilated pupils, elevated pulse, temperature, and blood pressure. Sedatives or narcotics can mean pinpoint pupils, slowed vitals, slower wits, and dulled senses. Either path can also lead to hallucinations, sweating, nausea, and vomiting. Untreated overdose can lead to shock (indicated by blue lips and pale skin), coma, convulsions, and death. See items **002** and **005 / Check Vital Signs** and **Treat for Shock** for more.

COUNTER THE CHEMISTRY

For a narcotic overdose such as heroin or other opioids, naloxone (Narcan) is the drug of choice to help clear their system, but too much can cause agitation, sweating, and elevated vitals akin to stimulant overdose. An overload of cocaine or other stimulants is generally treated with sedatives and antipsychotics.

TAKE SOME TIME

An overdose victim's systems take a serious beating: They may have long-term health issues involving heart, liver, kidneys, nervous system, or other parts of the body (or mind). Regardless, professional care is needed—and maybe a stint in rehab.

With the exception of folks like Sharma Salsa (see item **086 / Record a Race, Kyrati Films Style**), rarely have I seen anyone making movies in a combat zone. Director Guy Marvel, however, considers himself an auteur, willing to take risks to finish the production the way he wants it—sounds familiar, huh? A moviemaker after my own heart. When I heard his film crew was in Hope County, filming scenes for *Blood Dragon 3*, I leapt at the chance to meet my all-time film hero: Michael Biehn! Sadly, he was in Hollywood doing green screen work, but Marvel was still happy to hire me while filming at Grimalkin Radon Mine. (I'm one of the extras who gets eaten alive in the tunnel scene!) If you want to get into acting, being an extra is a great way to start. Here's how to get that foot in the film-room door!

HEED THE CALL

Open casting calls are one way to get a chance to be onscreen. Check online and any local social media or local film offices for announcements and follow instructions to the letter. If the director wants email applications titled "Extra Casting," don't say "Extras" even if it's grammatically correct. Submit current headshots and full body photos along with your contact info and bodily measurements, and bring extra (get it?) copies.

GET AN AGENT

A casting agency gets your name and any experience easily represented, especially in closed casting calls. You can sign with multiple agencies; they'll do the legwork for you while you practice trying not to mug for the camera (see below for more). But do your research first: Don't sign with an agency that promises your name in lights on day one or sounds too good to be true. If it seems like a scam, it probably is . . . especially if the agency has a black leather couch in a white room.

SUCCEED ON SET

If you're hired, clear your schedule and show up on time. Directors want extras who follow instructions; if you can't do that, your career ends before it begins. Don't improvise moves or lines or look at the camera unless ordered. Don't bother principal actors, either. They're hard at work on their craft. Wait till they approach you to request an autograph—yes, sadly, even if it's Michael Biehn.

126 LEARN TO BE A DAREDEVIL

Every place has its local legends, including rural Montana. Born in Holland Valley in 1941, Clutch Nixon seemed destined for greatness, starting with his first stunt in 1960: driving a flaming vehicle around an obstacle course and into a nearby lake. He survived the experience, and went on to perform even more insane—often improvised!—stunts for crowds over the next fifteen years. After hearing so much about him, I wish I'd had the chance to meet the man himself. Unfortunately, he disappeared in 1975 after making a BASE jump with an improvised wingsuit (see item **087 / Wing It (with a Wingsuit)**. He was declared legally dead after months, although his body was never found. Wherever he may be, living or dead, I still count him as an inspirational figure—and so do the people of Hope County, or anyone wishing to become a daredevil.

SHED YOUR FEAR

Daredevils are a special breed. If you're totally fearless, you're usually either dead or a psychopath; even a daredevil has some planning and at least a hair of caution. You need practice, training, and willingness to risk injury or death in the pursuit of immortality. We all check out sometimes, probably even Clutch Nixon, but glory is forever!

GET THE GEAR

With no props or stunt vehicles, a daredevil is just someone with a complicated death wish. Get a cheap, used motorcycle or car and trick it out: Add painted flames, real flames, high wire ballast weights, a souped-up engine, all-terrain tires, a roll cage, five-point restraints—half of being a daredevil is the wild rides you'll be driving (and sometimes crashing).

HOLD MY BEER

Now the fun part: showing off for the crowds! Once you have a stunt and the means to do it, invite your friends, your family, your favorite orthopedic surgeon or insurance adjuster—anyone and everyone who'll show up. Wear a really flashy jumpsuit, half-cape, and crash helmet; they'll look great on film and distract viewers from any incidental bleeding. Godspeed!

127 RIDE A ZIP LINE

Of all the various exhilarating things I've tried in my travels, zip lines hold a special place in my heart. With zip lines you soar without wings, and you don't need a parachute (see item **042 / Pull On a Parachute**) to guard against a sudden splat at the end. If the bottom is near an important destination (or escape route), you save the trouble of walking—especially important if the area between is patrolled by hostiles, whether pirates, a dictator's army, doomsday cultists, or angry chefs who spotted you stealing their culinary secrets through the kitchen skylight. (He was a dick, though, and his cheesecake recipe was totally worth it.) You can't just jump barehanded onto any rope, though. Here's how to be a zip line zealot!

DO A FAT LINE

Your best bet is a smooth steel cable or a thick, sturdy rope. It must be anchored securely at both ends and have no obstructions. Taking a ride on a loose, weak cord means you just went bungee jumping without the bungee.

GET SOME SPEED

Park zip lines generally drop 6 feet (2 m) per 100 feet (30 m) of travel; a potential line in the wild is likely much steeper, and tautness and angle mean higher injury risk. Too saggy or too level, though, and you'll grind to a halt mid-ride—and a pissed off patisserie chef might be waiting for you just below.

FEEL THE RUSH

No matter what you've seen in *The Goonies*, old Errol Flynn movies, or *MacGyver* episodes, you need to control your ride. A sturdy rope or cloth will only hold you up until friction burns through it. You're better off with a sheave: a small pulley with a built-in handbrake, purpose-built for zip lining.

MANAGE THE COMEDOWN

Hook the wheels of your sheave over the cable, and jump! Inertia and gravity will propel you relentlessly down the line, so control your ride with the sheave. As you approach the bottom, tuck your legs for the dismount.

Virtually every culture has tales of hairy-scary humanoids roaming the untamed wilds—the yeti in Kyrat, Bigfoot in North America, or Vaas Montenegro on the Rook Islands. While I was in Kyrat, I thought I saw one of the legendary beasts (see item **080 / Learn to Throw a Knife**), so when I was in Hope County I just had to keep an eye out for the American variety. No dice, even after days and weeks of looking around—but after seeing blood trails and evidence of a struggle near a cabin in the Whitetail Mountains, I was left wondering: Were Seed's people responsible, or Sasquatch? How do you hunt for cryptids anyway?

GO IT ALONE, KINDA

From California to Connecticut, humans have sought Bigfoot en masse for decades. But if there's one thing I've learned from journalism, it's that people can get in the way of the story. Move quietly (see item **024 / Move with Stealth**) and bring maybe one person to watch your back in case of bears.

GATHER EVIDENCE

In my college days, I took a solo backpacking trip to Scotland. As I walked the shores of Loch Ness one evening, I could have sworn I saw a long-necked reptilian head emerge near a rocky outcrop. But my camera had been broken in a Glasgow pub brawl the night before, so I had no proof. Even a companion may not convince everyone you two saw Bigfoot, so bring at least two cameras.

SET OUT A SPREAD

If there's a Bigfoot out there (maybe a whole species of Bigfeet), they've got to eat, and offering food is a nearly universal friendship gesture. My local redneck buddy, Darnell, said the Sasquatch likes sweets, fruits, and meat: berries, apples, donuts, raw venison, cooked bacon, and the like. (Then again, he does too—including the venison—and he said much the same about baiting bears.)

EMBRACE THE 'SQUATCH

Some folks, especially Native Americans, say you have to open your spirit to the idea of the mythical man-monster, and ask nature to guide you. After all I've seen, from psychotic pirates to honey badger swarms, I'm willing to believe, especially if it lands me the story of the century.

In Montana, the survivalist ethos definitely showed in people's nuclear paranoia; most Hope County residents have a bomb shelter on their property. With all the things I've seen and heard throughout my travels of the region, I'm not sure if they were paranoid or just smart. You start to believe a lot of things when you drink the water from the local well, especially if the local well is polluted with Bliss. If you find yourself feeling paranoid, here's how to build a bomb shelter just in case.

STEEL SARCOPHAGUS

The goal is to protect against radiation's rays, so the more the mass the better. Build the roof from steel, concrete, rock, soil, and wood layers and build your bunker at least 3 feet (1 m) underground.

THE RIGHT TOOLS

You're going to be down there for a while (ten days minimum), so you're going to need the basic necessities of your home, like a chemical toilet (which deodorizes waste) and a septic tank. You'll also want an air pump and filter, plus a periscope and Geiger counter so you can monitor radiation levels.

PREPPER STASH

Stock it up with all the food, water, medicine, and hygiene supplies you'll need for everyone hunkering down in a bunker with you. Estimate 1 gallon (3.75 l) of water per day per person, and gather canned and dehydrated foods (factoring in that you'll need water to hydrate them). Have a radio and extra batteries so you can stay up-to-date with the developments above ground.

130 SURVIVE A NUCLEAR APOCALYPSE

At first glance, a nuclear apocalypse may seem like an unlikely event to prepare for, but when your ultimate goal is survival you need to prepare for all of life's crazy, possible outcomes. And Montana has plenty of missile silos, each one holding its radioactive cargo for the big day everyone hopes never comes. It's a great mutually-assisted-destruction deterrent, but it also makes it a big target for other atomic-bomb-equipped powers. In case surviving Hope County wasn't hard enough, here's how to survive it during a nuclear gift exchange.

APOCALYPSE NOW OR NEVER

Okay, so you survived the blast, but I'm not congratulating you just yet. Now you have to survive the radioactive fallout. Don't leave your shelter during the first forty-eight hours after a blast to give the radioactive iodine levels time to decay, and plan to stay sheltered for ten days at minimum.

WASTELAND, WANT NOT

Nuclear fallout can be airborne for days and be carried by prevailing winds for hundreds, even thousands of miles. Inhaling or ingesting fallout can be lethal, so always wear breathing protection. Bear in mind, any covering that blocks falling ash and soot won't protect against deadly gamma rays.

SPIN-OFF ADVENTURE

A nuclear apocalypse is a survivalist's Mount Everest (aside from the actual Mount Everest). So if you keep your supplies stocked, your combat knife sharp, and your mind even sharper, you just may survive the collapse and emerge from the ground reborn into the sunlight of a new dawn. There may you find Prosperity.

FAR CRY 6

THE NATION
OF YARA

THE NATION OF YARA

After leaving Hope County, I retreated to the isolated Republic of Yara to finally write that novel I had been putting off for years. It's a beautiful island jewel hidden in the Caribbean, frozen in time and cut off from the rest of the world. It's the perfect place get away from it all because it's so hard to get to! Its vibrant people emanate the spirit of art and improvisational craftsmanship, restoring old 1950s hot rods and building everything they could need with a little creative scavenging. A contrasting palette of colors dot the landscape, washed in brushstrokes of the golden sun, setting through an aurora borealis of chemicals dancing in the skies over vast tobacco fields. And of course, some of the best damned rum in the world. But just as I took my first sip, after the seventeen-hour journey that included being smuggled into the country in an empty oil drum, a car bomb went off outside the cantina I was in, and I dropped it when the shockwave threw me against the back wall. I dusted off my white linen suit and clocked my jagged reflection in the shattered mirror behind the bar. Over the ensuing gunfire and ringing in my ears, I thought to myself, "Yeah. This feels about right."

This beautiful and isolated Caribbean island nation is run by Antón Castillo, a brutal dictator born with a C-4 spoon in his mouth. Raised to be a tyrant since birth, he seeks to rebuild Yara into a paradise and will do so by dispensing a particularly chilling brand of violence that earns him a top-four spot in the rogues' gallery of insanity I've encountered during my travels. He uses his military strength to suppress revolution by any means necessary—including kidnapping, torturing, and silencing anyone who opposes his sadistic regime. Getting to the island from the outside isn't hard . . . it's Master-level difficulty on account of the naval blockade that has been surrounding the island since the late 60s. Once you're there, plan on getting comfortable and staying a while. I probably clocked in a good several hundred hours exploring the island myself.

Castillo plans to profit from cultivating a cancer-fighting drug called Viviro, derived from a native tobacco plant grown on Yara's fertile soil. Antón Castillo isn't exactly known for charity, but this could be a game-changing level of drug dealing that makes Vaas Montenegro look like a pirate mascot for a seafood restaurant. But a band of outcasts known as *Libertad* are waging a David-versus-Goliath revolution against Castillo with hand grenades in their hearts, improvised poison throwers in their hands, and eyes set on the horizon as they peer through rifle sights made from sardine cans. *Libertad* has been getting louder at the capital city, and their numbers and support are growing. Always keep your eyes open and head up when moving throughout the island—unless you're being shot at, then keep your head down. This chapter will cover the tactics necessary to keep you alive while crossing the expansive and diverse landscape of Yara, from the war-torn capital of Esperanza to the alligator-infested swamps of Valle de Oro. This is recommended reading material while you're being smuggled into the country via cargo. If you didn't have a chance to prepare in advance, you might want to keep this survival guide holstered and ready to use at a moment's notice.

Bienvenido a la Republica de Yara!

It's usually a good idea to follow any lockdown orders when traveling to locales where civil and political unrest is the most active. Anyone seen outside of a lockdown can be stopped, imprisoned, or worse. Understanding the political climate of the region you're traveling to will go a long way in keeping you alive, so here are a few tips to help you sneak out of a lockdown when tensions start to boil over. No matter your methods, proceed with extreme caution.

DRESS THE PART

Always dress casual but dark, and be ready to move. Stay well off main paths and always be ready with a reason to be somewhere in the event authorities stop and question you. Castillo's military police will rarely, if ever, release a captive.

AVOID CROWDS

If you're traveling through a city, move away from crowds and refrain from constantly looking around or over your shoulder. Act too furtive, and you will stand out.

CONCEALED CARRY

Make sure any weapons you have are concealed and avoid carrying large rifles or military grade weaponry. Pistols are your best bet in this situation. (This is where a hidden compartment in your typewriter case really comes in handy!)

DO YOUR HOMEWORK QUIETLY

Knowing exactly when to sneak out is equally as important as knowing where to sneak. Watch police patrols to get a sense of their routes and know where guard outposts are so you know when to time your next move.

Sometimes protesters need to break some glass to be heard, and in Yara, I heard and saw a lot of smashing. On the other hand, you have the local authorities trying to maintain order using their own arsenal of riot-suppressing gear—and I saw plenty of that, too. Here are some crowd control hazards to look out for when things turn ugly.

BATONS

Move low to the ground and keep your head down. Keep your neck covered to protect your vertebrae.

SHIELDS

Not just used to protect from thrown objects, riot shields are also used to push crowds back. Try not to resist as you can easily lose your balance, putting yourself at risk of being trampled.

CONCUSSION GRENADES

Hunker in place and cover your head if one goes off near you. Use the chaos to your advantage by finding a break in the crowd to make your escape.

WATER CANNONS

If you're in range of a water cannon, don't stand up as you can be easily knocked over. Hunch down to protect your vital organs and face away from the cannon as much as possible.

RUBBER BULLETS

Curl up like a rubber ball and cover your face and arms, but never turn your back to a shooter. A rubber bullet impact to the back can be very painful and could temporarily paralyze.

ROCKS, BRICKS, AND BOTTLES

If any of these start to fly, watch your head and eyes. Duck and cover as you scramble to safety. Try not to run through broken glass. A slip and fall could cut you up.

MOLOTOV COCKTAIL

Run perpendicular to the trajectory of these improvised incendiary devices to avoid a third-degree burns, or worse.

TEAR GAS CANISTERS

These things are made to be thrown. Throw them back even if they're discharging their harmful contents, but wear gloves; they do get hot!

There's a good reason I put riot survival tactics first in this chapter: Things can escalate quick on Yara, especially when Castillo's military forces push the locals around. Here are some tips to keep you safe in a riot when the anti-Castillo revolutionaries push back.

GET OUT OF THE CROWD

As the bricks begin to fly, spectators can be injured. When trouble starts, keep your head up and your eyes forward. Avoid hotspots where riots typically occur: wide streets, parking lots, and city centers.

MOVE LIKE THE WIND

If you find yourself in the middle of an unruly crowd, move inconspicuously and steadily out of the center of activity, staying close to walls to minimize exposure. Find a place to hole up safely until the danger subsides.

STAY COOL

Maintain a level head and don't let your surging adrenaline make you do anything to put you in danger. Think rationally, pursue safety, and act as an individual, not as a member of the crowd.

AVOID THE AUTHORITIES

This is a good general survival tip to use when traveling to countries under authoritarian rule, regardless of rioting. Police tend to employ riot control agents like tear gas and pepper spray to deal with unruly crowds. Also be aware that running towards the police, even if seeking help, can be seen as threatening. (See item **131 / Sneak Out in a Lockdown** for more.)

134 DEAL WITH TEAR GAS

Where there are riots, there's bound to be tear gas. But much like rubber bullets, the name of this standard crowd control weapon can be somewhat misleading. Yes, it will irritate your eyes and affect your breathing, but wearing a bandana or simple face covering won't protect you from tear gas fully; it also coats the skin and causes chemical burns. If you're in a cloud of tear gas, leave the area as quickly as possible and breathe in short bursts through your nose. Avoid rubbing your skin or eyes to prevent the chemical agents from irritating you further. Once you're out of the chemical cloud and into safety, wash the tear gas off and pour milk in your eyes if they're still irritated.

Knowing how to blend in with the locals is a good tactic to employ when traveling, especially to regions not exactly warm and welcoming to outsiders—like all the places in this book! While you may not be able to conform completely, here are some ways I learned to apply a bit of cultural camouflage to help blend in.

CLOTHES

Like the old saying goes: Don't dress for the undercover gig you have, dress for the undercover gig you want. Avoid any pieces of wardrobe or flair that could make you easily identifiable as an outsider like ball caps, fanny packs, or tennis shoes. In other words, don't dress like you're a tourist visiting a theme park. Wear clothing similar in color to what the locals wear. A white linen suit in Yara sounds good in theory, but between the debris from explosions and the blood—yours and others'—it won't stay white very long. (If you happen to find a Panama hat near the city center of Esperanza, contact me.)

HABITS

Locals don't usually walk around reading maps, so avoid doing anything in public that makes you look like a tourist. The same goes for carrying a camera around your neck and constantly snapping pictures. Wait until you return home to post pictures on social media, so as not to give away your location in case someone is monitoring you. Shadow governments, man.

136 CROSS ROOFTOPS CORRECTLY

Avoiding the streets is a good survival tactic to employ when moving around hostile cities, and Esperanza is as hostile as cities can get. It can take some practice, but once you get the hang of it you'll find that rooftops can be a great alternative to getting past police patrols, checkpoints, or the aforementioned riots (especially if you happen to find a good zip line; see item **127 / Ride a Zip Line**). Here are some tips to help you stay low and high at the same time by crossing rooftops to stay out of danger.

SHOES

You'll want good, reliable footwear strapped to your feet when traversing rooftops. There will usually be a way to get up and down buildings, but there may be a situation or two that will require you to jump to get from structure to structure (especially if you're being chased)! Flip-flops will easily get you killed in this situation.

BE EDGY

Stay close to the edges of rooftops to both use the rigid frame under the roofing and to keep what's happening on the ground in your periphery. This also provides you with cover to crouch behind in the event you need to avoid the eyes of a rooftop sniper.

MAKE CONTACT

Getting up to a rooftop isn't the hardest part of climbing; it's the hard ground waiting below. Whether it's two hands and one foot or two feet and one hand, always maintain three points of contact at all times when climbing.

When it hits the fan and you need to make an emergency escape, the sewers may be your best option. City streets can become extremely dangerous in times of crisis, so having a subterranean substitute for your escape makes good survival sense—and it's yet another solid reason to avoid wearing a white linen suit. (Mine will certainly never be the same, even after multiple dry cleanings.) Here's how to navigate sewers so your chances of survival don't get flushed down the toilet.

WASTE NOT, WANT NOT

Most cities have a labyrinth of different sewage systems winding beneath them. Each is designed to manage and transport different forms of waste or runoff, and each has its own unique pros and cons.

RUNOFF

Stormwater sewers are great because there's no sewage and they usually lead to a body of water like a river or the ocean. But if a rainstorm or flood hits while you're down there, you'll drown.

SEWAGE

Behind door number two, raw sewage sewers are a great option because they run all over the city, but not so great on account of all the raw sewage. Even with waders and protective gear, there's high risk of infection, contamination, and choking to death on sewer gas.

COMBINED

Finally, there's the combined water sewage system that carries sewage, rainwater runoff, and industrial waste in the same pipes. It's unknown what types of toxic waste compounds lurk in these pipes, so using this option is a real crapshoot.

MAP IT

Yara isn't known for its immaculate record keeping, so locating an official city map will be a challenge. Instead, try making your own sewer map by walking proposed rainwater routes on the surface. This is also a great way to test your escape route in advance to make sure it can get you to safety in an emergency evac. Never pooh-pooh good survival prep!

Unless you have a satellite phone with enough minutes, cellular reception is hard to get when traveling through isolated regions. Add an ongoing revolution to the mix, and you usually have attacks on utility infrastructures and radio towers. That means more power outages and fewer places to broadcast a signal. There's also heightened monitoring for cell signals to eavesdrop and locate dissidents. Here's how to use a cell phone wisely in a revolution.

CONSERVE PHONE AMMO

Preserving the battery life of your cell phone is crucial as it can be your only lifeline in a survival situation. If your phone dies, you could be next. Keep it off or in airplane mode and only use it if you absolutely need to.

LISTEN FOR GHOSTS

Cell signals can be heavily monitored by local authorities, but also by anyone with technical know-how and access to a Radio Shack. (I hear they just opened a new store in Yara this year!) Avoid IMSI phone trackers, also known as "stingrays" within the ghost ops journalism community.

BE AN IPHONY

Use an empty backup phone with no personal data. Even if it's not able to turn on, it can still be stripped and mined for its data if you lose it or get captured. Spoof emergency calls to bad guys (especially if they're the bad guys who have official regime backing and an emergency services number) to confuse and disorient guard patrols. If you're using a Blume model phone, they come standard with CTOS. Hack enemy phones like a digital axe murderer!

Everyone has their go-to hangover remedy they like to use after a night of heavy drinking, peyote, and regret. But none of those things will help you if you're hungover in Yara. They brew a dark rum with some amazing herbal infusions, and I may have drunk more than a few bottles in my time on the island. It's like having a car bomb go off in your mouth, then being visited by an angel . . . followed by a devil wielding a flaming maul. Here's how to survive a Yaran hangover.

EAT A GREASY BREAKFAST

Kidding, it doesn't have to be greasy. I just wrote that to make the hungover people reading this nauseous. Despite what your appetite may be telling you, having a good breakfast (whatever you choose) when hungover will help raise your blood sugar levels and reduce hangover symptoms.

STAY IN BED

Lack of sleep can make hangover symptoms worse, so getting plenty of rest is important to allow your body to recover. Depending on your poison of choice, some of it may still be in your system when you wake up, so you might be seeing things that aren't really in the room with you . . . y'know, like the old woman crawling towards me on the ceiling. Best sleep it off.

OLD FAITHFUL

If you wake up on the beach the morning after a Yaran bender with duct tape on your wrists and a typewriter case tied to your ankles like an anchor, that's a sign you had a wild night. But you also lost plenty of electrolytes swimming to shore, so drink lots of water and stay hydrated. Mix in sports drink powder for added potassium.

In my time on Yara, I could easily see *Libertad* was outmatched in a straight-up fight with the regime. Asymmetrical conflict calls for asymmetrical solutions: What a guerrilla force lacks in size and firepower, they make up for in fighting with misdirection and sleight of hand. Yaran revolutionaries are tactical magicians who infiltrate the heads of their opponents while simultaneously infiltrating their stronghold to make a small force seem much larger. Here are some guerrilla magic tricks to help you fight dirty and smart, then disappear like rabbits.

TOE-TO-TOE A NO-GO

Never engage in a frontal assault. A guerrilla force going head-to-head with a larger military opponent will have a huge disadvantage. Indirect attacks from unusual angles will catch your opponent off guard. Guerrillas do their homework on a stronghold before an assault, knowing guard positions, patrol routes, ingress and egress points, and alarm locations. It's recommended you do the same.

HIT AND RUM

Launching an attack and quickly withdrawing from an engagement is a guerrilla fighting tactic designed to frustrate and wear down your opponent. Get in, make some noise, and get out before they even know what hit 'em. Constant movement is key—give yourself three seconds, three hits, or three stolen bottles of Yaran dark rum in your loot bag, then disengage. Do not linger in any given position.

STAKE OUT THE FLANK

Attacking from a dominant position gives you more options and your opponent fewer. Coming in from the side forces your opponent to adjust their attack. You'll have a few extra seconds to get a shot off before they do, so be quick on the trigger.

SABOTAGE AND AMBUSH

A guerrilla classic, sabotage is great for destroying enemy resources and equipment, disrupting supply lines and infrastructure, and making Viviro labs explode. But you can also sabotage your opponent in combat psychologically by surprising them with an ambush attack. Be aggressive and continuous to overwhelm them when they least expect it.

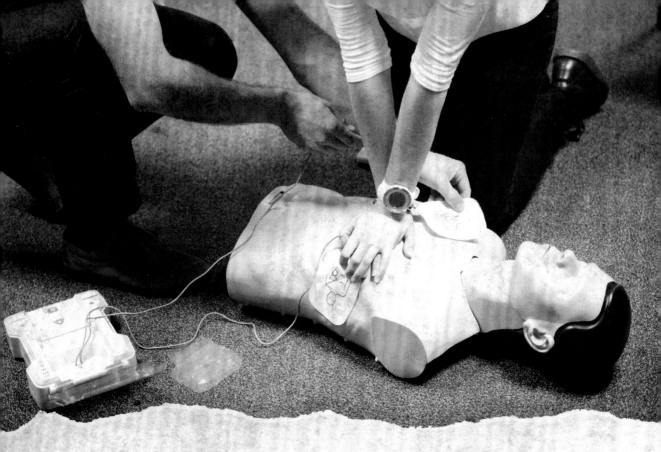

141 SAVE WITH CPR

CPR: We've all heard of it. We've all seen it performed in movies and workplace comedies enough to think we know how to do it. But loss of blood flow to the heart and brain can be fatal, so when someone loses their pulse and it's up to you to find it, you want to know exactly where to look and quickly. Here's how to perform CPR—because when someone is dying, you don't have time to say "cardiopulmonary resuscitation!"

STEP 1

Any situation needing CPR is life-threatening, so the first step is to always try to get medical assistance immediately. This is easier said than done on Yara, but *Libertad* does have some medical resources. Seek them out.

STEP 2

Place the heel of your hand in the middle of the victim's chest just above the bottom of the sternum and stack your other hand on top of it.

STEP 3

Begin compressions on the victim's chest, pushing 2 inches (5 cm) down while keeping your elbows locked. Put your full weight over adult victims—the more force the better. Go lighter if it's a kid; for infants, use the pads of your fingers and compress to an inch (2.5 cm).

STEP 4

Pump at a rate of one hundred beats per minute and continue until the victim recovers. You'll tire easily, so switch off with anyone nearby to maintain steady compressions. There's no time to rest like the lazy jerk you're trying to resuscitate who's just lying there.

STEP 5

If you're CPR certified, stop after thirty compressions and gently tip the victim's head back to open the airway for breathing business. Pinch the nose and seal your mouth over the victim's mouth, giving two deep breaths. Keep repeating the entire process until help arrives with a medic backpack.

Yara is practically built on *resolver*—the local slang for basically "making do with what you have." And unless you're in the Castillo regime, you don't have much. Luckily, Yaran guerrillas excel at improvisational warfare by crafting unique weapons and explosive devices out of whatever they can scavenge. Traveling to Yara by barrel meant I had to skip first aid supplies, but *resolver* also includes getting creative with field medicine, because when you're low on supplies, you have to improvise. Here's what I learned about being a medical MacGyver, using objects scavenged from abandoned buildings or looted from corpses.

SOCK YOUR ARM

Cut a hole in the bottom of a (preferably clean) tube sock and use it as a bandage cover. This handy sleeve is especially useful if you have to move a lot after being bandaged—and running from gunfire just happens to be a top Yaran sport.

GET SPANDEXTEROUS

Cut a Lycra shirt in a spiral pattern or cut the sleeve or leg from a Lycra garment to get various lengths of stretch material that can be used in place of bandages to stabilize sprains or tie splints in place.

USE A BANDANA-AID

Use a bandana or scarf as an arm sling. Regular scarves can be used to secure the sling to the torso more comfortably than a belt and come in an array of fashionable colors and patterns.

TAMP DOWN BLOOD

Clean and absorbent, tampons and sanitary napkins are good stand-ins as trauma dressings for gunshot wounds. They're also great for splint padding or stopping a nosebleed, and you can use pads as eyepatches.

DISINFECT INTERNALLY

Alcoholic beverages like vodka, whiskey, or rum can be used as a disinfectant for equipment and hands. While drinking alcohol isn't designed to disinfect wounds, it can be used if there's no other option.

SALT THE WOUNDS

Epsom salt is a great topical treatment for soothing insect bites, stings, sunburns, blisters, and poison ivy. If you're lucky enough to be holed up in a building with running hot water, pour some in a tub and luxuriate.

Whenever I travel to dangerous and isolated locations, I carry fake IDs like my janitor father carried keys—I've got one to open any door. But when not used to hide someone's identity, ID cards can also be used to patch a bullet wound in an emergency, like when gunfire erupted at another cantina where I was drinking. In between exchanging gunfire with a Yaran military captain, I found time to help a local who took a round between the ribs. In the event of a piercing wound to the torso (like a gunshot), the victim's chest may fill with air if a lung is punctured. This can cause a sucking chest wound, and it really sucks to get one. Here's how to patch it up with an ID card so you can make it suck less.

STEP 1

Get your ID card and something to keep it in place. I think you know where this recommendation is going: sturdy, reliable duct tape.

STEP 2

Cover the wound by securing the edges, leaving one open. If done correctly, indrawn breath should keep the seal over the wound, while exhaling should relieve some pressure from the lung.

STEP 3

Get immediately to medical care—especially if all that's keeping you breathing is an expired Blockbuster card.

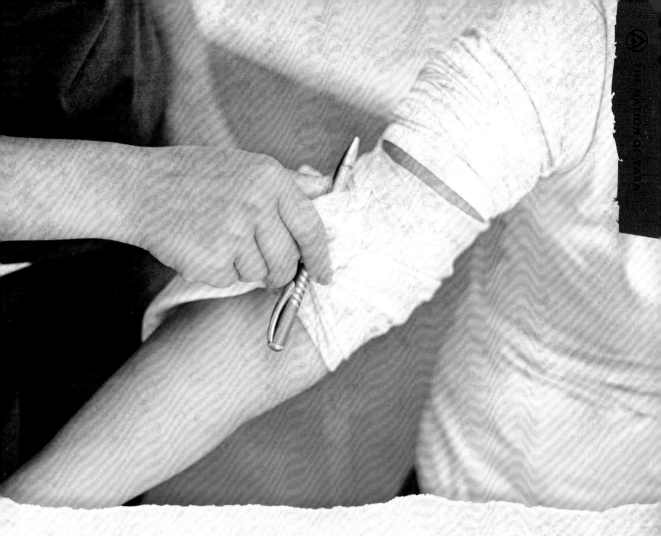

144 RIG A TOURNIQUET

Castillo's speeches sometimes referred to the people of Yara being the lifeblood of the country. It's ironic that so many of them were being bled dry thanks to his regime. If you need to help keep an injured victim from bleeding out and you don't have a proper medical tourniquet, here are a few really great entry-level options for the amateur guerrilla field medic or hobbyist.

TOURNAMENT OF TOURNIQUETS

Any broad, flexible, or sturdy substance can be fashioned into a tourniquet cinching band: a leather belt, a rolled-up shirt, the rubber inner tube from a unicycle, braided lengths of paracord, and so many more. Ensure the material isn't thin enough to cut into the tissue and cause more bleeding.

Wrap your tourniquet of choice firmly around the limb and tie it off with an overhand knot.

TWIST AND SHOUT

Use a rigid object like a wooden spoon, metal rebar, or a screwdriver to apply torsion. Any sturdy object about the size of your forearm will do. Place it against the cinching band that you've made and tie it in place with a square knot. Much like my ex-wife turning the knife in my heart, twist until the bleeding stops.

LIFE AND LIMB

Record the time the tourniquet was applied and seek professional medical assistance immediately.

145 HALT AN ELECTROCUTION

The Yaran military does a lot to get information out of hostages. One method guaranteed to get words, or at least a scream, out of a quiet captive: electrocution. But simply halting one may be a bit of an undersell. In order to save a friend or fellow revolutionist from being electrocuted, you'll likely have to storm a compound, guns blazing and preferably in squads. But what do you do after dispatching all the guards and clearing the room? Follow these simple steps when you have to halt an electrocution.

OUT OF THE FRYING PAN

Don't attempt to touch the victim with your bare hands. Human bodies are good conductors of electricity and if the victim is still connected to a power source, you could be electrocuted as well. Use a wooden object if you need to move them.

INTO HOT WATER

Electricity and water are a dangerous combination. Keep water away from the electrocution site to avoid conduction.

DO THE ELECTRIC SLIDE

Castillo's soldiers are known to use car batteries when electrocuting hostages, so look for those nearby but don't rule out other power sources. Check to make sure power is completely switched off. When that has been confirmed, begin hostage extraction, and get out of there.

RECITE YOUR ABCS

Remember the ABCs of survival? (See item **002 / Check Vital Signs.**) Check the victim's vitals to assess their medical condition.

Paracelsus once said, "The dose makes the poison." I myself once said, "There's a time and place for everything, and that's after I get a doctorate in journalism." From Hope County's hallucinogenic Bliss to Yara's chemically infused tobacco fields of Viviro, it wouldn't be a survival excursion across the borders of insanity without a drug trip. Sometimes you'll need meds to numb the pain along the way, and if you're unable to loot any extra strength aspirin, why not repurpose some of that cocaine?! Here's how to turn a good times stash to legitimate medical use so you can feel no pain when bad times loom.

MDMA

This so-called "party drug" treats PTSD and has other therapeutic purposes. It's also being studied as a possible treatment for Parkinson's disease.

COCAINE

This 1980s Wall Street vending machine staple was once used as a topical anaesthetic in surgery and dentistry because if you take enough, you won't be able to feel your face. Leaves from the coca plant can be chewed to treat nausea and altitude sickness—something I'll keep in mind should I ever return to Kyrat (see items **051** and **052 / Train for the Mountains** and **Conquer Altitude Sickness**).

BLISS

That's right: Hope County's own answer to hillbilly heroin, Bliss, can be ingested in both liquid and powder form and is typically harmless in very small doses. However, the plant does contain alkaloids like scopolamine that some theorize carry mind control properties. Small amounts of Bliss can work as a short-term antidepressant. Excess doses will fry your brain and give you angel wings.

CANNABIS

If medicinal drugs had a mascot, it would probably be a cute cartoon joint. Legal in many countries for its medical use, cannabis has been approved to treat nausea, "chronic" pain, anxiety, and even epilepsy.

LSD

When used in low does, acid and 'shrooms (see item **037 / Sprout Killer 'Shrooms**) have been proven effective in treating cluster headaches, migraines, and severe pain. Warning: If used in high doses, you'll be slaying Blood Dragons like a champ instead.

HEROIN

An opiate painkiller more effective than morphine, Vicodin, or Oxy, and more likely to kill you as well.

AMPHETAMINES

Useful in treating severe allergic reactions as well as narcolepsy and ADHD. Also great for staying up several nights in a row watching for Castillo's *policia* and spotting the shadow people by day.

Somewhere between a knife and a sword is the machete, a versatile cutting tool used by jungle explorers to hack through dense foliage. And if you swing it just right and keep it sharp, it's great for protection. I've usually carried knives when I travel (see item **079 / Choose Your Blade**), but the machete was my melee weapon of choice on Yara: Its heavy razor edge cuts Kevlar as easily as jungle vines. Here's how to swing a machete like a goalie-masked killer.

SLICE WITH SAFETY

As with any cutting or gutting tool, use it with caution to prevent injury to yourself. Be mindful of where your blade will land if you miss your intended target, so make sure any body parts you want to keep aren't in the vicinity.

HANDLE IT

Always hold the machete handle with a firm grip. You can customize your machete by wrapping the handle with duct tape to give you a better surface grip. I enhanced my writing wrist guard with extra padding in the palm to grip weapons. (I also gave it a metal knuckle plate and a retractable wrist blade, but that's a story for another time.)

STAY SHARP

Make sure to always keep the blade sharp, and never let the edge strike the ground or it will get dull. Use a side-to-side sweeping action if you're clearing vegetation, and as tempting as it may be, avoid making kung fu noises while you're doing it so you don't give away your position.

As I got to see firsthand by spending a few weeks in a farmland camp, compounds in the rural hinterlands of Yara were an essential safe haven for *Libertad* revolutionaries to recoup, unwind with a friendly game of dominoes, improvise chaos devices, and strategize their next move. Compounds need to be functional, heavily armed, and defensively positioned to hold up against surprise attacks. Here are some tips to build a guerrilla compound that might win you some resistance points.

GET HIGH

Elevation is key for defense. You have the tactical advantage if the enemy has to climb or run up steep inclines to attack you. Alternate dirt and berms and fencing (concertina wire works great).

DEAD END

Keep the exit and entrance simple. Give wannabe bunker busters the fewest options possible to infiltrate your compound. A single driveway with a sturdy gate is what you want here. A cattle guard also provides a solid base to brace your gate closed. Use sturdy metal poles to reinforce the gate even more.

HEAVILY FARMED

Surviving on Yara means living on your own for the long haul. Planting a vegetable garden and fruit trees can provide you with vitamins and minerals year-round, and you can preserve any excess stock for later use. Windmills and solar panels will give you a steady stream of electricity when you're living off the grid. Build a barn for the animals. Add ramps to structures so even the little wheelchair-assisted dog I met, dubbed "Chorizo," or other pets can have access.

EYE IN THE SKY

Take advantage of having the high ground by always keeping a watchful eye on the horizon. A watchtower or two is a good idea. Add floodlights and a stationary machine gun for some added flair that screams "Keep out!"

GOPHER BROKE

If you need an escape plan, a buried school bus makes a great DIY bunker, and while you have your shovel out, why not dig a single underground escape tunnel? Camouflage and reinforce the exit.

149 IMPROVISE TOOLS

No tools? No problem! The resourceful and imaginative Yaran guerrillas can craft all manner of wild and destructive weapons of chaos from anything they find. But before you can craft your own supremo backpack or a gas pump flamethrower, you need the right tools for the job. Here's how to improvise tools like the Yarans do.

AXE

Scavenge a piece of thick, flat metal (try scrap or copper) and a hefty oak or hickory branch. Much like branches of Anton Castillo's military, the more crooked it is, the better. Position the metal at a 90-degree angle at the limb's bent end and wrap lashing around it to hold it in place. Grind the blade against a stone to sharpen it. Substitute stone or granite for your axe head if metal is scarce.

SHOVEL

Try nailing an old milk crate, a plastic tub, or a large tin can to the end of a broomstick if you need to dig an emergency escape tunnel, improvise a hilarious melee weapon, or bury bodies.

BOW SAW

If you have a wire saw from a basic survival kit or a garrote from a basic assassin kit, you can make a lightweight bow saw that can cut through saplings and small PVC pipes. Get a slightly curved stick about 3 feet (1 m) in length and 1 inch (2.5 cm) in diameter. Carve notches in the ends of the stick and string your death cord between them. Ease the saw's end rings into the notches. You can also use it as a weapon to strike the violin strings in an orchestra of chaos!

Yara offers a delicious bounty of food for the modern survivor to harvest—from plentiful fish and game to wild herbs and exotic fruits and vegetables. Unfortunately, gathering ingredients and finding an adequate (or functional) kitchen to cook them in is a dangerous aspiration at best and deadly at worst. So, much like staying alive on Yara, if you want to prepare a meal for yourself or your squadmates you'll need to pack heat—and I don't mean a .45 ACP. While some of these items may seem like a luxury, you'd be surprised what you can scavenge from the backpacks of missing thrill seekers and abandoned Viviro labs.

■ STOVE

- Burner camp stove (Viviro labs are a good place to scavenge these)

■ COOKWARE

- Pots
- Large frying pan (can double as a melee weapon or be stashed in your waistband if you're trying to cook up some bullet protection)
- Measuring cup/mixing cup (again, Viviro labs)
- Coffee pot and extra mugs (FYI: Yaran coffee keeps you up for days. There must be something in the soil.)

■ UTENSILS

- Knife (sub for combat knife or machete)
- Mixing and serving spoons
- Metal tongs
- Stackable plates/cups

■ CLEANUP

Typically you want to clean up after a meal, but you tend to eat and run on Yara fairly regularly. Save the item space in your loot bag.

- Camp sink
- Biodegradable soap
- Quick-dry towels
- Pot scrubbers
- Trash bags

■ MISCELLANEOUS

- Strike anywhere matches
- Bottle opener
- Corkscrew
- Can opener
- Collapsible water container
- Aluminum foil
- Thermacell

Crocs may be fast and hungry, and while they aren't prone to chasing people down on land, it has been known to happen. Just ask my Yaran friend, a metal worker and farmer named Federico who was attacked by one. In the water, they're absolutely terrifying and can even propel themselves upward out of the water with their tails. The crocodile land speed record, meanwhile, clocks in at about 10 miles per hour (17 kph)—Federico confirmed this after he began conducting speed trials to gather calibration data for the home-brew croc-claw gun he was improvising out of scrap to catch one—so they can easily be outpaced.

Ideally, stay at least 20 feet (6 m) away from any croc at all times. But if you're like me and don't respect personal space or boundaries, know that crocodiles strike in powerful bursts and burn a lot of energy, so they tire quickly. If you dodge the initial attack and it decides to give chase, don't bother running an evasive zigzag pattern. It doesn't work and just serves to slow you down—the exact opposite of what you want to do. Federico's tactical data on crocodiles recommends running for your life in a straight line as fast and hard as you can. If the situation is dire, drop gear to lighten your feet and increase your speed.

Crocs have the home field advantage in the water—they're stealthier, faster, and they can maneuver better than you can. My good friend—and crocodile tamer—Federico suggests if you're wading through the swamps of Valle Luzcano and a croc approaches, get to land fast or get ready to wrestle even faster. Here's how to stack the odds in your favor to win the one-hundred-meter crocodile freestyle and avoid becoming a post-workout snack.

CROC AND ROLL

If a croc gets ahold of you and goes into its famous "death roll" beneath the water's surface, you could become human sashimi if you don't act fast. Never try to fight the direction of the revolution, as the croc will tear off bite-size pieces of your body (and crocs take big bites).

CROCODILE "M" FOR MURDER

Try to gouge out its eyes or thrust your fingers (or even better, your combat knife, machete, or any impaling object like a nearby branch) into its snout. This should drive it away. If all else fails, try punching and kicking the crocodile in those general areas. (Insult-to-injury points if you happen to be wearing croc skin boots while kicking it. Even more points if you wear Crocs.) But if you've previously hunted and skinned crocs for cash in those waters, you've likely killed its family, so it may be dead set on a winner-takes-all revenge rematch. (Just hope it's not a tag team match.)

A crocodile is a swamp-holiday feast big enough to feed a dysfunctional guerrilla squad on Christmas. The best part is the tail meat, and lucky for you, it just so happens to be the easiest to get to. Grab that newly sharpened machete; here's your recipe for success to prepare a mean tail like Federico, the expert guerrilla crocodile chef.

CROC LOBSTER

Start by cutting through the thickest part of the tail (the underbelly) all the way to the bone. Cut along the tail from the hip, then work the point of the knife down between the bone and the meat to separate the two.

A CROCODILE MEAT TALE

Look for the tenderloins inside a larger chunk of tail meat separated by a layer of fat. You should be able to reach in and pull out these tender cuts with your bare hands.

CROC CUTLET

Cut the fat and the connective tissue from the remaining meat for a feast of lean, delicious croc steaks. Even the small crocs can yield several meals' worth of that sweet crocodile meat. If you prefer a darker meat, cut from the midsection. Crocs on Yara have a diet consisting mostly of guerrillas and Castillo's soldiers, most of whom wear grenade belts, so slice into the belly with caution.

154 READ A DOG'S INTENTIONS

Once you've spent some time observing wild animals in their natural habitat, it becomes easier to identify the triggers of aggressive behavior and avoid them. And when it comes to man's best friend, they can be just as wild and dangerous as their wolf cousins—even the little wheelchair-bound dachshund named Chorizo. Here are some warning signs to observe before you go in for a belly rub on that stray doggo. If you play your dog poker just right, you may just make a new friend and battle buddy.

THE BARK SIDE

Dogs bark in various tones and registers to communicate, but a low, guttural bark is their way of giving a warning or threat. Likewise, growling or snarling are good indicators that it may not be the goodest boy.

READ DOGGY LANGUAGE

Body posture is another useful indicator. Watch to see if its ears are pulled back, lying flat against the head, or if the dog becomes very still. Approach slowly as any sudden movement could make the dog see you as a potential threat and attack.

AVOID THE BITES

A dog's primary weapon is its mouth, but it may also use it to gently grab someone to establish dominance without biting or shoving with its muzzle. If this behavior escalates to warning shots in the form of light nips, back away and get out of the situation before the aggression level raises to a ravenous hail-fire of bullet teeth.

155 FIGHT OFF A DOG ATTACK

If a persistent pooch is chasing you down, relentless in its bloodlust, and you've tried everything you can to escape a bad dogfrontation, what do you do now? Dogs have two more legs than you do, so you can't outrun them on foot. That just leaves you with one final option: Fight! Here are some non-PETA-approved methods you can use to let the fur fly and fight off an attacking dog when you just can't get away.

ARM AND LEG YOURSELF

Dog attacks can be deadly, and you should fight with whatever means you have in your fleshy arsenal if you find yourself without a weapon to defend yourself. Much like the mouth being a dog's natural weapon and defense mechanism, we humans have those too: arms and legs. Punching and kicking followed up with some assertive yelling commands will show the dog you mean business.

DOG POUNDS

You're likely to have the size advantage in a dog brawl. Use that to your advantage by wrestling the dog with your full body weight to subdue them into tapping out. I was in a wrestling match with a dog on Yara for two hours straight before we both got tired and gave up. We developed a mutual respect for each other, so if you meet a dog named Hunter in Yara, pour a little whiskey in a hubcap for him. He's a good boy.

156 DEAL WITH ANGRY DOGS

Pretty much everything on Yara is aggressive and wants to injure or kill you, even the dogs! Whether it's a pack of wild canines, or one that a Yaran *policia* just sent off the leash and in your direction like a furry heat-seeker, they can all be handled similarly. Here are some tactics for handling an angry dog attack.

STAY CALM

Dogs will react less aggressively to you if you're calm. They will also react less aggressively to you if you offer them a treat.

AVERT YOUR EYES AND TEETH

Dogs may see this behavior as you challenging them. You also want to avoid smiling, as bared teeth are also an aggression signal among animals.

HOLD YOUR GROUND

Any sudden movement could trigger a predatory response that leads to a chase or attack, so remain still even if the dog approaches you.

USE SLEIGHT OF HAM

Offer a stick or other object within reach for the dog to chew on. If you're being chased down, throw a food item so the dog becomes distracted, and use the opportunity to disappear.

BARK LIKE AN ALPHA

If the quiet approach is ineffective in deterring a dog attack, speak in a deep, confident voice and let it know it's being a real bad boy.

BE AN UP DOG

Dogs aren't good climbers, so if being chased, run towards something in the environment that can elevate you off the ground: a parked car, a torched car, or an overturned car.

NO LEG BONES ABOUT IT

Dogs love bones, but if your canine pursuer loses interest in chomping down on your tibia, slowly and carefully leave the area.

Nothing beats the feeling of invincibility you get walking around with a rocket launcher slung over your shoulder—except maybe the feeling of sneaking into battle with a rocket launcher and six hundred pounds of angry, snarling grizzly bear at your side. Sadly, grizzlies are hard to come by on Yara, and Cheeseburger (see item **104 / Survive Grizzlies**) is nowhere near, but the island has its own ferocious bestiary. You just have to know how to tame them. Like many places in the Caribbean, chickens are everywhere, and cockfighting is among the popular underground blood sports. Here's how to tame a rooster so you can add its razor-sharp claws to an arsenal of insanity.

PUNKY ROOSTER

Roosters are naturally aggressive and prone to attack in order to assert their dominance. A rooster will usually give you a warning by lowering its head, puffing out its chest, and performing a ritualistic blood waltz to summon the power of rooster Satan. If you see this, do not walk towards the rooster or stare it down. These can be considered acts of aggression and enrage it further, and you don't want that mojo.

COCKY BALBOA

If the angry rooster attacks and starts swinging its wing fists and kicking its heel spurs, you have a few defensive options. Crouch down and try to feed the rooster to show it you're not a potential threat. Eventually it will calm down, and you've taken a step closer to commanding a rooster to dispatch a soldier for you.

COCK BLOCK

Assert your dominance by grabbing the rooster on both sides and pressing it firmly to the ground, holding its wings pinned. Repeat this every time it tries to act out. This will make the rooster feel embarrassed around the hens and remind him who's boss. Eventually, you can reward him by picking him up and parading him around to the flock.

There's a reason the power of car engines is measured in horsepower, but in Yara, sometimes the horsepower I encountered was literal, especially in the boonies. If you need a fast ride and don't have wheels, a horse is a hard option to beat. Here's how to ride an OG mustang like a guerrilla Steve McQueen.

MAKE A GREAT ESCAPE

Nudge your horse in the ribs simultaneously with both heels to get it going. The harder the nudge, the more urgent the command. To stop your horse, pull back on the reins until it halts. Pull harder if you get no response and ease up until you come to a complete stop.

RIDE THE BULLET

Bridle reins are a kind of steering wheel. A well-trained horse will "neck rein," moving away from the rein pressure on his neck. To neck rein, hold both reins in one hand (typically your weak hand, leaving your strong hand free to lead a packhorse or shoot at bad guys). To turn your horse, move the reins to the side, putting pressure on the side of the horse's neck.

WIN THE TRIPLE CROWN AFFAIR

You can also turn your horse by steering with your feet. To turn the front end, swing your foot slightly forward from its normal position and nudge it with your heel. To move the back end, swing your foot to the rear and nudge. Repeat this for as long as you need to keep the horse moving.

BEAT THE BLOB

Don't slump in the saddle. Maintain a straightened posture while riding, staying relaxed to move with the horse and stay balanced. If you're riding uphill, keep your torso upright by leaning forward. If going downhill, lean back.

159 DRIVE SAFELY IN DRIVING RAIN

Like many parts of the Caribbean, Yara is hot, humid, and has no shortage of rainfall. There's no such thing as "safe driving" in Yara on account of those slicked streets and muddy mountain roads—that, and all the military vehicles and hot rods with flamethrowers. So the least you can do is try to drive safely in the rain. You probably have heavy explosives in the trunk and you don't want to crash into anything, so here's how to keep the wheels of the stolen vehicle you're driving from flying off the road like a hydroplane.

HAIL HYDRO!

When tires encounter more water than the tread grooves can dissipate, the tire essentially floats on a layer of water. That's when you're hydroplaning, and that's not good.

HYDRO-SPLAINING

When hydroplaning, the engine's revolutions per minute (RPM) rise sharply and the wheels have no traction. A good defensive driver will feel it in the steering wheel and know how to adjust accordingly. Make the vehicle an extension of your body.

RAT ROD WATER SKIER

When your war wagon becomes a battleship, don't turn the wheel or hit the brakes; both will cause a skid. Hold your course and ease off the accelerator, allowing your vehicle to slow down and the tires to penetrate the water layer. The weight from the heavy artillery in the trunk will act as an anchor.

160 STEER THROUGH A SKID

The first sign the drugs have kicked in is that you suddenly lose control of your vehicle and end up driving sideways down the highway. That's also the first sign you're in a skid. But it may not come until the moment you lose control of your vehicle, so you'll have to react fast. Here's how to take control of the situation when your vehicle starts to lose its grip on the ground.

BRAKE FREE

To steer out of a skid, you need to have the tires rolling, not locked up. Resist the temptation to hit the brakes; the only thing it will break is your face on the dashboard when you spin off the road and crash into a tree.

BE BILLY THE SKID

Turn the steering wheel in the direction of the skid. Do this gently, without overreacting. Try not to shoot from the hip. If your wheels start to skid in the opposite direction, lasso gravity by turning the steering wheel into the skid. Be prepared to straighten the wheel as the vehicle returns to its normal trajectory. Apply very light pressure on the gas pedal to help the vehicle regain its equilibrium.

With so many hazards I saw on the roads of Yara—from rusty nails to improvised explosives—it's inevitable that you'll eventually blow out a tire at some point. And because most people have to drive fast to avoid getting shot on this Caribbean jewel, you may need to keep your escape vehicle on the road with a blown tire. Here are a few tips to help you steer clear of a tree.

RUBBER HORSESHOE

During a tire blowout, the vehicle will be pulled in the direction of the flat. So, much like piloting a skid in the rain, fight the urge to overcorrect or slam the brakes. Remain calm and hold the steering wheel firmly at ten and two o'clock, and ease off the accelerator.

BRACE FOR IMPACT

Switch on your turn signal and start moving toward the shoulder of the road. Once you've made it to safety, consider your location before activating an emergency flasher or GPS beacon—this is Yara after all. Always have a finger on a trigger and an eye on a rearview mirror if making roadside repairs while stranded at night. Approaching headlights may not be friendly, but if your draw is quick enough, you can save repair time by just taking their ride.

Snipers are everywhere on Yara, always scanning the horizon for some long-distance target practice. But as Federico told me over rum and a guerrilla campfire, you can use the environment for cover to move stealthily and evade their precision eyes glazed over with boredom. Here's how to avoid getting rained on with sniper fire when infiltrating an enemy stronghold or just moving through the capital city streets.

KEEP YOUR SCOPES UP

Rule number one when moving through any war zone or former outlet mall turned military outpost is to never stand still. Move quickly between vehicles and buildings. Alter your pace and direction; moving erratically makes you harder to track. If infiltrating a stronghold or base, scout the area with binoculars first to mark the sniper posts. Knowing where they are when they don't know where you are gives you the tactical upper hand.

STAY IN YOUR LANE

Castillo's snipers like to brag about long-distance kills to each other so avoid open "fire lanes" where a sniper can get a clear shot, even from a distance. Cover and concealment are always your two best infiltration buddies (cover is physical protection; concealment is moving within shadows or other environmental camouflage). If you're caught in the open, get low and crawl like a snake. Make yourself a hard target to make the shooter lose his or her money in the company sniper pool.

Getting caught behind enemy lines with a squadron of rifles pointed at you is not the most pleasant situation to find yourself in, especially in Yara. Staying alive means moving with stealth as you make your way to friendly forces and that can require a little know-how and a lot of patience. Here are a few tactics to help you slip past the enemy.

GET COMFY

Sometimes lying low and waiting for the battle lines to shift is the best way to avoid being spotted. Monitor guard movements and await backup. If you've assessed your situation and you'll be holed up in a spot for a while, take the opportunity to further your survival education by reading this book (especially on stealthy movement; see item **024 / Move with Stealth**) if you have some time to kill.

SILENT BUT DEADLY

If you feel you have to move, don't hurry, or you'll make mistakes and give yourself away. Avoid normal travel routes; they'll be monitored. Also avoid lines of conflict and stay low when moving for silence and flexibility.

SHADOW DANCER

Travel at night wearing dark clothing and avoid using a flashlight or torch. Scan every area carefully and thoroughly when moving between cover. When you've confirmed the coast is clear, make your stealthy move.

UNDERCOVER WEAR

If you know friendlies are nearby, signal to them in broad daylight. Wave a white flag (or your tighty whities) and come out with your hands (and pants) up.

The guerrillas of *Libertad* are really good at building their own arsenal, but if your rebellion needs some heavy artillery in its garage, sometimes it's just easier to steal it. Thankfully, Castillo's military has a well-stocked panzer pantry, and after a little gearing up, a walk-along with Federico and company one night turned into a ride-along I'll never forget. (Note to self: Ask for a down payment on a tank as my next advance.)

SHOP SMART

Know the location of the tank and scout the area in advance. Note how many guards there are, their positions, and the type of firepower they're packing. Corruption is rampant in Castillo's military ranks, and sometimes a bribe to the right underpaid soldier can pay out in big tanky dividends. Eavesdropping on drunken soldiers in cantinas can also be a great source of intel.

GRAND THEFT ARMOR

Before you attempt a risky tank theft, you might want to make sure the tank is fueled and ready to roll first. Bring a few gas cans' worth of diesel with you just in case. If you end up not needing it, it can be used to improvise Molotov cocktails to raise some hell over the alarm bells. Tanks can consume $1,000 per hour in fuel, so be prepared to assault a petrol station or two to get you safely from point A to point B.

TANKS FOR THE MEMORIES

Infiltrating a military base to steal a tank can be done stealthily but getting out can't. Draw ALL the attention by starting up your newly acquired turbine-powered metal beast and letting the engine roar!

ROAD WARRIOR

Fire the ignition switch to get it going, shifting gears with your left foot like a motorcycle and throttling up with your right. Steer with the left and right tread-control levers, and brake with the hand lever. It's like driving a 1970s station wagon with a cannon—and the gas mileage is just as bad!

165 OUTSMART KIDNAPPERS

Kidnapping is just another tool of the tyrant trade Antón Castillo's military employs to terrorize any opposition to his regime. Hopefully, it never happens to you, and it didn't happen to me, but plenty of Yaran rebels have ended up as torture fodder this way. If you find yourself in the back of a trunk with a burlap sack over your head and your wrists betrayed by your good friend duct tape, you should attempt to play your captors to your advantage.

CATCH THEM NAPPING, KID

Keep track of how many captors you have, noting their names, physical appearance, mannerisms, and where they fall in Castillo's hierarchy (soldiers wear name bars and rank insignias on their uniforms). Hopefully, you've picked up enough Spanish while on the island to eavesdrop on their conversations. You may be lucky and pick up a clue as to your whereabouts or destination.

BE ENEMIES WITH BENEFITS

Try to establish a rapport. Yes, they're kidnappers, but getting your captors to see your human side might make them view you as a person rather than a valuable commodity. Once you've successfully accomplished that, it opens up the possibility to bribe your way to freedom.

TAKE MENTAL NOTES

Memorize your captors' schedules and keep track of the passage of time. If you don't have a room with a view, pay attention to changes in temperature at dawn and dusk. Listen for any sounds outside your room like bustling in a hallway, any conversations, and your handlers' general alertness. If it looks like they need coffee, it just might be morning.

CARPE DIEM

Keep your eyes open for patterns of behavior that you can use to your advantage. If your captor leaves to take a smoke break, you might have enough time to slip free (see items **167–170 / Escape Handcuffs**, **Break Out of Rope Bindings**, **Slip Free of Zip Ties**, and **Liberate Yourself from Duct Tape**), albeit with potential fighting, and make your escape at breakneck speed.

166 ENDURE TORTURE

Unless your name is Rex "Power" Colt, you probably won't be able to resist the cruel and unusual torture methods dreamed up by the twisted minds of Antón Castillo's military. If you have information they want, they'll push your body beyond its pain thresholds to get it.

GIVE AN AWARD-WINNING PERFORMANCE

Don't challenge your tormentor's authority or try to act tough. (Leave that for Rex.) Instead of going all Michael Biehn, try Meryl Streep. Exaggerate your agony and pretend they're really hurting you before they actually do. Make them think they're killing you and maybe they won't increase the voltage, so to speak. You can also pretend to be enjoying it—which will definitely throw them off.

FINE-TRUTH COMB

Don't lie and claim you know nothing at all, but what you tell them should be plausible misinformation. Make them believe what you're saying. Tell them you only know a fragment of what they're looking for and stick with that. Avoid shifting gears and

telling them more or giving them a different story. They'll see you were lying earlier and crank up the abuse.

TAKE A MENTAL VACATION

Close your eyes and whisk yourself away to another, more pleasant mental destination—like the warm and tranquil beaches of the Rook Islands, or the picturesque mountain scapes of Kyrat.

TAKE A SALVATION VACATION

If you're religious, prayer and contemplation can be a valuable mental weapon for enduring torture. The strength you can develop from it won't make the pain and stress go away, but it will help carry you through it.

TRY A DIFFERENT ACTING METHOD

If your Streep can't stop the electrical heat, switch up to Bertinelli and take it one day at a time. Stay strong and remember the day will eventually come when the torture gets canceled.

Duct tape is a great budget option for binding wrists, but larger, more well-equipped military forces tend to have the cash to spend on actual handcuffs. Luckily, you're in Yara and the resourcefulness of the locals will certainly come in handy if your wrists ever get shackled. If you're even luckier not to be locked up in Yara, you can still use this knowledge. Here's how to escape handcuffs to amaze your friends—or captors.

CREATE YOUR KEY

Find a paper clip with a thick gauge to it; it'll need strength. Unbend the paperclip to give you the length and leverage to work your guerrilla magic.

BE A LOCKSMITH

Inspect your cuffs. You might notice a gap near where the cuff locks into itself. If you can insert the paper clip into the gap, you can shim the cuff. Use the clip to hold down the lock bar keeping the cuff's teeth in place. Presto! Your cuffs are open! But if you only have a keyhole to work with, it's time to proceed to the next step.

HARDLY HOUDINI

Insert the paper clip's end vertically into the keyhole, then bend it to form an "L" shape. Remove the clip and reinsert it into the notch of the keyhole with the bent part facing away from the center. Now give it a careful but firm twist counterclockwise. You should be able to feel the paper clip bump into the double lock bar. With a little finesse, you may even feel a click as it gives.

WINNER, WINNER, CLICKIN' DINNER

Now turn the paper clip clockwise, and this time you'll feel it bump into the single lock bar. With a little work, you should be able to disengage the single lock and make the cuffs fall right off. Now that your hands are free, I recommend putting a weapon in them immediately.

Whether you're in Yara or anywhere else unsafe, duct tape, handcuffs, and rope are all tools of the binding trade. Each has its pros and cons, and each has its own unique methods to escape it. Here's how to escape rope bindings if you find yourself unable to reach your trusty combat knife and must rely on your sharpened wits to free yourself.

FLEX ON THEM

Let your captor tie your wrists all they want but keep your arms close to your sides and muscles clenched in your forearms and hands. If your torso or legs are being bound, hold your breath and flex every muscle you can.

TRY ROPE YOGA

Once your captor puts the bow on their new hostage and their attention is elsewhere, rotate your wrists together, exhale, and relax your body. You should get a little bit of slack in all your bonds.

SWEAT IT OUT

Now that things are a little loosened, work your wrists (or any other bound limbs) back and forth, around and against each other. As you do this, the rope should stretch out a little. Luckily for you, you'll likely be perspiring in this situation, and the sweat will help reduce friction between you and the rope!

ENDURE ROPE BURN

If you can get your wrists up to your face, you can use your teeth to help work loose the bindings and pick at any troublesome knots. Once the ties are loose enough, slip out of your binding and taste that freedom!

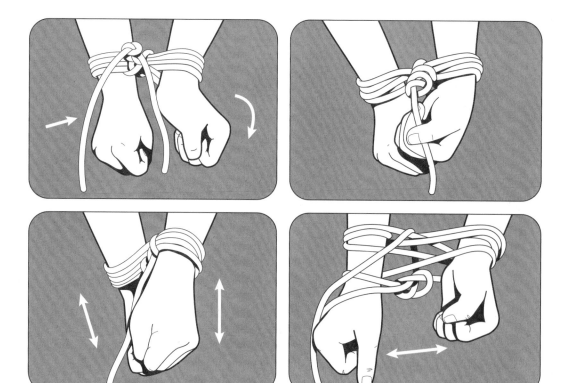

169   SLIP FREE OF ZIP TIES

Quick and easy is the name of the game zip ties play. They're an effective means of restraint and the preferred happy medium, especially by the Yaran riot cops, when handcuffs aren't available but duct tape is. As easy as they are to carry and deploy, they can be just as easy for you to escape.

HAVE AN ESCAPE PLAN

Before being tied, try to keep your fists close together horizontally with your muscles clenched as much as possible and your elbows flared out. After the tie is on, rotate your palms to give you more space to wriggle out.

PICK THE PLASTIC LOCK

Something small and rigid can lever the ratchet mechanism off the plastic strip. The corner of a credit card or tip of a pen could do the trick. A Swiss Army knife can also work . . . if you have one and can reach and unfold it with your hands tied behind your back.

GIVE IT THE BOOT (LACE)

A simple cord can cut through zip ties. Slip a shoe or bootlace around the tie and pull it back and forth rapidly while concentrating on one spot. Keep going and the pressure and friction will release you from your plastic wrist prison.

HAVE A SMOKE

Use a lighter or lit cigarette still burning in the ashtray next to your typewriter to heat the cord and melt through it. A heating element like a coil in a stove or a Bunsen burner in a Viviro lab will also work. (Use caution so you don't singe your wrist as you free yourself, Heisenberg.)

TAKE UP SLACK

Tighten the tie around your wrist as much as you can (plot twist!) then lift your arms up. With your hands overhead and elbows past your hips, bring your arms down hard and fast while pulling your hands apart to snap the ties and end your plastic wrist curse.

170 LIBERATE YOURSELF FROM DUCT TAPE

Remember that hilariously titled last escape tip in the zip tie section? It also works on duct tape! One of the most well-known uses for this tacky vinyl miracle is a quick and convenient restraint, known by some as "abduct tape." If you find yourself hobbled and bound with duct tape, don't stick around to find out what your captors plan to do to you. Here's how to free yourself and fast.

PLAY ALONG

Be compliant: Hold your hands out together and allow yourself to be bound. Keep your feet together, you need your wrists and ankles to be as close as possible for this to work.

SLACK OFF AGAIN

Just as with zip ties (see item **169 / Slip Free of Zip Ties**), you can tear duct tape with enough swift force. Done right, escape will be a snap (of tape)!

R.I.P. THE TAPE

Once again, lift your arms up above your head and then bring them down, hard. Follow through on the downward swing, and when your elbows flare outward, the sudden impact should tear through the tape like a zip tie. (Duct tape fun fact: In Yara, a live grenade duct taped to a wrist is known as a ramillete, or corsage!)

DO THE SPLITS

For your leg bindings, put your hands together with the palms facing each other and slide them between your knees, forcing your hands and forearms down the length of your shins. The sudden force should split the tape.

"When it comes to *resolver*," as I heard from Federico and other rebels, "you make do with anything and everything you can—everything." Words to live by, literally. Sometimes your back is against the wall and your gun is out of ammo. Sometimes a poison thrower runs of juice, or you lose your machete because you swung so hard it got stuck in a clavicle, and the only thing left in the bag of grenades is the smell of gunpowder. Now there's only one thing left you can do to survive: resolve to put your fists up and fight.

DODGE

You can evade an incoming blow by thrusting it aside with your arms or legs, a move called parrying. Effective blocks follow a circular motion either inward or outward depending on where the threat is coming from. Use your arms and hands to parry attacks from punches, high kicks, and melee weapons. Parry with your legs to deflect kicks or low strikes.

PUNCH

Out of real grenades? Throw some explosive fist power! Bring your fist to waist level with your elbows pulled back. Step forward with the opposite foot as you punch, landing the blow as your foot hits the ground. Aim for vulnerable targets like the nose, throat, or the center of your enemies' pain universe: the solar plexus. Follow through like you're trying to punch a hole in them, and they'll feel like you just did!

KICK

It can take some practice and finesse to swing your foot-hammer right. Concentrate on delivering powerful leg kicks to lower targets by raising your foot to knee level and thrust into the gut, groin, or knee of your opponent. Step into it and follow up with more punches and kicks; be relentless! Don't stop until your attacker tastes pavement or is stunned enough for you to make your escape!

It is possible to break your thumb if you throw a punch incorrectly. Punching with your thumb tucked inside the fingers is a no-no-brainer. You always want to keep your thumb on the outside of your fist, primed and ready to join the fight. First, you want to hold your fist loosely and strike with the knuckles of your first two fingers. Now you're punching with power. Here are some weak points to aim for as you pursue the fine art of pugilism:

ADAM'S APPLE

Drive your fist into your attacker's throat as hard as you can and mash it into Adam's applesauce. Make your escape as they roll around on the ground struggling for air.

UNDERARM

A well-placed punch to an exposed underarm can temporarily impair the entire arm. It's an effective move to gain an advantage over your attacker but depending on their personal hygiene, you do risk getting a case of stink fist.

NOSE

Strike hard on the bridge of the nose to cause whiplash, bleeding, or confusion. (Fun fact: Yarans love baseball and hitting someone in the nose with a bat and causing all three of these conditions with one swing is called a *triplica*.)

173 CLUTCH A ROLL OF QUARTERS

Looking to pack more face-tenderizing power in your punches and you don't have a pair of brass knuckles? Try copper and nickel knuckles instead! Yarans use money just like everyone else, and that includes coins. Their version of the quarter is a little denser and flatter, but it's close enough for discomfort when a coin roll collides with a soldier's jaw. Tightly grip a roll of coins before a brawl and you'll feel like you're in the western movie *A Fistful of Dollars*! The solid support inside your closed hand will make your fist feel like stone, with the added weight giving your fist guns the stopping power of a five-fingered LMG. The extra weight will also give you reinforcement to prevent injury to your hand, allowing you to continue wailing on your attacker for extended periods of time.

Bonus tip: You can use the quarters afterwards to do a load of laundry and wash the blood off your clothing! Optional: Here are a few zingers you can use to taunt your opponent right before punching them with a roll of quarters in your fist that would make Rex "Power" Colt proud: "Ten bucks says I can kick your ass." "Wanna see a coin trick?" "Pain is my currency."

"Special offer: twenty-five cent rhinoplasty. Today only." Or, toss the roll of quarters on them as they writhe on the floor holding their broken and bloody nose and tell them to "keep the change." If you can't lighten the mood in these dangerous places, you're bound to go insane.

I've been punched more times than I can count—but I'm still here, typing, punching, and shooting away when the times call for it. Holding your own in a fight means more than just throwing a devastating barrage of attacks, it also means knowing how to take them, whether the barroom brawl is in Yara over a spilled army officer's drink or anywhere else with any other antagonist. Here's how to take a licking and keep on punching and kicking. (To take the blow of a hangover instead, see item **139 / Survive a Yaran Hangover**.)

TAKE A FIST

If a fist is coming your way at high speed and you can't escape, brace for impact. Clench your jaw and move toward the attacker to lessen the extension of their arm. You can also duck to take the blow on your forehead instead of the more breakable parts of your face. For a blow to the gut, flex your abdominal muscles and exhale so your wind doesn't get knocked out.

GO CLUBBING

Getting hit with a blunt weapon is like getting punched, just with a harder object and way more painful. Try and close the distance between you and your attacker and take the blow in soft spots like large muscle masses on the thigh. Avoid taking blows to bones, which will shatter.

GET ON A RIDE

In a car-versus-pedestrian fight, the car will always win if you stand your ground. Roll into the impact if you're about to be struck to take the weight off your feet. Aim your landing for the center of the hood and let the momentum carry your body through the impact and over the windshield and roof like a rag doll.

CUT IT OUT

Don't try to close the distance on a knife-wielding attacker. Instead, fight outside the critical distance zone which is about two-thirds the length of the attacker's arm. Try to move your body in the direction of the slash to minimize resistance.

BE A LEAD SPONGE

Most lethal gunshots are to the head, neck, and back so protect those vulnerable areas. Turn your body to face your attacker, then drop to the floor with your legs together and your knees drawn up to protect your torso. Place your arms together in front of your head, resting your palms on top.

Your goal when facing off against an armed assailant is to escape injury and above all else to survive. You should always submit to demands for your possessions, unless someone is making the fatal mistake of trying to steal your typewriter case—like the guy outside the cantina who wanted mine, and was too drunk to understand both English and Spanish words for "no" and "drop it now" and "I will shoot you." He eventually relented, especially since I had the .45 and all he had was the typewriter. But if escape isn't an option when being attacked by an armed assailant, and all you have to defend yourself are your arms, you can even the playing field by disarming your attacker.

KNIFE

If your attacker is wielding a knife, stay back to remain out of its range. When you have the opportunity, grab the attacker's wrist to angle the blade away. Bonus tip: If your attacker is wielding a machete, disarm them and then with a nice hard swing, use it to dis-arm them! (See item **147 / Clear the Way with a Machete.**)

CLUB

Move quickly to reduce your attacker's ability to swing a club. To release their grip, push the attacker back, grab their wrist, and twist it violently. (If you hear the sound of a snapping celery stalk, it means you did it right.)

GUN

Much like when firing a gun (see item **117 / Shoot in the Right Stance**), pivot out of the line of fire by turning sideways rather than facing your attacker head-on. Gain control of the shooter's wrist with one hand and their gun with the other. Twist the gun away from your body and down to disarm.

TYPEWRITER

If someone grabbed your typewriter case to try to steal it and is now trying to fight you with it, the joke's on them, because sticks and stones may break my bones but words will never hurt you. While the two of you are grappling, press the secret release mechanism to slip out the hidden M1911 and correct the situation with a red ink obituary.

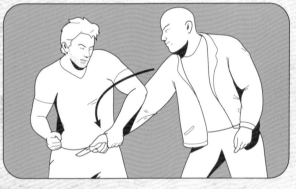

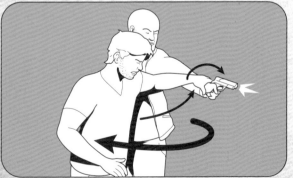

176 HIT WHERE IT HURTS MOST

Thanks to my travels and experience in Yara (and elsewhere), you should know how to throw a punch, swing a club, and take a hit like a champ. Now it's time to learn some anatomical intel to direct the fury of your fists (or aluminum baseball bat) to your opponent's body for maximum effectiveness. Targeting specific fragile areas of your attacker's body could stun them enough to give you time to escape—but use this information wisely. The TL;DR version? Only swing for the potentially fatal areas in encounters that call for it. Shots to the groin, meanwhile, are always acceptable and hilarious.

177 THROW A TOMAHAWK

Federico's lessons in guerrilla warfare weren't just about the philosophy of Yaran resolve or how to steal a tank (see item **164 / Steal a Tank**), but about doing as much damage as possible with the smallest means you can. He and the band of rebels I journeyed with didn't have Tomahawk missiles, but a tomahawk can be just as deadly . . . kinda. The best part? They're as deadly when thrown at a target as when swung at close range. If you know how to throw it properly, that is. If you have knife throwing experience (see item **080 / Learn to Throw a Knife**), it's even a transferable skill!

SHARP SHOOTER

If you can't find a tomahawk, scavenge an old hatchet. They're easily found at most farms (at least, they were in Yara). Search around chicken coops and barns and check for a comfortable balance and weight. Now it's time to take it for a spin.

THROW IT ALREADY!

Is what I shouted to my ex-wife when she was fumbling with a grenade during that shoot-out on our honeymoon. Eye the spot you want your 'hawk to hit. Staying focused on your target, swing your throwing arm behind you, then back up. When the axe blade passes your head, bring your arm forward again, like throwing a grenade.

GRAB THE AXE HANDLE

Is what I whispered to my wife as an armed mercenary was slowly approaching our hiding spot on her birthday trip that one year. Grip your tomahawk tight like it's a mythical hammer. Make sure the axe head is perfectly straight, otherwise you'll have a crooked flight. Try placing your thumb on the top of the grip if you're getting too much spin on your throws.

KEEP IT DULL

This was the last thing my ex-wife said to me as she slammed the divorce lawyer's office door. It also happens to be good advice for anyone looking to maintain an edge when throwing an old blade. It doesn't need a razor-sharp edge to stick in its target. Keep it dull so it won't easily cut you when you throw it.

Knives are a great weapon for protection (see item **079 / Choose Your Blade**), but it wouldn't be my first weapon of choice to take into a knife fight. If you're being attacked by a knife, you likely won't have time to draw your knife to fight back, and your attacker won't give you time to level the playing field. So if you must pack sharp steel, go with a sheath knife. You'll eliminate the extra steps of unfolding or extracting the blade—but the scar on my hip recommends you spend some time practicing your quick draw.

TAKE MY KNIFE, PLEASE

Fights don't typically break out; they escalate. You don't want to be the guy expecting a knife fight against a gun or flamethrower. If you have to rely on a knife, be quick enough to get the drop on your opponent before they pull out their weapon and turn up the heat.

BECOME A BLADE RUNNER

There's always a better option than going with a knife. Your opponent will attack unpredictably, so even if you "win" you'll still sustain injuries and flamethrower burns. Depending on your unique survival situation, a serious wound could spell the end of your day off real quick. Most modern knife fighting combat techniques have evolved from martial arts, so unless you're a skilled martial artisan, your best defense is running as fast as you can.

179 DIY ANY WEAPON

In guerrilla combat, you need to do a lot with a little. If you need to defend yourself and you don't have a weapon or enough components to craft a nail gun rifle, all is never lost on Yara when you know how to turn trash into thrash and weaponize your environment like the rebels do.

STOCK YOUR KILL KITCHEN

Hiding out in a kitchen and need to make your escape? Look for any nearby knives or forks you can quietly reach. Rolling pins, pots, and pans can be used as melee weapons to cook up a successful escape! Wield a melon baller or grab some cayenne pepper to blow in your enemy's eyes like a Yaran ninja with a complete disregard for vision insurance deductibles!

GO TO THE DIE-NING ROOM

If you're crouching quietly in a dining room and in need of a weapon, look for silverware or broken dishes. The jagged edge of a broken china plate can be an effective cutting weapon and ideal for a stealthy takedown.

TRY THE LIVING DEAD ROOM

Any long, rigid object will make a great melee weapon. Look for mop or broom handles and fireplace pokers. **Bonus tip:** If there's a fire burning, heat the end of the poker until it's white-hot. Wrap a brick or other heavy object in a sock or pillowcase, then swing to strike from a distance. The possibilities are endless! Don't be afraid to get creative! You're only limited by your own destructive imagination.

A FARTHER CRY BEYOND

Everywhere I went to try and get a desperately needed mental respite, insanity always seemed to find me. After failing so many times, there was only one place left for me to go for a little peace of mind—another dimension.

I gathered every drug and narcotic I had crafted and smuggled during my world travels—from the mind-numbing Bliss, to whatever that was that Reggie and Yogi gave me in Kyrat—and consumed everything over a weekend bender that became a week-long fever dream.

One night I made blades and bows next to a fisherman named Eh'di from a tribe of primitive warriors who called themselves the Wenja and fought saber-toothed cats and wooly mammoths in a primeval forest. I woke up the next morning on the floor of the Natural History museum. That night I made a lovely Coq au Vin using Earnhardt's cave mushrooms and sat down to watch one of my favorite Michael Biehn films, and that's when the Blood Dragons showed up. Then Rex Powercolt himself sent me to Mars where I had to fight killer robots, alien spiders, and the urge to not shoot Hurk Drubman Jr.'s severed head that wouldn't shut up.

When the trip started to fade, I passed out in a Bliss crop I was cultivating in my backyard and when I awoke the next morning with chocolate smeared all over my mouth and a Mars bar wrapper stuck to my face, it started all over again. I was in an apocalyptic wasteland with purple flowers blanketing the horizon as far as the eye could see. I crafted a saw gun and tracked a monstrous-looking buffalo that was secretly judging me. We talked for a while about love, the universe, and the virtues of ranch dressing as a dipping sauce, then it flapped its tiny wings proportionate to its large body and flew away into the night.

When I woke up covered in discarded chicken wing bones and buffalo sauce two days later, I realized I had even more to write about. (I also never got to apologize to Eh'di for hitting him with a bag full of angry bees by accident. Sorry, Eh'di.) I thought a lot about all I'd learned and how I could apply the knowledge practically: How would I craft a sling or spear, or stare down a grizzly? How much radiation can I withstand? Will I explode in a transporter accident to Mars? This section might give you the knowledge to survive in pretty much any territory or timeline you may find yourself. Just in case you end up taking a trip to somewhere far out.

No humans knew how to survive better than the ancient people of the Mesozoic period around 10,000 BC. They had to fight off mammoths and saber-toothed tigers with nothing but spears, rocks, and arrows. Those who were skilled enough with a weapon could then fight hypothermia with the hides of their kills and good old-fashioned fire—and they had to do it without the aid of modern weapons or equipment. Here's how to channel your primal ancestors so you can conquer fire.

STEP 1

Pick an open spot free of foliage or flammable objects with protection from the wind and precipitation on dry ground.

STEP 2

Three types of dry fuel are needed to make fire: tinder, kindling, and large pieces of wood. For tinder, bundle dry grass into a bird's nest shape and gather splintered wood pieces for kindling, which can range from the diameter of a matchstick to the size of a wood pencil. (When you're a survivalist journo, you learn to save worn-out pencils for such an occasion.) Small, dry twigs or splintered pieces of wood snapped from a tree also work. You also want to get shattered or split wood between the size of your finger to your forearm for the larger pieces.

STEP 3

Arrange your kindling into a pyramid shape and place a bundle of tinder beneath it. Keep it loose; the fire will need space to breathe.

STEP 4

Using your body as a windbreak, light the tinder bundle and begin feeding kindling to produce a strong blaze. Start gradually adding wood starting with the smallest pieces first.

181 FIRE UP A PRIMITIVE TORCH

You know that feeling of invincibility that surges through your body when you're walking around with your newly painted gold assault rifle glistening in the sun? That's exactly how our primitive ancestors felt carrying a torch for protection—they were both sophisticated pieces of firepower for their times. Here is my firsthand primal knowledge on firing up a torch, translated for the modern survivor.

GATHER YOUR STICKS

Assemble everything you need: 50 feet (15 m) of toilet paper; half a cup (120 ml) of any cooking oil; and a green wood stick about an inch (2.5 cm) in diameter and 2 feet (60 cm) long. The stick has to be green to ensure the torch head won't burn through.

A MAMMOTH Q-TIP

Wrap the toilet paper around the end of the stick. Twist the toilet paper slightly to get more of a white rope as you wrap it, and tie off the end with an overhand knot. You should now be holding an elephantine cotton swab.

A PRIMITIVE FLAMING SWORD

Soak the newly wrapped end in oil, absorbing as much as possible, and light with an open flame. It will take a few seconds to light, but once the torch head is engulfed in flames you should get a good twenty-minute burn.

A good all-purpose knife is an essential survival item to have any setting. Top five, even. Not only is it a versatile tool for crafting or cutting your way out of a dangerous situation, having a good knife in your gear bag will give you a fighting chance over the vicious fanged and clawed predator bearing down on you. (They also come in handy if you're squeamish about snapping a neck for a stealthy takedown.) Blades will break and not everyone is lucky or prepared enough to have one in the first place, but the good news is there area lot of options for

crafting one in the wild. Here's a method you can use to craft a bone blade.

Get a leg bone from a medium-sized animal like a small deer, or member of the Canidae taxonomy like a wolf. Tap the bone slightly with a rock until it begins to show hairline fractures. Now, twist for the spiral fracture! Find the sharp edges and use as a knife. It won't be as strong or durable as a metal bladed knife, but will be a nice understudy until you can craft a stronger one out of stone (see the next item).

183 MAKE QUICK STONE BLADES

Rocks have proven to be useful tools to distract someone, but they can also be great for dispatching them if your survival skills are sharp enough. Here's how to turn a rock into an edged weapon and become a prehistoric stonesmith.

A CAUTIONARY TALE

In addition to the numerous bee stings all over his body, Ed'hi the Wenja fisherman was missing an eye and a finger or two from various stonework accidents he'd experienced over the years. Trial by fire was the only way to learn anything back then, and he was a master of his craft to be sure, but I would suggest taking modern-day precautions by wearing heavy leather work gloves and glasses to protect your hands and eyes from stone chips.

GATHER YOUR STONE STICKS

You'll need three different sizes of rocks. The biggest is placed on the ground to act as your anvil to hammer upon. Stand your smallest rock atop the biggest one on its tallest axis like you're trying to stand an egg made of rock upright. Once it's stable, use a medium-sized stone at least four to five times larger than the small one, and hammer down hard on it. After a few good wallops you'll hopefully have broken off some nice sharp stone shrapnel.

184 MAKE STRING IN THE WILD

Cordage is like the throw rug that ties your survival equipment together nicely. With so many practical uses—from assembling weapons to making a tourniquet to binding the hands and feet of captives—some sturdy string is the must-craft item this survival season. And if you're resourceful you can recycle your cord. I once made a garrote, then later used it as a bow on a gift.

GATHER YOUR STRING STICKS

Collect all the strongest fibers you can find. These can be flax, hemp, or any fibrous inner bark. Also be on the lookout for wild plant stalks. (I recommend dogbane.)

GET KINKY

Grab a small length of fiber and twist until it kinks. Then grab the kink and keep twisting each bundle. If you started twisting in a clockwise direction, maintain the same direction while allowing them to encircle each other counterclockwise. The opposing force will help to strengthen your cord.

THE TIE THAT BINDS

For extra length in your cordage, continue to splice in new fibers using the same twisting pattern.

Hide glue has been made from animal parts for thousands of years as a strong, all-natural adhesive binding for tools and arrows, and works great for all your general survival adhesive needs. Using scrapings, de-haired scraps of animal skins, sinew, tendons, descaled fish skins, defeathered bird skins, and basically any other animal part you decide not to throw into your frontier stew, here's how to make hide glue to help keep you out of sticky survival situations.

GATHER YOUR GLUE STICKS

Collagen and elastin are the fibrous proteins you need to extract from animal parts (aka glue stock). Start by cooking your glue stew in water without boiling it, as temperatures above 180°F (82°C) will break up the proteins. For a strong adhesive, simmer the stock between 130°F and 150°F (54°C and 66°C) in two parts water for several hours until the water becomes gelatinous, and replace any evaporated water in the process.

PLATE AND SERVE

Filter the glue stock remnants through a cloth and squeeze out excess liquid. Simmer this gluellabaisse until it has a thick, maple syrup–like consistency, and your home brew glue is ready to use! Chef's kisses!

ENJOY LEFTOVERS

Hide glue needs to be dried for storage and later use. The two best ways to achieve this are as a glue stick or as glue chips. Dip a stick into the glue and blow on it so it can cool and gel. Continue this process until you have something resembling a glue lollipop, then set it aside to dry. When you're ready to use, just dip the glue stick in warm water, and it will reconstitute and be ready for use. You can also let your glue syrup cool until it becomes gelatin, then slice into sheets and dry. Reconstitute in warm water for a nice spreadable glue butter, but remember: Don't let it boil.

Pitch glue (aka the vegan survivalists' adhesive) is made from the sap of evergreen trees such as pine, spruce, fir, and cedar. As opposed to the hide glue option, this type of adhesive is ideal in wet conditions but can easily melt in the heat. Here's the recipe to make a craft pitch brew to impress your hipster survivalist friends with.

GATHER GLUE STICKS

You'll need sap and pitch from evergreen trunks and branches for your gluten-free glue. You want the clearer, softer pitch over the dark, harder pitch, which contains impurities. You'll also need a vessel whose last job will be this glue pot because you'll never get all the glue out again.

BREW YOUR GLUE

Once you've broken the news to your pot that it will never be filled with soup again, heat the pitch to about 200°F (93°C), at which point the volatile oils and turpentine evaporate. As the sappy broth cooks, the gasses released may catch fire, so keep a lid handy to cover and extinguish the flames.

SERVE WARM

Once cooked, the pitch will have notes of pine and charcoal, and can be used as is, or you can add charcoal dust up to half the volume to stretch your supply. Pitch glue hardens as it cools, so whatever you intend to glue must also be hot or you won't get a good adhesive. Making pitch brew is thirsty work, so have a kombucha; you've earned it.

What was once an ancient hunting tool used to slay small game and even a weapon of war was eventually sold as a children's toy and popularized by several hooligan cartoon characters. Whether you grew up breaking windows or are just now taking your first rock shot, slings are easy to make, effective to use, and hard to master. Here's how to make your very own sling if the environment you're trying to survive in doesn't have a toy store.

STRING

Hey, remember that cord you learned how to make (see item **184 / Make String in the Wild**)? Cut two lengths at 2½ feet (75 cm) each. Tie a bowline knot in the end of one line with a big enough loop to slip over your thumb.

Tie three or four other knots at the end of the other line. Figure eights or overhand knots will do.

PAD

To make a sling pad, cut an oval-shaped piece of cloth (preferably leather for durability) at a size slightly larger than your palm.

SLING

Pierce a hole in each side of your sling pad and tie the unknotted ends of each cord in place. If your sling pad is leather, dampen with water and shape it with a stone by squeezing for a few minutes for a custom fit. Congratulations! Your sling is complete, but your sling training has just begun!

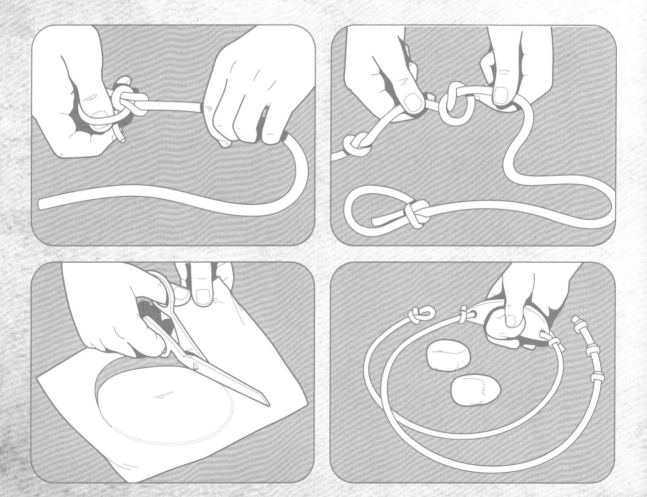

Building a sling and building a reputation as a lethal sling murderer are two very different skill sets. Truly practiced slingers can accurately fling everything from marshmallows to Molotov cocktails, so spend some time practicing your rock shots or you'll likely return from your next hunting trip with an empty hand and an empty stomach. (You also want to be ready for a sling fight if anyone suspiciously nicknamed Goliath shows up.)

GET A ROCK

Place the bowline loop on the thumb of your throwing hand, and hold the knotted line between your palm and thumb. Now load some rock ammo into the pad and grip with your palm so the stone is cradled level and even.

WIND IT UP

Start with some easy underhand throws by releasing the knotted line to give your rock the power of flight. Eventually you'll get a feel for the proper timing of your release and you can try throwing overhand. Add more energy to your throw as you get comfortable slingin' rocks.

GET GOOD

Instinctually calculating the azimuth and zenith of your target with your brain scope or knowing how much strength to put into your shot with your slinger finger will require time and patience to master. Remember, slingin' rock stars aren't born; they're made. In order to nail the solo of this particular stringed instrument of death, you must practice—and practice a lot.

If a sling isn't your string thing, perhaps a bow can scratch that ranged weapon itch (and can also double as a back scratcher)! A timeless classic of human ingenuity, the bow has been used since the dawn of man and is still used by hunters (and the hunted) to this day. Here's how to carve a bow if you find yourself in either situation.

A BOW TO PICK

Before you go carving any old wood, know that a good bow requires the right wood. Some of the better species suited for bow carving include Osage orange, yew, ash, sycamore, black locust, and hickory. Most hardwoods such as oak and maple can also work.

BOW DRY

Get a relatively straight piece of sapling or branch free of imperfections. You'll need a piece about 6 feet (2 m) long and approximately 2 inches (5 cm) in diameter. If you find yourself in a hurry and need to use your bow immediately, the wood should be dead and dry. Otherwise, let your stave dry out for a few months before use.

GOOD BOW STRUCTURE

Stand the bow stave straight up. Holding the top loosely, push down, letting the natural bend of the stave guide you. Mark a handhold on the inside middle of the bow (the belly) about 3 inches (8 cm) from the center in both directions. The area above the handhold is the upper limb, the area below it is the lower limb. Mark these points for reference when carving.

RHINBOWPLASTY

For proper balance, mirror the way the branch grew with the thicker base on the bottom. Bend carefully and begin removing the stiffer parts of the belly with a knife, leaving the back untouched. Check the limbs as you carve to ensure they bend equally.

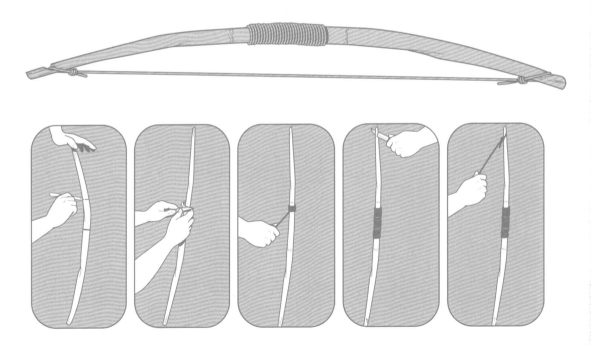

190 DON'T BREAK IT

There are plenty of ways you can break your newly crafted bow, like using it as a melee weapon when you run out of arrows, or combustion from a faulty explosive tip on an arrow, among other things. But much like your spirit, things will inevitably break when trying to survive the inhospitable wilds you find yourself in. Not all hope is lost! Here are a few tips to keep your hard-earned bow nice and functional even though your will to live may be starting to crack.

DON'T CHOP

Novice bowyers who are eager to get their bow up and firing often chop too deeply from the belly of the bow.

Maintain the strength of your bow by carefully shaving or slicing the wood instead of going full lumberjack. If your bow is too thin it may break when drawn, and with nothing to protect you, your blood likely will be drawn.

WATCH YOUR BOW SIX

Don't do anything to damage the back of your bow. Don't carve any cool designs or kill count hash marks. This is the side under the most tension when the bow is drawn and if the integrity is compromised, you get a broken bow.

I once used a feather quill to pen an elegantly worded death threat to a Kyrati Royal Army colonel, then used that feather to craft the arrow I shot him with. But I digress. Here are a few tips to put the aerodynamic in your arrows.

STICK TO DRY WOOD

Collect branches that are at least 30 inches (75 cm) long with a diameter between 3.8 inches (around 10 cm) and ½ inch (around 1 cm). Carefully peel the outer bark and set the wood aside for a few days to dry. If you're prepping in advance, tie the shafts in a tight bundle and set aside for a few months.

FIRE + WOOD = ARROWS

Sand the shafts to smooth the edges, then straighten them by bending over an open fire (but don't let it change color or burn). Once the crooked area is heated, bend a little past straight and hold that position until it cools. This may take a few rounds of heating and bending to get it just right.

NOCK NOCK

Cut a notch for the bow string (the nock) about ¼ inch (5 mm) deep into the end of the arrow shaft. Use caution when doing this so as to not split the arrow. Tie a string around the shaft below the nock for sturdy reinforcement.

STICKS AND STONES

Arrowheads can be crafted from thin iron, bone shards, or chipped pieces of stone. Form into a triangular shape about 1½ to 2 inches (4 to 5 cm) in length and about 1 inch (2.5 cm) wide. Glue the arrowhead into a notch and wrap with cordage. Seal the wrapping with more glue to secure into place.

TAIL FEATHERS

Gather bird tail and wing feathers and split them in half. They need to be from the same wing for each arrow so don't mix and match. Trim to about 4 to 5 inches (11 to 13 cm) long and about ½ inch (1 cm) wide. Glue three feathers equally spaced around the arrow, and secure with cordage.

192 CRAFT A BLOWGUN

If you've mastered the sling and arrow, and want to add another projectile weapon to your string and stone arsenal, might I suggest a nice blowgun? Here's how to build your own Death Loogie spitter.

BAMBOO SHOOTS

Get a piece of bamboo approximately ½ inch (1.2 cm) wide by 5 feet (1.5 m) long. Much like modern-day rifles, the bigger the blowgun, the more powerful and accurate the shot. But if it's too big, it can be both unwieldy and a strain on your lung power.

OLD SCHOOL

Heat a steel rod about a foot longer than the bamboo over a flame. Insert the rod into the bamboo to hollow and smooth out the inner joint membranes.

M1911BC

You can also make a blowgun out of PVC pipe. Cut a 3 foot (91.5 cm) length of ½ inch (1.2 cm) wide PVC pipe and sand the edges. Attach a ½ inch (1.2 cm) mouthpiece adapter on one end of the tube to serve as a mouthpiece. Add a rubber washer into the mouthpiece to prevent the dart from falling out.

A WORK OF DART

Any hardwoods or bamboo skewers you find in the wild are suitable for dart construction, but to make fletching, you should swap the feathers from the blow dart's bigger cousin the arrow for fur. Thistledown and rabbit fur are the ancient materials of choice, but cotton balls are a good modern-day substitute. Using a thread approximately the diameter of dental floss, tie a knot around your dart about 2 inches (5 cm) from the end of the shaft. Begin stuffing shredded cotton ball material under the thread wrappings while spinning the dart, then tie or glue the end.

BONUS DART TIP, TIP

If you're feeling adventurous and want to elevate your blow dart game, try experimenting with coating the dart tips with various toxins or venoms you may come across in the wild.

Sticks and stones may break some bones, but string and stones can slow them (specifically the ones in the ankles and legs). A bola is a great two-way weapon: a lucky strike from the weights can stun or kill your target, and with a lucky throw the cords can ensnare their legs so you can move in and deliver the killing blow. (You can also take this opportunity to deliver a killer one-liner before you dispatch your target, since they're not really going anywhere). Here's how to build a bolas and throw strikes like a bola champion.

CUT THE CORD

Assemble three to five cords, each about 24 to 32 inches (60 to 80 cm) long. Use an overhand knot or figure eight knot to join them together.

GET REALLY STONED

Gather stones about ½ pound (0.25 kg) each. Sharp edges can cut through rawhide, so try to find ones with rounded edges if possible. Wrap the stones in wet rawhide and pierce holes in the edges to fasten each cord. Let the rawhide dry fully to properly shrink and harden.

ENTER A WHIRL OF HURT

To throw, hold the knot in your dominant hand and whip the weights in a circle to build up speed. When you've lined up your target, give it your best hurl. Though the bolas is a low-fi weapon option, it can still make a good whistling noise when you rev it up, so be aware of your surroundings.

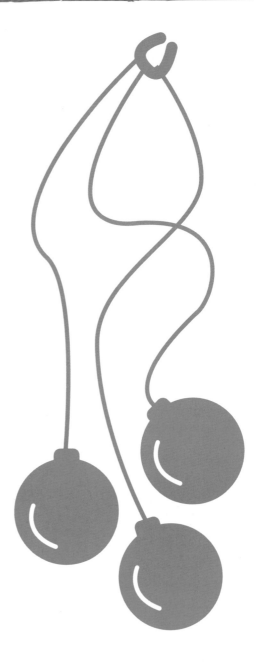

194 MAKE A POULTICE

Older than old school, a poultice is as simple as survival medicine can get. Even if you've grown accustomed to crafting your own medical syringes in your travels as I have, sometimes you end up in places (or alternate timelines) where it isn't practical or feasible to do so. Here's how to make a poultice to get the medicinal benefits out of the abundant supply of colorful plants that seem to grow everywhere you go.

MAKE PASTE

Crush the plant material into a pulp or paste. Even a pulpy paste will do! You can also chew the plant to get the desired texture so long as ingestion is also safe.

SPREAD

Take your plant pulp and apply directly to the affected area. Keep in place with a bandage or dressing. Replace a few times a day until your wound has ripened (aka healed). If the plant material is deemed nontoxic, the poultice material can be held in the mouth for gum or tooth pains.

PLANTAIN THE PAIN AWAY

Plantain is a great poultice for wounds, especially insect bites and stings, with some even reporting relief in minutes. Plantains are equally great for treating hunger pains. Just take several of those sweet, leafy greens internally until full. Other good options are curly dock root, comfrey root, and yarrow leaf.

Drugs manufactured in a lab are great, but the healing power of nature cannot be understated. Plants grow in all different sizes and colors, and aside from looking pretty and smelling good, some have medicinal properties to heal many different ailments. Know what grows before you head to your adventure destination, and you'll always have a pharmacy at your blistered and bleeding fingertips.

YARROW (*Achillea millefolium*)
A common plant found all over the American West, its white flowers and fern-like leaves can be brewed into tea to treat colds, the flu, and fever. Crushed into a poultice and rubbed on the skin, yarrow acts as a mosquito repellent.

PLANTAIN (*Plantago major*)
Found all over the world, this miracle weed is a cure all for most common ailments. Crush into a poultice to treat insect bites and stings. It also works wonders on abrasions.

MULLEIN (*Verbascum thapsus*)
The dried leaves can be rolled and smoked to treat a bad cough, but use in moderation. They can also be plucked and used as a comfortable substitute for toilet paper. You'll laugh now, but you won't be when you need TP.

WILLOW (*Salix genus*)
One of the essential first aid plants that grows in the wild, its twigs and bark can be seeped into tea or chewed to reduce inflammation in joints and as a pain reliever for headache.

STINGING NETTLE (*Urtica dioica*)
Also known by its stage name Urtica, the stinging nettle has a reputation as being a prick in most botany circles. But don't let its pointed name dissuade you from taking advantage of its healing properties. It's edible, and the leaves can be cooked and added to soups.

OSHÁ (*Ligusticum porteri*)
This high altitude herb is extremely effective at treating sore throats, bronchial inflammation, altitude sickness, and viral infections. The only problem is, it can sometimes be confused with water hemlock, which is extremely effective at killing you instead. Osha roots have a brown covering; hemlock roots are usually light-colored. Don't use or ingest any plant unless you can positively identify the species.

196 ADDRESS INTERNAL INJURIES

Sometimes the injury isn't visible, but the pain is there—like when Eddie the Rakyat fisherman laughed at me for falling in the riverbank and getting tangled in fishing line that one time. That's an internal pain you can easily walk off after you've removed the fishing hooks stuck to your face. But for other more serious injuries beneath the surface, like abdominal pain or bleeding from parts that shouldn't be bleeding, you'll want to seek medical assistance. Here are some signs to look out for.

ABDOMINAL INJURIES

If you've had a slip and fall off a rock face or been rammed by the lowered head of an angry ram and walked away from it with all your bones intact, there's still a chance you may have suffered an internal abdominal injury and don't know it. If you experience shock and your abdomen is becoming distended about an hour after experiencing blunt trauma, you may have a ruptured spleen. Get to the nearest hospital immediately, or you could be dead within hours.

INTERNAL INJURIES

Any internal injury can potentially be life-threatening if not identified and treated immediately. After a fall or experiencing blunt force trauma, monitor for signs of shock, distended belly, and abdominal pain. Look for blood in vomit, stool resembling black tar, or urine with a red or pink hue. Any of these signs point straight to a hospital.

IMPALEMENT

This one is serious and requires immediate medical help, but an important note when dealing with this type of injury is to never remove the impaled object. It could accelerate the bleeding and therefore accelerate death. Try to gently secure the object in place with bandaging, and get to a hospital as soon as possible.

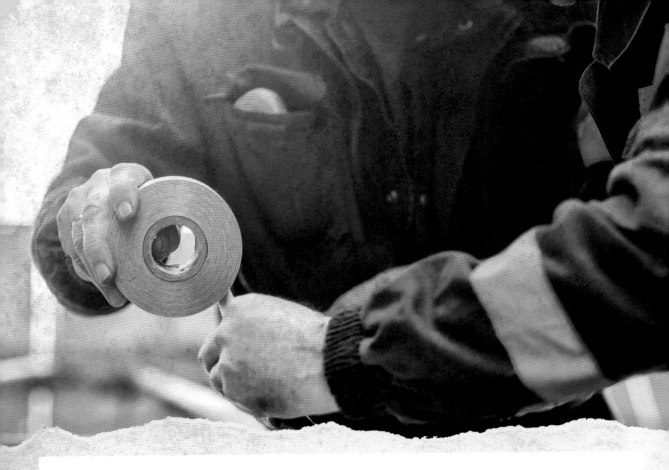

197 BE A DUCT TAPE DOCTOR

Is there anything duct tape can't do? You can fix just about anything with it, bound and gag a hostage, and I suppose . . . repair ducts with it? I don't know; I only pretended to be an HVAC tech so I could put a mic in a restaurant kitchen in Hope County, Montana to learn a venison bourguignon recipe for an article I was writing. But gastro-espionage aside, this flat and sticky Swiss Army knife also has a number of useful medical applications. Adhere to these duct tape tips to keep your body in tip-top shape.

TAPE THAT SCRAPE

If you're sporting an injury and don't have any bandages handy, grab some gauze and hold it in place with a little patch of duct tape. (If you're high on mushrooms or using a genetic memory analyzer and find yourself in an '80s retro-future, try wrapping your exposed body parts in duct tape to try to pass as a cyber soldier.)

TWEEZER BURN

Need to remove a splinter and you don't have tweezers handy? Duct tape works great in a pinch! Apply duct tape to the affected area and give it a peel to remove it.

SPLINT TAPE

Use cardboard, sticks, or any other rigid stabilizing item to support an injured limb, then give it a good tape wrap to hold everything in place.

DUCT SLING

Make a triangle of duct tape strips with each side as long as the patient's forearm. Keep adding more strips inside the triangle to form a net to hold the injured arm. Reinforce those strips with more tape to keep them from sticking, and secure around the arm and shoulder.

198 SUPERGLUE A WOUND

Keeping your body held together is obviously an important survival tactic when everything you encounter in your wild adventures wants to tear you open. You've heard the healing tale of the tape, but superglue is also effective at mending rips in your skin bag should the necessity arise. However, you'll want to proceed with caution; unlike the stuff they might whip out in an ER, store-bought superglue isn't approved for medical use and should only be used in a no bandage, no tape, no hope-type situation. When desperate times call for desperate measures, answer with superglue. (Be sure the wound is properly cleaned before applying glue to avoid infection.)

PREP

Apply a topical anesthetic if available, then clean and dry the surrounding skin thoroughly. As noted in previous sections, booze can be easily scavenged and makes for a great internal anesthesia if you're squeamish.

LACE

Close the wound shut with your fingers and gently apply the adhesive to the laceration. It's important to make sure no adhesive gets into the wound.

LAYER

Apply three layers of adhesive while keeping the wound held together for at least sixty seconds after the third and final application. Optional: Apply glitter to the wound for artistic flair.

DRESS

Once the superglue bandage has completely dried, apply a dressing and avoid touching, scrubbing, or soaking the wound until the adhesive naturally peels off between five and ten days.

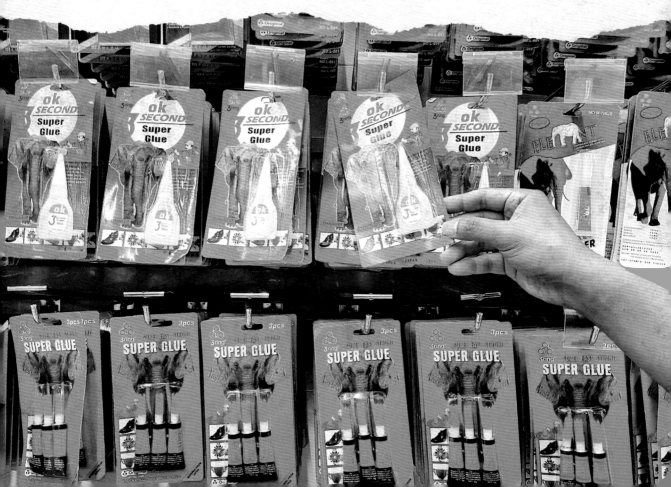

Impalement isn't usually a very common injury, but the places you're visiting aren't exactly the most common to survive in, either. You could easily take a spill onto a sharp rock while traversing a cliffside on the Rook Islands, land on a sharp fence post running from the Royal Army in Kyrat, experience trauma from a high-speed vehicle collision in rural Montana, or get shot by a shredder in Yara. Being prepared for anything that comes your way (whether towards you or through you) is essential for survival. Here's how to lend a helping hand to the impaled.

DON'T TOUCH

Do not attempt to remove the object. This could result in additional tissue damage, a sucking chest wound (see item **143 / Patch a Gunshot with an ID Card**), or might expedite the bleeding. Instead, try to stabilize the object so it doesn't move when the victim gets transported to a hospital or medical facility.

GIVE IT A CUT

If you're in a remote setting (which, if you're reading this book, you just might be), cut the object a few inches from the wound to make moving the victim easier. This is usually easier when dealing with more slender objects, like that arrow I accidentally shot into Eddie the fisherman's leg that one time.

DRESS IT UP AND APOLOGIZE

Apply a bandage or dressing to the wound to further stabilize the object so you can get the victim to a hospital (or Dr. Earnhardt in the case of my dear friend Eddie—a bottle of scotch and a lot of Rakyat profanity later, he was totally fine).

200 CAUTERIZE A WOUND

There's nothing quite like the sensation of a heated knife blade searing an open wound. A method to heal wounds also used as a method of torture by Rook Island pirates, this extremely painful and risky procedure should only be attempted in extreme circumstances, if you're days away from medical professionals—or if you happen to be in an isolated area far enough away from danger so the danger can't hear your screams of searing pain. If you've heeded this warning and still want to heat that blade and cauterize that wound like an '80s action movie hero that never did it for real, here's how.

HEAT THE BLADE

Stick your knife blade in an open fire until the steel is red-hot. Don't be a bonehead and use a bone blade for this.

BITE THE BULLET

As with most painful and risky field medical procedures, consider having a generous dose of your favorite over-the-counter eighty proof painkiller. Hold the red-hot knife blade to the wound for about five to ten seconds. Remove the blade and repeat this process until you have a nice crispy sear on the wound. Charred on the outside, raw on the inside is what you're looking for.

BANDAGE THE WOUND

Dress the wound with whatever bandage options are available to you, and make sure to inspect it for infection and change the dressing daily. Drink whatever liquor you have left in the bottle.

Some species of bears are scary, while others are simply terrifying. But all species of bears have different behavioral patterns and if you know what to look for, you can get a good gauge of just how much danger you're in when a 300- to 800-pound (135-360 kg) mass of sharp teeth and claws is bearing down on you. Here's how to avoid getting your torso torn open and its contents devoured like a pic-a-nic basket.

GRIZZLY

Weighing in at 800 pounds (360 kg) and standing tall at 7 feet (2 m) on their hind legs, this mighty species of bear has brown fur and a distinct hump at the shoulders. Their angry faces feature a dip between the forehead and nose and have small, rounded ears. Grizzlies are at their most, well, grizzly if they're surprised or threatened, especially if it's a mother protecting her cubs. If you encounter one, back away slowly and don't run. If it charges you, your best bet is to play dead and hope it's not in preparation for your upcoming role as devoured corpse number one at a bear dinner theater show.

BLACK BEAR

Don't let the name fool you; black bears are 300 pounds (135 kg) and 5 feet (1.5 m) of fur ranging in various colors from blond to brown to deep black. Their faces are straight from the forehead to the nose with long and pointed ears. As with any bear encounter, don't run, as it can be a sign of aggression that instigates an attack. Instead, face the bear and make yourself a bigger person by flailing your arms high or shouting compliments at the bear despite its pettiness in trying to eat you.

202 READ A BEAR'S MIND

Peering into the mind of a bear to understand its innermost thoughts and feelings is the ultimate defensive tactic to survive an encounter with this unpredictable predator. But until I can perfect the mind-reading machine I'm building from 1978 Buick parts, all I can do is speculate about what their next move is. Still, we can sometimes see what's on a bear's mind simply by reading its body language. Understanding what they're trying to communicate to you could mean the difference between walking away from a bear encounter unscathed and ending up as bear stool.

BEAR IN MIND

A bear in a defensive posture will appear stressed and unsure what its next move is while pacing about and popping its jaws. Talk to it in a very calm voice and never throw anything. When it is no longer moving towards you, begin to move away from it slowly. If the bear continues to approach, stop and stand your ground, continuing to talk calmly. If the bear charges, use a rifle and wait until the last possible moment before you kiss the dirt.

BARRELING DOWN

A predatory bear isn't intent on rendering you harmless as it peers at you through its angry, furrowed brow, but rather rendering your body into paste with its razor-sharp claws and jagged teeth. If a bear approaches you in a nondefensive or casual manner, it's time to get loud and serious. Speak in a loud and firm voice, like Vaas Montenegro monologuing. Maneuver out of the bear's direction of travel but stay calm and slow. Make yourself appear larger by standing on a rock or moving uphill. If it continues, keep shouting, but remember that telling it you have a gun won't ameliorate your situation. Ready your rifle and prepare for a charge.

An electromagnetic pulse (EMP) is what my science fiction poetry will ignite in robot hearts. It also doesn't actually blow anything up, but what it lacks in physical destruction, it makes up for in its ability to fry electronic devices. From household appliances to entire power grids and communication systems, an EMP is a weapon designed to inflict mass chaos, cripple large populated areas, and revert society back to a lawless version of the 1800s like civilization's off switch. Here's what you can do to protect yourself after an EMP attack in a world where everything relies on electronics.

PARTY LIKE IT'S 1799

With no communications, no internet, and no working vehicles with electronics, you'll need to live like your ancestors. Keep hand tools at the ready and have the supplies you'll need for repairs, carpentry, and gardening. Rely on your experience hunting game in dangerous locales (like the Rook Islands or Kyrat), and learn to preserve meat without refrigeration. Forage plants for food and medicine, and stock up on food that has a long shelf life. You'll also want water and a filter system, medical supplies, seeds, firearms, and ammunition. Avoid confrontations and live quietly so as not to draw attention to yourself, but be prepared to defend yourself if marauders arrive to take the supplies you worked so hard to stockpile.

LITTLE DEAD CORVETTE

Remember, an EMP strike will render vehicles with electronics inoperable, so have an analog transportation option ready to go in case of an emergency. Have a plan to get to a remote location on foot, bicycle, sailboat, or other vehicle without electronics.

Fallout sucks. Like, really sucks. It's terrible and nobody should ever have to experience it. Surviving the aftermath of a nuclear bomb strike is a chilling thought to process, but if I've learned one thing in my travels to dangerous and unpredictable locales these many years, it's that you never know what to expect. Since your decisions along the way will always change the outcome of your adventure, being prepared for anything and everything is essential for survival. But before you can survive any danger, you should have a good understanding of what the danger you're facing is capable of. In the case of a nuclear fallout, there's a lot to cover.

SEEK SHELTER

Radioactive fallout can stay airborne for days and spread over a wide area. Any contact will result in radiation poisoning and contamination. Get to a secure bunker and hunker down.

STAY PUT

Stay sheltered for at least ten days, more if you can. Radioactive iodine needs time to decay to a safe level, so don't leave your shelter for the first forty-eight hours following a nuclear blast. Other elements have longer decay periods and are absorbed into the ground, making animal and plant food sources dangerous for decades.

STAY POSITIVE

Carelessness can kill; nobody is safe living in the aftermath of a nuclear bomb strike. But keeping your hopes up will keep your mind focused on surviving so you can avoid a postapocalyptic slipup.

If you're lucky enough to survive a nuke, let's hope you've saved some luck to deal with fallout. Radiation isn't great for people, despite what comic books told us about superpowers. Learning how to handle it makes you a survival superhero, but know the risks. According to a handy chart I peeled off the wall of an old fallout shelter in Hope County, Montana, you're likely to live through 300 rads or 3 grays (Gy) in modern terms, but you'll feel like hell: You'll be nauseous, weak, and low in blood cell count, a little like my first day in Kyrat. Past that, more radiation equals more disintegration; 4 to 6 Gy means hair loss, bleeding, infections, and possible death without treatment. Any higher and death is ever more certain—and agonizing as you kinda liquefy from inside out. Now that you've assessed your radiation situation, it's time to decontaminate.

STRIP DOWN

Outer clothing layers carry most of the fallout. Strip in layers, don't shake off any fallout on the material, and put it all in a sealable container or bag, then store out of the way.

WASH UP

Shower or rinse off with warm water, then gently wash with lots of soap and shampoo. Don't scrub or scratch yourself and cover any cuts or abrasions.

WIPE OFF

If you're low on water, clean your hands, head, or anywhere you were uncovered. Use as much water and soap as you can; if you can't do that, use a wet cloth or baby wipes. Gently blow your nose and wipe your eyelids and ears. Put the used wipes in a trash bag and store it with the clothing.

COVER UP

Change into clean clothing. If you can't find any, shake your previous outfit off somewhere you can do so safely, keeping your mouth and nose covered—then dress again and search for a noncontaminated outfit.

206

MAKE THE MOST OF A SHOTSHELL

Shotgun shells are the umami in a survival spice rack; they have many different flavors suitable for many different survival palates. You can make fire using the wadding for tinder. The buckshot can be melted down and formed into other calibers of ammunition. The gunpowder can be useful in starting fires or to reload other empty shells. The casing can be used to smuggle drugs or small gems or be fashioned into a lipstick case and gifted to your revolutionist lady friend. You can also make a chest explode by firing a shell from a shotgun. Whatever part your situation calls for, here's how to perform a shotshell autopsy and donate the organs.

CRACK IT LIKE A CRAB SHELL

Hold the shell by the brass end and, using a knife, cut through the crimped end. If your loot bag is lucky enough to have one in it, you can also try to pry the shell open with a pair of needle-nose pliers.

POUR, PULL, POUR

Now that you've cracked the shell open, it's time to collect that sweet shotgun shell meat. Turn the shell over and empty out the buckshot. Use your fingers or those needle-nose pliers to remove the wadding, then turn the shell over one more time and dump out the gunpowder.

I'd like to hope the friends I made in Montana would approve of the battle wagon I dreamed up. There are so many factors to consider: Do I want to sacrifice durability for speed? Am I driving in the desert or the mountains? Do I spend the extra money to bulletproof the windows? Consider some emergency extras along with a few nice upgrades to turn that former rental car into the star of the next dystopian action film!

SUV

A robust ride is great for when you need to get off the blacktop and hit the back roads, and easy to drive while shooting. Find a full-frame, full-size model with four-wheel drive and avoid small to medium SUVs. Get one with a two-speed transfer case to give you the gear options to enhance your traction.

HEAVY TRUCK

When you want horsepower, high ground clearance, and ample towing capacity, the heavy truck is a top choice for driving in bad conditions. It can tow twice the weight that a full SUV can pull (20,000 lbs/9 metric tons) and has plenty of space to mount a heavy machine gun turret in the flatbed.

VAN

Perfect for carrying cargo or a squad of soldiers, the size and covered cargo room of a van is hard to beat. If you plan on transporting a large haul through bad weather, the reasonable gas mileage could make this your best option. Get one with a sunroof so someone can fire RPGs.

Once you have your sweet adrenaline mobile up and pumping, you'll eventually want to add some sweet upgrades. Sharma Salsa assured me the checks would come flowing in from helping distribute Kyrati Films, but until then, here are some thoughts on how to spend your own royalties to give your ride the edge in a winner-take-all race to survive.

BRUSH BAR

Mounted to the vehicle's frame, the brush bar protects the vehicle in a front-end collision and can push vegetation and debris out of the way when driving off-road. A must-have when driving through an apocalyptic wasteland.

SNORKEL INTAKE

With a snorkel intake equipped to your engine, it can take your off-road adventure into the water, enabling you to drive across floods or rivers. Hurk Drubman Jr. had one, but not on his truck; he used it as a bong.

ELECTRIC WINCH

Great for pulling vehicles or large objects out of jams, a sturdy front-mounted winch is the accessory you want when your truck is stuck in a hole. When being used to free a heavy truck in the desert, it's referred to as a Ram sand winch.

HIGH-FLOTATION TIRES

Wider, higher-flotation tires provide enhanced traction when off-road driving in loose sand, snow, or deep mud. A wise option to consider since you'll likely be driving across those more than actual paved roads.

TOW HOOKS

Attach these hooks to the frame to give cables a sturdy location to lock onto when towing. They also prove useful if you're the one being towed.

209 ADD SOME FLAIR

You've rigged your ride with the latest and greatest in useful tech and accessories, now go even bigger and weirder with some added flair! Here are some things you might not have known could make the difference in a roadside or middle-of-nowhere emergency.

HIGH-CAPACITY FUEL TANK

Fuel prices be damned, consider upsizing your 15-gallon (57 l) gas tank to a 20-gallon (76 l), or even the beefy 25-gallon (95 l) tank to keep your war wagon blazing forward! It will cost you twice as much to fill up but will get you twice as far.

TOOLS AND SPARE PARTS

Your spare tire will only get you so far, just like your tire iron will only club so many zombies before you tire. Keep a full tool kit and a full-size spare, along with a plug-in air compressor to reinflate it, and you can make critical repairs to your ride—like after hitting a bharal or two on a road in Kyrat.

ELECTRICAL POWER

Engines weren't designed to be portable electrical power generators, but that's pretty much what they are. Electrical inverters with outlets can be plugged into the vehicle, allowing you to run small appliances. They can also be hardwired into the vehicle's electrical system if you're fancy like that.

ADD SOME FLARE TOO

While you're adding flair, maybe stash an emergency flare gun in the glovebox. It won't get you any roadside assistance, but it will set a pirate on fire if you're approached while stranded on the side of the road.

210 PATCH A RADIATOR

Radiators are the circulatory systems that keep your engine cool and prevent it from overheating. If the radiator fails, so does your engine. If your engine fails, so could you . . . at surviving. And since most of the danger you'll encounter on travels like mine are faster than you, here's a method to patch a leaky radiator that requires no tools, no automotive knowledge, and no auto parts to make sure your engine is always running in tip-top shape. That way you won't find yourself running from danger when you could be driving away from it at high speed.

First, find an egg. If your refrigerator is empty, try your luck at scavenging. Chicken coops are a pretty standard feature at a farm too, so if you find one you're in luck. Give it a crack and empty the egg whites into the radiator opening. The egg white proteins will solidify from the heat as the embryonic fluid circulates through the radiator, eventually finding the leak and acting as a patch from the inside. It's not suitable for large cracks or holes, and making a radiator soufflé should only be used as a last-ditch effort when you have no other options, but it can get you where you need to go—such as the closest place to fix or replace your radiator.

211 HACK A
VEHICLE BATTERY

Sometimes just having access to a limited yet reliable power supply can make all the difference in a survival situation. I saw a few acquaintances in Yara hacking a car battery for power, and it worked, but keep this in mind: If you want to use this system indoors, use an absorbed glass mat (AGM) battery; the traditional lead-acid types can produce harmful fumes. You can pick up a 55 Ah (ampere-hour) 12-volt battery at any home improvement or boating store. You can also repurpose one from a boat, RV, or other vehicle. You'll also need to scavenge a battery wall charger, a cigarette lighter adapter, a cell phone car charger, and a voltmeter (like the one I found on a table in an abandoned drug lab on the Rook Islands) to test the setup. Wear safety goggles and be careful messing around with batteries. AGM batteries may be less toxic than lead-acid batteries but they still contain acid.

CIRCUIT BREAKIN'

Use your voltmeter to ensure the battery is fully charged. If you store your battery, check on it every three months and keep the charge above 12.4 volts so it's ready to go when the power goes out.

SMOKE MEANS YOU DID IT WRONG

Attach the cigarette lighter port to the battery by attaching its jumper cable–like alligator clips to the wires. Plug in your phone and charge it up. Your results will vary depending on the number and capacity of devices you're charging and the total capacity of the battery. Most modern cell phones will recharge about twenty-five times on a typical car battery charge, and even more on those larger-capacity marine batteries.

CIRCUIT BREAKIN' 2:
ELECTRIC BOOGALOO

Use your voltmeter to periodically check the voltage. You don't want to run your only power source down too far. Never let the voltage drop below 12.4 volts when in storage.

212 STRAP ON A JETPACK

You really do feel like the lead in a badass spy movie after successfully sticking the landing of that first jetpack flight. Technically, it's several days after you stick the landing when you wake up in the hospital wearing a lower body cast. This experimental piece of solo transportation tech has been experimental since it first debuted sixty years ago. But despite humanity's inability to master jetpack flight, we're still fascinated with the idea of strapping a turbine engine to our backs and pushing a button that says "FIRE." Even if you're not soaring over the dust of Mars, you can still perform desperate escapes, missions to midnight base infiltrations, and trips to the hospital trauma ward. Here's how to strap on a jetpack and take to the sky!

PREFLIGHT

The jetpack attaches to the pilot via a five-point safety harness. Try wearing it around for a few days to get used to the weight. Just go about your daily routine, but in a jetpack. You may have to make an emergency landing on terrain you didn't account for, so make sure to wear sturdy footwear when you gear up on game day. Add earplugs to protect your hearing from the screeching whine of the jet turbine or your own involuntary terrified whining.

LIFTOFF

Start the engines by pressing the "fire" button on the control arm to achieve lift. Once airborne, the pilot has full control over altitude, speed, pitch, and yaw utilizing the throttle on the control arm. As you pilot the jetpack, use your body to bank turns by leaning in the direction you want to go, like flying a hang glider. You can track your fuel level, engine RPM, battery status, and exhaust temperature readouts with a screen on the control arm.

LANDING

Return to ground by easing off the thrust to descend slowly and gently into a Halloween party wearing a tux with a white dinner jacket accented with a red carnation; sip a martini, like the first place costume contest winner you are.

213 SURVIVE BEING SPACED (MAYBE)

I've been all over, but there's no place on Earth more hostile to humans than outer space. It's dark, empty, lifeless, and if you find yourself stranded in it, I'm sorry to say your chances of survival are slim to none out in the void. If you were ejected from a spacecraft airlock without a space suit, you would die from ten different things in less than a minute. You'd pass out in about ten seconds and asphyxiate shortly after. Holding your breath won't help you either, as the absence of external pressure would rupture your lungs—and that's a tear duct tape can't fix. Here are the gory details of what will happen if you find yourself embarking on an unplanned spacewalk.

Tears and saliva would evaporate and turn to frost. Your body fluids would expand to swell your soft tissue, eventually bloating you to twice your size—kind of like how I found out I had developed a shellfish allergy after the last Rakyat beach party I attended.

If you miraculously managed to survive all of that (you probably wouldn't), you would now be exposed to extremely high doses of radiation. You could also be struck by small particles of space dust or micrometeoroids traveling tens of thousands of miles per hour, killing you instantly like a hailstorm of celestial bullets.

But if you followed the call to adventure all the way to a space station in the future, and you find yourself starring as an alien in a live pirate-hostage performance, exhale completely before getting blown out of the airlock. Now close your mouth and eyes, curl into a ball to protect yourself as much as possible, and hope to get rescued in ninety seconds. That's how long you have to survive.

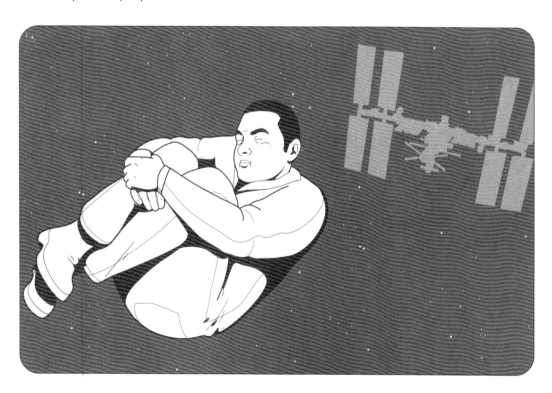

INDEX

INDEX

INDEX

TITAN
BOOKS

144 Southwark Street
London SE1 0UP
www.titanbooks.com

 Find us on Facebook: www.facebook.com/titanbooks

Follow us on Twitter: @TitanBooks

Published by arrangement with Insight Editions,
PO Box 3088, San Rafael, CA 94912 USA. www.insighteditions.com

A CIP catalogue record for this title is available from the British Library.

ISBN: 978-1-78909-758-0

Publisher: Raoul Goff
VP of Licensing and Partnerships: Vanessa Lopez
VP of Creative: Chrissy Kwasnik
VP of Manufacturing: Alix Nicholaeff
Designer: Allister Fein
Senior Editor: Amanda Ng
Editor: Ian Cannon
Managing Editor: Lauren LePera
Senior Production Editor: Elaine Ou
Senior Production Manager: Greg Steffen
Senior Production Manager, Subsidiary Rights: Lina S. Palma

Special thanks to Cédric Decelle, Jean-Alexis Doyon, Médéric Ellul-Gravel, Dan Hay, Navid Khavari, Marie-Pier Michaud, James Nadiger, Marie-Joëlle Paquin, and Sandra Warren.

All illustration by Conor Buckley/And Them Design. Special thanks to Liberum Donum, Hayden Foell, Lauren Towner, Robert L. Prince, & Christine Meighan for previous illustration work.

Insight Editions, in association with Roots of Peace, will plant two trees for each tree used in the manufacturing of this book. Roots of Peace is an internationally renowned humanitarian organization dedicated to eradicating land mines worldwide and converting war-torn lands into productive farms and wildlife habitats. Roots of Peace will plant two million fruit and nut trees in Afghanistan and provide farmers there with the skills and support necessary for sustainable land use.

Manufactured in China by Insight Editions

10 9 8 7 6 5 4 3 2 1